Bri[illegible] Lives

A Bristol Broadsides Book

Acknowledgements

Thanks to: South West Arts, Bristol City Council Avon County Council, Workers Educational Association, Adrian Smith, and Leslie Johnson. For help with 'Our Ron, That Chlöe' Ron Glade thanks 'The Feeder', Novvy Allen, Tessa Jones, Bob Sharples, Tim Bickell, Dave Edwards, Gurmit, Nazleen Nathoo, Nemeet Nathoo, Tina, Pat and Joan Sullivan and regulars at The Hillgrove Public House and sisters – Doreen, Betty, Eileen, Dorothy and Freda.

Published by: Bristol Broadsides (Co-op) Ltd
108c Stokes Croft
Bristol BS1 3RU
☎ (0272) 40764.

Produced by: Pia Ltd
37 Charles Street
Cardiff CF1 4EB
☎ (0222) 222782.

Cover Design: Rob Mackay at Springboard Design.

Photographic copywork: Will Guy

Bristol Broadsides is a member of
the Federation of Worker Writers and Community Publishers.

ISBN 0 906944 38 4

Further Reading

After reading **Bristol Lives** you might like to read some more stories of Bristol's people and their history. Bristol Broadsides' books of reminiscence and history are listed below in full. However, you may have a story of your own to tell. If so, why not get in touch with us – at Bristol Broadsides, 108c Stokes Croft, Bristol BS1 3RU, ☎ (0272) 40764.

Bristol Picture Book Part One and Two both £4.95 (80p p&p)
Tales Of The Rails Ernie Ross £1.95 (50p p&p)
Bristol's Other History £2.75 (60p p&p)
Bristol As We Remember It £1.20 (30p p&p)
Arthur And Me Jo Barnes 50p (30p p&p)
Tears And Joy £1.20 (40p p&p)
St Pauls People Talking £1.25 (40p p&p)
City Pit Fred Moss £2.50 (60p p&p)
Celebration Of Differences £1.95 (60p p&p)
Placards and Pin Money £3.95 (60p p&p)
Black and White On The Buses Madge Dresser £1.95 (60p p&p)
The Dinner Lady And Other Women £1.50 (60p p&p)
Our Joyce Joyce Storey £3.50 (60p p&p)
Fred's People 60p (30 p&p)

All these books are available by post from
Bristol Broadsides, 108c Stokes Croft, Bristol BS1 3RU.

Contents

(Parts of 'Our Ron, That Chlöe' have previously been published in 'The Feeder'.)

Introduction

This book contains an enormous variety of memories in different styles to produce a fascinating insight into the lives of Bristol people. There are stories of childhood, first jobs, family life in city and country. For one writer the memories are of wild flowers and summer days. For another they are recollections of being cold and hungry. So what links and motivates all these authors? One possible answer is expressed by a contributor who says "As one grows older past years ...... nostalgically cry out for remembrance."

Some of the authors recall characters and conversations, descriptions and details of 50, 60 and 70 years ago. Stories of being in-service, working at a psychiatric hospital or fighting fires in a blitzed Bristol. Tales such as an epic journey with an 18 foot pole will make you smile, while others, for example a strike at a local bakery, you may find uplifting. Some stories are more harrowing, written by people who have spent most years of their lives in institutions. The reader may sometimes feel uncomfortable at being allowed into lives once private but now made public in print. However, the impression is that we are welcomed by the writers who wish to share their happiness and sadness, their humour and seriousness.

Bristol Broadsides can be congratulated for continuing in its declared aim of democratising history and providing access to print for Bristol people. This book continues the series of complementary publications such as Bristol As We Remember It, Bristol's Other History and The Bristol Picture Book.

Hopefully you too will be inspired to put down your memories and experiences on paper or on tape. Reminiscence is not the sole preserve of the elderly, as this book shows. All our experiences are important. Perhaps they may not be published tomorrow or broadcast next week, but in years to come they may provide part of a unique record of Bristol and its people. So look to your local Writers Workshops, Community History Projects and Local History Groups. Memories shouldn't just leave us to wallow in the past but give us the experience with which to change the future for ourselves and all Bristol People.

Bob Pitt

THE GOOD OLD DAYS
BY ALICE E PRICE AS SPOKEN TO VIOLET SIMPSON AND B PRICE

I was born in June 1899, at No. 1 Avonvale Road. My mother, Alice Emily Fry, had six children before me, and several more afterwards. My father sired many others, a typical Victorian.

Father was the son of a blacksmith, Edward Fry, and seemed to have relatives all over Easton, St. George, Conham, and St. Pauls. As he was an itinerant lead smelter, we seemed to move about a lot. In fact none of my brothers and sisters were born in the same house, except the twins in 1900.

It was only years later, long after his death in 1918, that I realised that his erratic behaviour, and even cruelty, were possibly due to the slow lead poisoning, which eventually killed him.

Amongst my earliest memories were being taken to my granny (Mary Ann Hawkins) who kept a millinery shop at 64 Bloy Street, and later at 64 Chelsea Road, Easton. This shop went on down to her daughter, also Mary Ann Hawkins (Aunt Poly), who maintained the business until the early 1920's.

During my visits I was allowed, as a treat, to help my Cousin Lily Hawkins sort out and tidy the cottons and threads. Their beautiful colours were like a magnet to me, as I had never seen anything like them before.

As a child I got used to the domestic upheaval caused by the effects of father's 'illness'. When mother got advanced warning of father being on the rampage, she collected the youngest children together and made straight for an uninhabited house. There we would sit in the dark, or twilight, to await the passing of father's displeasure. The strictest of instructions; "Stay away from the windows", was only broken once; by me – and I never did it again. The other girls, and our brothers, fled to relatives or hid where they could, until he had "slept it off".

My father's disposition for wandering always surfaced when threatened by the Rent Man, or any other financial difficulty. He just ran off, leaving mother to tackle the Poor Relief, Guardians, or sympathetic neighbours and relatives.

On one occasion the police returned him, and then charged him with failing to maintain his family, thereby making us a charge on the Guardians. Their solution was to send him to Horfield Gaol, where he could not, under any circumstances, contribute to our existence.

Whilst a prisoner in Horfield, he was allowed out with a working party, to help in the construction of the pond in St. Georges Park – his memorial?

When I was six and we were living in Procter Street, Redfield, my twin sisters died within ten days of each other. It was only many years later that I began to appreciate the almost unendurable agony my mother must have felt returning to the grave of one infant, to bury the twin, within ten days.

When not in one of his moods my father would take me to see Aunt Charlotte Fry, a maiden aunt, who kept a general store and Off Licence, in Deep Pit, near Holly Lane. I would walk excitedly along Rose Green to Deep Pit, thrilled by the fact that I would be near forbidden territory, and would be warned not to "go out the back", where the miners would be drinking – illegally. Children would not, being talkative, have been welcomed. Aunt Charlotte gave up this business some time before the First World War. The old shop is still an Off Licence (1986).

At other times he would take me to the ferry at Conham, near Bees Tea Gardens, where I remembered him once introducing me to a relative, his brother I believe, who, when I told him my name was Lily, picked me a bunch of Lilies of the Valley, for me to remember him. I still do.

In 1908 my married sister, Ellen Hemmens, of 35 Philip Street, St Philips Marsh, died, at the age of 21, in childbirth. Although very young, I realised that this hit my mother really hard. The surviving baby, after being fussed over for some months, went to live in Barton Hill (Bradhurst Street), with her father's family, but in later years we maintained a contact.

Father "settled" to an erratic employment at Lysaghts Farm – opposite the "Penny Terrace Bridge", where he continued to work on the lead which was killing him.

My brother Albert, who was four years older than me, used to take me with him when he went to take father's dinner down to Lysaghts. Sometimes we were allowed to watch the Smeltermen and the other metal workers. After, we would pretend to leave for home and spend our time playing by the Feeder Canal.

I would edge my way fearfully along the coping stones of the bank, some 12 inches wide, with the water nearly touching my feet. If a barge passed by then the ripples went over your feet. Albert would race ahead, leaving me, terrified, to follow right under the bridge, from one end to the other. Later, I was to remember this amusement.

On the 24th of April, 1911, my mother, worn out by family cares and father's tantrums died, aged 47. As the youngest surviving child (aged 12) I mourned not only for her, but also for myself. I realised with the clarity of a child's vision, that no matter how hard life had been, that there was now no one to take the brunt of father's moods. I hadn't long to wait to find out.

His moods deteriorated, and his imagination began to create all kinds of images. Two of my sisters were married, and out of it, my eldest brother at sea, the three sisters dead, and my youngest brother showing signs of interest in the Royal Navy, as an outlet.

On the 7th of November, 1911, application was made for a copy of my Birth Certificate, for the purpose of "Employment". I was to leave school and go to work.

Alice Price (right standing) in 1909

About this time my unmarried sister, showing signs of rebellious youth, refused to render an account of all her comings and goings to father. In his fury he seized a knife and threatened and then tried to cut her throat. In the confusion she escaped and never returned.

I now had to work at any job available, and keep house, and prepare meals for father. If anything, particularly food, didn't suit him it was thrown at me, if I was present, or at the wall, if I was not. I then had to clean it up whilst he went to the pub.

This situation lasted for about a year, when my brother was notified of his acceptance for the Royal Navy. I did not relish the prospect of father's company. He had already, two or three times, in that year made attempts at suicide. He tied heavy flat irons around his neck, and then dropped the irons. He did not throttle himself, but his sore neck made him almost evil, for a while.

My brother left for the Navy, and I made my survival plan. I had grown very quickly since the death of my mother, and was preparing for the break. One particular Saturday night he was in a foul mood and began to throw food, china, cutlery and anything else that came to hand, at me. I recognised the mood as dangerously close to the tantrum he'd had when he tried to knife my sister. I dodged him and fled, terrified, out into the street, anywhere to escape.

It was late evening and I had to get somewhere to spend the night. To have stayed in the vicinity of Procter Street meant he would find me, neighbours fearful of his temper would not assist me.

Suddenly I thought of the Pinny Terrace (Marsh Lane) Bridge. On the Barton Hill side, in Herapath Street there were some wash houses which backed on to the Feeder. I knew that some of these would be unlocked and made for them.

Here I slept rough for two nights – it was a cold autumn – and on Monday morning I presented myself at the Cotton Factory. To my surprise, I was taken on, mainly for my cheek I think, at the pricely sum of three shillings and sixpence. But I still had problems. The clothes I was wearing was my entire wardrobe until I could sneak back and get some more. I had not eaten since Saturday, except for bread thrown out for the birds (Barton HIll had well fed birds); payday was a long way off, and I was homeless.

I was fortunate in that I hadn't to start work until 7.30 am. so it was possible for me to stay fairly late in the wash houses, and with luck until payday. Some of the Loom women gave me left over food and tea, which held off actual starvation, and I was able to last out for a while, I was also able to sneak back and get more clothes, which I had bundled up for a quick departure.

Payday seemed an age in coming but it came at last. Clutching my money tightly in my fist, thrust deep into my pocket and my bundle of clothes slung over my back, I left the Cotton Factory gate and walked up the road, straight into disaster.

My father's heavy hand grabbed the back of my neck, and he demanded my wages, at the same time spelling out the punishment I would get for running off. Unknown to me, I had been betrayed and he had just waited his chance, till I got paid, and then struck.

I shouted and screamed for help – and it came. A solid body of women from the Looms bore down on us, pulled me out of his grasp, and tore into him in a combined fury, which matched anything he could muster. He retreated, shouting, cursing, threatening – but he went. I never saw him again until after his death in 1918.

One of the women spectators came over to me and questioned me; it turned out that she was an aunt by marriage and knew my father. She took me by the arm and off I went to live with Mary Ann Fry in Corbett Street, her husband Sidney was my uncle.

Here I stayed, living the life of the rest of the poor working community, but at least I was free of violence, and father's tantrums. It was relative bliss.

I was happy with Mary Ann, but War changed that. Sidney Fry volunteered for the Army, and had the unfortunate distinction of serving some three weeks before being killed, in an accident. The effect on the family was shattering, and I felt I was an intruder. A lady living across the road offered me a room with them, and I went to stay with Laura Wagland, and her family, again kindly and free of fear, it was so different.

On February the 1st, 1918, my father, who had gone to live with a married sister in the Dings, finally succumbed to the lead, and died. I felt sorry for any suffering he had had, but I also felt free, completely free.

Some time after his death I went to live with this sister, who was as kind and welcoming as her heavy Victorian husband would allow. He believed that he was entitled to be waited on "hand, foot and finger" and we clashed, frequently and noisily.

In 1921 I married and went to live in the next street. My husband's family had mostly been connected with the Phoenix Bottlehouse in Avon Street, for nearly a century, and had their roots deep in the Dings. The household was run by their sister, Edith Jessie, who was TOUGH. She, like myself, had been left at the age of 12 to cater for a father and five brothers, ranging in age from 14 to 2 years. They were all terrified of her.

Nobody was rich, but Edith Jessie's pride and joy was her "Table". For the first time, since my mother's death ten years before, I felt full and no longer hungry.

We had one initial clash and I thought I was about to leave this earth in a puff of blue smoke, but I stood my ground. She offered me one privilege, which had never been granted to anyone else – she relented. Staring me straight in the eye she said, "You are the only one who has ever stood up to me. You must have had it hard." We remained on good terms for the rest of her life.

But my real acceptance came when I came across old Danner Price, sitting in the small yard, talking to his pigeons, and bemoaning the fact that none of his sons were any good with pigeons, they couldn't even open and close the "************ loft".

I listened for a while and then offered to climb up and work the loft trap for him if he would tell me how it was to be done. He told me what to do, I did it, and it worked. "Thee bis' alright. Thee's do," he said.

From that moment on, my troubled childhood began to recede, and go back into the recesses of the mind where the bad memories are slowly buried by the good.

A BRISTOL SON
BY GLADYS POWER

I began to know my Father from the time I went ashore in Malta in 1928. I had been in hospital most of my tender years which was the reason for our family joining him there. My Father had served two of the five years in the Navy he had to do already, and this is how it all began.

He was born William Russett, one of eight children in 1892. He hated school and played truant most days. There wasn't a School Board then to ensure a regular attendance. He seemed to have done pretty much as he liked in his early years, doing odd jobs to earn a few pence. At the age of twelve, he walked every inch of the way to Wales, where he was befriended by a soft-hearted miner who took pity on the very hungry, thirsty and desolate young boy. My Father stayed with the miner and his wife who looked after him as if he were her son. He went to work in the mines for the next few years and saved a few pounds. Then he began to get homesick to see his family and decided to return to Bristol.

It wasn't long before he realised he had made a mistake; money all gone, no work and no prospects. Feeling sick at heart he wished he'd stayed where he was. Then he met a friend who had joined the Royal Navy. Listening to his glowing tales of the life, he decided to join too.

Unfortunately he was failed, as he wasn't tall enough for his age. Not to be deterred, he returned later with his brother's birth certificate (as his brother was two years his junior at sixteen). My Father passed, but had to do boy's service, thus started his career.

He entered at the time of sailing ships when boys were still whipped up the mast. Many the tale I heard of the sadistic P.O. who had made their lives a misery, as with nothing on the lower part of their legs in freezing conditions, and with legs and feet bleeding from his inhuman treatment, they clung on to the riggings. One day, it seems he beat one of the boys so badly he died. My Father never forgave him. He swore if ever he met him in later years he would kill him. Perhaps it was as well for him he never did. After this, the first leave he had, he jumped ship, but having accepted the King's shilling he was soon recaptured and was posted to China for 2½ years. During this time he went ashore for the evening and got into an argument with a Chinaman who produced a knife and gashed his throat. When at roll call he was missing, a search party was sent out thinking he'd jumped ship again. They found him unconscious, slumped in a doorway and rushed him to the sick bay. He had lost an awful lot of blood and the knife had barely missed his jugular vein, but after a time he recovered. He decided at this stage to get the best out of the life he had chosen, and whenever his chores

William Russett – a Bristol Son

would allow, he returned to school. On returning to England he entered the Royal Navy College at Dartmouth. From then on he never looked back.

My Father qualified as a deep sea diver before World War I. During the war he served on H.M.S. Erin, and H.M.S. Vanguard when in 1916 it was blown up. At the battle of Jutland he was senior deep sea diver, and never tired of telling me about the time the German fleet surrendered. There was a picture that hung in our dining room showing the positions and types of each ship, i.e. Battle, Cruiser, etc. At the top of the picture, written in German, were the words 'Der Tag'. I remember asking, as a child, what it meant and being told 'The Day'.

Qualifying in Physical Training after the war, my Father held appointments at Dartmouth Royal Navy P.T. School as Squadron Physical Training Instructor. By this time however, he had decided to get married. Now came the day of reckoning as, in his own words, "I had to go to my Commanding Officer and confess I had joined the Navy under false pretences." There was now another Richard Russet of the same age, as his brother had followed him into the Service. After a silence that seemed never ending, the Officer asked my Father what the hell he expected him to do about it. Fortunately he quite respected my Father and after saying "You silly ..." he would see what he could do. With the minimum of trouble, the Commanding Officer pulled strings and managed to sort everything out amicably.

In 1918 my parents were married in St. Mary Redcliffe Church. Two years later, in August 1920, they were blessed with me, to the disgust of P.T.I. Russett who had looked forward to a son. He need not have worried though, because eighteen months later his wish came true, and I had a brother. My Father at this time was stationed at Portsmouth and ran the Royal Navy Sports Centre there. My health, from then on, deteriorated. I had swallowed a fish bone which, it was later discovered, had punctured my right lung. I spent the next few years of my life in hospital.

In 1924 my sister was born. As soon as she was old enough and whenever possible, my Mother joined my Father wherever he was stationed, leaving me to my Grandmother's care. When I was six years old my Father was posted to Malta. During the next two years my life was often in the balance, until my Father was finally sent for. After hearing he was stationed in Malta, the medical profession had come to the conclusion that, if I was to have a chance of survival, a warmer country may be the answer. In light of this information he set about making the necessary arrangements. This is how our family came to be embarking on the P & O Liner, The Raj Putana. The ship's surgeon was in despair when he saw me as we boarded and told my Mother I wouldn't reach Malta. I must admit I don't remember too much of the first half of the journey, except a raging thirst. Once we passed the Bay of Biscay I began to take notice. The sickly child that had to be carried aboard was able to stand to greet her Father. Although it was dark on our arrival, the air was warm. The lights from both ships and shore made the Grand Harbour of Malta appear, to a child's imagination, like Fairyland.

William Russett and other P.T.O.'s in 1921

The first few weeks were spent in Valetta. We had furnished rooms with a very nice Maltese lady. I remember being taken to the harbour wall and gazing down on the fleet as they stood at anchor; those beautiful proud ships and their crews who were to form our lives for the next few years.

My parents rented a house in Casapoala and that is where we lived for the remainder of our stay. In the next eighteen months I grew quite robust. We spent a good deal of our time in the warm Mediterranean Sea. My Father sent my brother to The Dockyard School – a very high-graded educational centre. He was in despair at what to do about me. I could neither read nor write as, in those years, no education was given in hospitals. The only tutoring I'd had was the alphabet that my Grandmother had so beautifully embroidered for me. I used to lay in bed and go over and over the letters until I knew them by heart. When I tired of this I learned them backwards. This limited knowledge was not enough to carry me through life. My parents knew something had to be done, but what? Not only was I sub-standard educationally, but I had two pieces of rib removed in the course of my operations. As only skin covered the wound in my back, they feared in the rough and tumble of school the other children wouldn't know this. By now I was ten-and-a-half years old. My Father finally decided to see the headmaster of the school my brother was attending, after investigating the possibilities of others. He thought if he explained the situation perhaps something could be worked out; thus started my education. I remember the excitement of the first morning. At last I was going to be able to read, (my greatest ambition). Oh, the excitement didn't last long! I still remember to this day the misery, as in a class of children half my age who could all read the first reader I was handed, I couldn't make out even the most simple word. I can't remember how long or when I first began to piece the letters together. Certainly I can remember being delighted to show my Father how clever I was and asking how long it would take before I would be able to read properly. There was a Miss Evans, I recall, who was one of the finest teachers I have ever been privileged to meet. She wouldn't give any quarter. If it wasn't right the first time, you did it over and over until 'you jolly well got it right'. I have a lot to thank her for. I have never been brilliant, but whatever I achieved was due to this lady and her patience.

My Father, at this stage in my life, was Chief P.T.I. on the staff of Commander in Chief, Mediterranean. I learned, as time passed, he had been the instigator of a sports complex named the Corodina Grounds, for which he was presented with a bronze discus thrower on a stand. On the base was a little silver plaque engraved with his name and his achievement. As each week passed, I grew stronger. I was never given any margin though! My Father expected me to toe the line just the same as my brother and sister. I was always in awe of him. It stayed with me all my life.

We children had the time of our lives. We were invited to all sorts of functions. I remember the Christmas pantomime Aladdin, performed by the crew of H.M.S. Resolution. I have seen this heaps of times since, but not one has had the magical effect of the first time I ever saw it. Then there was the time we were invited to the Corodina Grounds to hear my

Father and another member of the crew, singing a duet in the concert hall. I loved the whole evening! It was so exciting.

There was, in the square at Casapoala, a building named Carabots. To us children it seemed massive. It contained the cinema, a bar and a dance floor on the roof. We had our photograph taken in the foyer. We were as brown as the natives. Whilst our parents were socializing in the bar with ship-mates and their wives, we children would enjoy a film. All those Oldies of bygone days. So each day passed with trips in gaily coloured Dicoes to different parts of the island, to picnics or swimming in the bays and drying off in cool caves. We paid visits to the Sports Centre and there was a million and one other things to do. It would take too long to write down. I was into all the mischief other children got into, for which I was reprimanded by my very stern Father. I was alive and strong! I'd lost my dreadful cough and the world looked a good place to me.

So the years passed and except for the days when we had the rainy seasons or when the mosquitoes managed to find their mark, our stay came to an end with no mishaps.

Came the time to return to England and Bristol. It was in March 1932 we said farewell to my Father to go aboard the Passenger Ship. He had to stay and wind up his business and sail on H.M.S. Resolution. At the end of the next year, he had served his twenty-one years and was to be a reserve. During this time he had to face what he would be doing in Civvy Street.

Postscript

After other travels my Father finally returned to Bristol in 1970 to live at Holly House, Lawrence Weston. This is where he died at the grand old age of 89, in 1981.

I REMEMBER WHEN

(four extracts from a full length autobiography)

BY REG MIDDLE

Blackhorse. This was the hamlet where I was born, about one and a quarter miles from Mangotsfield on the Westerleigh Road. It had some twelve or fourteen cottages and three farms. A mile further on towards Westerleigh was a pub, the "Beaufort Arms", known by all the local people as the "Folly", not because it was a folly to go there, but because it was beside the bridge that went over The Folly Brook. Our house was the last down the road, and about one mile from the pub. It was a tall house, rather taller than the others in the road. It was a narrow house, being a single fronted two up and two down, with a wash house outside the back door and the lavatory next again. It had a very large garden with a stream at the bottom, which used to flood in the winter. There were three pig-sties, a stable for the horse and two other sheds, one for storing the cart and farm produce in, with a workshop at the other end. On Mondays, Wednesdays and Fridays Theophilus, my Father, would go round the district for about twelve miles radius, buying any produce he could not grow himself, collecting eggs, poultry, and fruit if it came into season. What vegetables he couldn't grow enough of or couldn't grow at all, he would buy from the farmers. Tuesdays, Thursdays, and Saturdays he would go into Bristol and sell what he had collected on the other days. While in Bristol he would buy in much larger quantities than our family would require salt, jam, soda, sugar, candles or anything that would keep and these he sold to the neighbours. It wasn't exactly a shop but we sold most things, including paraffin and coal, which he fetched by the cart load from the Colliery at Coalpit Heath. The other people who lived at Blackhorse were only too pleased to be able to buy bits and pieces from us because the nearest shop was one and a half miles away.

I'll take you for a walk up the road and introduce you to the other residents of the hamlet. Next door to our house was a very pretty old world cottage with a well in the front garden. (We had to get our water from here as well). The cottage was very small, with a porch over the door and little casement windows. It only had one room up and one room down, with a kitchen at the side. The lavatory was outside and to get to it you had to come out of the front door (there was no back door), turn left, go past the front of the house, then turn left again and walk the length of the garden. This brought you to the bottom of the boundary hedge with our garden, I tell you all this because there is a story about this lavatory later. The people I can first remember living here were a Mr. and Mrs. Sid Willard. Mrs. Willard was very deformed. She had a large hump on her back and she was only able to walk by having some assistance. I don't know whether this difficulty in walking was constitutional or whether it was from the strain of nursing her daughter. Her daughter was an imbecile and lived all her life in a long spinal chair. She was about sixteen but, was like a baby of six months. She got so big and heavy she had to be put in a home, soon after the Willards went away. When my Mother and Father came to live next door to the Willards, Mother thought they had a lodger and she used to wonder how all those people could live in such a small house. Why she thought they had a lodger was because every morning someone would say, "Good Morning Sid". It was a long time before she found out that Mr. Willard had a tame Magpie, that could talk.

The cottage was soon taken by a brother and sister by the name of George and Hanna Tandy. They had a white pony and a two wheel cart, which they used for collecting rags, bottles and bones. They would then come home and sort out all the cotton from the wool and if there was anything that was not too bad they would sell this to the second hand shops in the poor parts of Bristol. I have never seen a house decorated inside quite like theirs was. The wood work was painted all different colours, for if they found a drop of paint they would use it as far as it would go. So the finished article looked something like this: a red door inside, green skirting board, blue shelves, yellow windows, the stairs door white and door into the kitchen pink. But these colours would change overnight if they found some paint of another colour. The walls changed also, but in a different way. They were papered, not with wallpaper but with the picture pages out of newspapers and magazines, any paper that had a picture on it. As any picture became available, it was stuck on the wall, so the scene was always changing. There are many stories I could tell about them, but there are two that always come to mind when I think of George and Hanna.

Their brother Joby came to stay. Now Joby was blind. He lost his sight while working in Sodbury tunnel, where there was an explosion when they were building the Great Western Line. This was at the same time that my father was working on the line. Soon after the accident Joby left his wife and was now living with a woman called Maggie. Joby and Maggie would walk into Bristol begging, he with one hand on her shoulder and the other holding a cup. On his chest he had a little notice saying how he had lost his sight and that he had no other means of making a living. Maggie, before she set out on these journeys, would strap a large pad around her waist so that she looked as if she was in the late stages of pregnancy. She carried a large basket on her arm filled with what was supposed to be roots of herbs. These consisted of sprigs of sage, mint, thyme, etc. with lumps of clay on their stems. When they had walked the six or seven miles into Bristol, Maggie went off to sell her herbs, leaving Joby standing on a street corner with his cup in his hand and the notice on his chest. He would sing hymns very softly as if singing to himself, but loud enough for the passer-by to hear. Then sometimes he would have a change, and quietly stand and thank God for his blessings that he had only lost his sight and not his life. This used to touch the public's heart and the pennies would start dropping into his cup. These he always took out as fast as they went in, so that it looked as if he was having a very poor time of it. Coming home they would stop at certain pubs and have a drink. They would also fill Maggie's basket with bottles of beer, which they would share with

George and Hanna later in the evening. One night, after one of these pub crawls, they were at the "Lamb Inn" at Mangotsfield and something dropped off the front of Maggie's basket. As she stooped to pick it up, something dropped off the back and this kept repeating itself. Then the other people in the pub started to laugh and Maggie started to swear, which made things worse. Joby didn't know what was going on because he couldn't see, but knew it was something to do with Maggie, so he said, "Why can't you leave the poor bitch alone, she's only pregnant. Can't you see she's ill, she can't help it?"

On another occasion when they had come home drunk and had shared the bottles in the basket with George and Hanna, they had a quarrel, there was a lot of swearing and shouting, Joby and Maggie were lying on the floor, Hanna was sitting on a chair by the table, George was staggering about in a temper. Mother, Doris and I were in our front garden pretending not to notice that anything out of the ordinary was going on. George decided to turn Joby and Maggie out, so he started by picking up their belongings and stepping over Maggie and Joby on the floor and pushing past Hanna, who had to hang on to the table to stop from being knocked off the chair. He would first take out a cup and then a saucer and then something else, all singly, and with the same performance each time of stepping over and pushing past, he would walk the length of the garden path, or rather stagger, then stand by the gate and throw the articles across the road into the ditch on the other side, and with each thing thrown he would shout, "Out you go, you buggers". The next morning they were all out in the ditch looking for their crockery so that they could have a cup of tea.

I said I would tell you a story about the lavatory. I have already given you the location. Well, this lavatory was built of wood, about four feet square and about six feet six inches high with a galvanised iron roof. I think the first thing that happened was the door fell off or was taken off to use for something else. Then if George or Hanna wanted wood to light the fire, they would take a bit off the side. Then one day in a storm the roof blew away, so it was quite easy then for the other sides to fall down. All that was left now was the lavatory pan standing on its own in the garden. Joby must have had an idea, because he planted withy branches in a circle round the pan and although he was blind made quite a good job of it. These branches very quickly took root and made quite a thick hedge. During the summer it was very effective, the leaves on the hedge giving a certain amount of screening, but in the winter they might just as well have been out in the open. In any case if it rained and they wanted to use the lavatory they sat there with their umbrella up. From the time the lavatory fell to pieces until the hedge grew Joby always used the lavatory pan. Well, I suppose if he couldn't see, why should other people worry? We lived next door and we didn't.

(As Reg Middle grew up the First World War raged and his Father's life and temperament mirrored a harsher and more serious world.)

Dad would go for a walk with us on a Sunday evening sometimes in the summer, but these were very rare, since he and Mother were always working. I don't think I ever saw Mother sit down with folded arms, and Dad worked from daylight until dark and after. He was a very quiet man, he had no friends and wanted none. He didn't like people very much so he didn't do much talking to anyone, not even to us children. Mother was the apple of his eye, she could do or say no wrong. I think he loved her more than we ever realised. I am sure that his world revolved round Kate. Other than being with her he liked his own company and was quite happy to stay at home smoking his pipe and working in the garden while Mother took us on any of the outings that were going on. I never once heard him sing or even whistle. He could see a joke and would laugh at one but he wasn't a jocular man and detested practical jokes.

He was a very kind man and had great concern for the welfare of his horse and any other animals that were in his care. He was also much more generous than Mother. When Dad gave you anything it would be the best he had. I don't know what his politics were, but I would say he was a Communist. His idea was that you should only have what you worked for. Nobody should own large areas of land, especially land that was only kept for hunting or shooting over. Any land that wasn't farmed properly and made the best use of should be taken over by the state and then relet to tenants who would get the most out of it. Anything taken from the land such as minerals and rock should belong to the state, so that everybody would benefit and not just a few. He had no use at all for the idle rich. He said their riches hadn't been come by honestly and fairly; somewhere in getting them somebody had been exploited or cheated, and in all cases it was the sweat of somebody else's brow that allowed them to have this life of ease. Three other lots of people he didn't trust and recommended you should keep away from : clergymen, solicitors, and doctors, in this order. I can't say if his ideas were from deep thinking on his part, or if it was how he felt, seeing the hard life he had had from a boy and was still having.

One morning while it was still quite dark, I heard a kind of chopping noise outside in the garden. I got out of bed to see what it was. There was Dad with a lantern hanging on a branch of a tree, hoeing the cabbage patch. If Mother wanted to keep him in after tea in the evenings for company, just before he'd finish his meal she would either pick up the daily paper or a book and start reading. He would then sit and smoke his pipe and listen to her reading as he loved being read to. As a matter of fact this was our usual Sunday evening entertainment in the winter: Mother would sit and read while we sat round the fire listening. I have known her to read herself hoarse and even lose her voice altogether. We had a huge book like a bible, called "The Boys of Marford" which we as children liked her to read. It was filled with stories of boys in a boarding school.

After the war had started and had been going for some time, things began to get very bad. The men went into the army and some of the women went out to work or to auxiliary nursing. Dad's round got so small it wasn't worth doing. He got himself a job at Yate when they were building the prisoner of war camp there and only did the round on Saturdays. Mother collected from the farms what was required for the smaller round. She also went to Coalpit Heath Colliery for the coal, assisted by me when on holiday from school, evenings and weekends. Between us we looked after two large gardens, the horse, three goats, and about a dozen fowls (the pigs had gone by now). When we were working in the garden at Kendleshire, we would go for the day. Mother would pack up some food and off we would go, sometimes with the horse and cart, but more often walking, as it was nearer to walk than take the horse.

We would stay there all day weeding, hoeing or gathering the crops when they were ready. Dad dug or ploughed the garden and got it ready for us to plant. There was a Mrs. Marshall who always brought us a jug of tea to have with our dinner. We always seemed to spend a lot of time walking to and from everywhere. We sold quite a lot of coal to the neighbours who didn't work at the Parkfield Colliery, so this meant fetching it fairly frequently from Coalpit Heath Colliery. When I was at school Mother went alone. When I was on holiday from school I would go with her. We couldn't fetch coal on Saturdays as Dad had the horse and cart to do his greengrocery round in Bristol. It was quite a long journey and the horse only went at walking pace.

From Blackhorse to the pit head would be all of five miles, but it wasn't the journey that took the time, it was the waiting at the pit for the coal. You could get small-coal quite easily and quickly if you shovelled it up yourself; it was the best lump coal that you had to wait for. After the drams of coal had come up the pit shaft, they were pushed along a track. This track then divided. One line would go to the railway trucks and the other to the waiting carts. As the railway trucks were filled they had to be shunted down the line, so that another truck could come under the chute that the coal came down, and it was while this was being done that the drams which came to the surface went round to the waiting carts. It needed two and the part of another for one ton and there were very few of the carts that took less than this. When you got to the colliery there would be a long queue of horses and carts large and small already there. It was nothing to wait for six to eight hours before you got a load. In the colliery yard was a small hut with a wooden bench seat all round the walls. This was where the drivers waited when the weather was cold or wet. Some of the drivers couldn't leave their horses if they were restless and would have to stand by them for all these hours. Mother was lucky: our horse was very quiet and, providing she had a nose-bag full of food, and a couple of sacks put over her when it was cold, she would be quite content for Mother to go into the hut. Mother always took some knitting with her, usually socks, either knitting new ones or putting feet in old ones. One day while she was knitting, one of the men waiting there in the hut, Jimmy Nixon asked her what she was doing. Mother said that she was putting some new feet into some old socks. He then said that he had had a pair of socks for twenty years when he was a boy. His mother would put new feet when they were needed and then put new legs when they were wanted. "That was the beauty of hand knitted socks. They would last for ever." At the time he was talking, Jimmy Nixon didn't need any socks as he had two wooden legs. Both of his legs were cut off by a railway truck, at the same time as Joby Tandy lost his sight. He was working in the Sodbury tunnel with his legs across the railway line doing something to one of the sleepers. The explosion started the truck moving and before he could get out of the way it had run over his legs. He was now in business on his own, doing light hauling and coal delivering. He had a cart and two donkeys which he drove tandem and which he didn't treat with the greatest of kindness. Many times he was before the Courts for over-loading the cart, for beating the donkeys, for using them when they were lame, or for not feeding them. Another thing was being drunk and disorderly. He never answered a summons but always waited until the police arrested him. He never paid a fine but would rather go to prison. The artfulness of the man was that when the police came to arrest him, to make the charge worse he would stick his two wooden legs into two holes in the floor in a corner of his living room, which he had made for this purpose. Now with his back in the corner, his two wooden legs stuck in the holes, a heavy walking stick in each hand, he would defy the police for hours. As they came forward to get him he would hit out first with one stick and then with the other. When he tired of resisting arrest, he would undo the straps which held his wooden legs and then wherever they wanted him to go from then until he came home again, the police would have to carry him.

At these times Jimmy Nixon had an arrangement with a crony of his to turn the donkeys loose on Chipping Sodbury Common. A story about him when he was in prison once: one of the prison warders who was looking after him when he was doing a turn of hard labour, said that he wasn't picking enough oakum. Jimmy told him he was doing all he intended to do and if he wanted more work done he must recruit more labour. Although he had two wooden legs he could load small coal better than people with two good legs. He would stick his wooden legs into the heap of coal and put his back against the wheel of his cart and shovel the coal over his shoulder into the cart. But he always had his eyes open for a stranger. As soon as he spotted one, he pretended to be very helpless and would approach him with, "Just take my donkeys over there", "Just back the cart up to the small coal", "Just shovel a bit of coal into my cart for me", "Just take my donkeys and the load over to the weigh bridge and get it weighed", "Just help me up on to my cart". Then off he would go not having done anything himself, and not so much as a thank you. Other women besides Mother went to the colliery to fetch coal. One of the others I remember was a Mrs. Kettey from Chipping Sodbury. Her husband had to go into the army and leave his coal merchant business. There was nobody else to do the work, so it either meant closing the business down or doing as she did, run it herself. This included delivering coal by the sack as well as delivering it by the load. All this entailed a lot of heaving and lifting, a job not much enjoyed by strong men and she wasn't a very big woman either. She kept the business going on her own until he came out of the army after the war.

(After leaving school, and against the wishes of his father, Reg Middle became a farm labourer. He worked for Bernard Early on his small farm at Kendleshire.)

Once in the Spring when Bernard and I were in the fields hoeing in between the mangols (the first hoeing when they were very small seedlings) a man came up to the wall of the field and asked Bernard if he required any help. He was carrying a kind of holdall-cum-carpet bag and was wearing a dirty grey mac. After a few questions about what he could do and when he could start and such like, he said he could start straight away and jumped over the wall and started hoeing. He said he lived at Chipping Sodbury, I can't remember his name and if I could, I don't think it would make any difference because I don't expect it would be his real name, so for this story we will call him George.

During that afternoon he told us a lot of things about himself, about how he was courting a girl at Chipping Sodbury and was saving to get married. He also asked if, provided he was the kind of man that Bernard wanted, he could have a permanent job at the farm. The night when he finished work, he didn't do any milking, so worked on in the field until six o'clock. He asked Bernard if he could have a sub from his wages so that he could ride on the bus to Sodbury, Bernard gave him some money but told him he didn't like doing this and would rather pay him properly at the end of the week. Next morning he arrived while we were milking, and when I had come back from delivering the milk to Staple Hill and was having my breakfast, Bernard came in to me and said, "Have you seen George's bike? If not, you had better come and have a look." I went with him to the barn and there standing just inside the door with George's carpet bag hanging on the handlebars, together with his grey mac, was the most magnificent bike you ever saw; a dark green, three speed, oil chain bath, Sunbeam, just about the most expensive bike you could get in those days. When we went out to work in the field where George was working, Bernard asked him whose bike it was and he replied, "It's mine. I had a little talk to the girl and she agreed that I should spend some of the money we've been saving to get married and buy a bike, as this would be easier and cheaper than catching buses."

The next morning there was a different bike in the barn and when we asked him where the Sunbeam was, he replied that the three speed had gone wrong going home the night before and he had taken it back to the shop where he had bought it, for them to put it right. The strange thing was he never came to work on the same bike all the time he worked for Bernard, but he always had his carpet bag and grey mac.

On another day when we were working together, Bernard asked him whereabouts in Chipping Sodbury did he lodge, and then he told us a story which I think was the only time he told us the truth. He said he stayed at a lodging house at the bottom of the street, and for a bed only it cost him four pence a night, but if he wanted he could sit in a chair for two pence, or if he was late getting in in the evening and if all the accommodation was taken (as there was no advanced booking) he could hang on a line. This line was put across the room between the beds. This would cost him one penny. If he wanted to use any of the cooking utensils, which consisted of one kettle and one saucepan, which had to be used on the one and only open fire, this would cost him an extra penny. He said he always did his level best to have a bed to sleep on, but even then he had to sleep in his clothes, with his mac wrapped round his carpet bag for a pillow and the two legs at the bottom of the bed standing one in each boot, so that nobody could steal any of his belongings, and any money that he may have rolled up in his shirt sleeve underneath his jacket. If he slept in a chair he wore the lot and sat on his bag, and on the rare occasions that he had hung on the line, he had tied the bag to his back and put his mac on top. He said he had known things go from one bed to another and the real owner steal them back again all in one night.

One morning he came to work in a very bad temper. He said he hadn't had any tea or breakfast as someone had stolen it. It appears he went to his lodgings at night and had taken with him some bread, butter and some eggs. He intended to have boiled eggs and bread and butter for tea; but, knowing the kind of people that lived at this lodging house, which should he do first, cut his bread and butter and then boil his eggs or boil his eggs first? He decided to boil his eggs first, so he got the saucepan and water and put it on to boil. This is really important, you must put your eggs in boiling water. If you put them in cold water and then turned your back someone would take them out, but they couldn't do this if they are in boiling water, or so he thought. When the water was boiling he put his eggs in and then looked in his bag for his bread and butter. It was gone. Someone had taken it while he was getting the saucepan. This meant he would have to eat his eggs without any bread and butter. He made a few polite and a few impolite enquiries, he accused one or two, then the others threatened to give him a good thumping if he didn't shut up, and told him he wouldn't be allowed to stay there anymore. So he turned to the saucepan for his eggs, which would have been hard boiled by now, and lo and behold, the eggs had gone. Hence his bad temper. No bread, no butter, no eggs, no tea or breakfast.

But this gave Bernard an idea. He put two and two together and came up with the answer, a different bicycle every day and eggs for tea and breakfast. He would steal the eggs from the farm before he went home at night. So every night after that, Bernard would either drop George's bag on the floor or do something so that if there were amy eggs in there, they would be broken. He would also do something to get him to do something so that if he had any eggs in his coat pockets they would also break. Bernard said this was the best way, as he didn't want to accuse him and that be the very night when he wouldn't have any, and he wasn't going to pick his pockets and have him accusing Bernard of being a pickpocket, in any case he didn't intend to have him working there much longer.

Time was getting on and the days were getting warmer, we had hoed through the roots once, and had gone through them again bunching them out, this was drawing the hoe across the rows of young plants, leaving them in bunches ready to single out when they had grown a little bigger and this was what we were doing on this particular day. The sun was shining and it was hot, Bernard and I were working in our trousers and shirts and still the perspiration was running down our faces as we bent two double pulling out the smallest of the plants and just leaving the biggest and best to go on growing.

George was still wearing his jacket and a collar and tie, he was red in the face and the perspiration was running off of him as well, but he wouldn't take his jacket off. I'd never seen him with his jacket off, he'd put his mac on and off to go to his lodgings but he'd never take off his jacket. Bernard suggested he took it off on this particular day, he said he would feel better. But George refused, he said he was alright, he could work better when he was warm. Then Bernard started to work faster and we had to work faster to keep up and this made us hotter but still he wouldn't take his jacket off. Dinner time came and Bernard and I went back to the farm to have our meal, George stayed on and had his dinner in the field.

When we got back to start work for the afternoon session George was under the hedge in the shade fast asleep, and then we knew why he wouldn't take his jacket off while we were with him. There he was lying on his back on the grass, his shirt done up to the neck, his tie in a nice tight knot and pinned down to the front of his shirt. Beside him on the grass was his jacket. When he heard us coming, we were only a few yards away, he reached for his jacket and got up to put it on and then we saw he had no back to his shirt at all, his shirt consisted of only the collar and the front, but when he had his jacket on it looked as if his shirt was a perfect garment. Bernard asked him if he had had an accident, and he replied this wasn't his shirt, somebody had nicked his and left him this one. I don't think he was telling the truth, I'd never seen him in any other shirt and he always wore his jacket. That night Bernard gave him an old one of his, a complete one, and the next day in the field the three of us were working in our shirts and trousers.

(After farm-1abouring Reg Middle went to work as a motor mechanic in the village of Westerleigh; a community whose people Reg Middle describes:)

On the Monday morning that I started work at Minster and Reed's I rode my bicycle, as the motor bike was now a heap of old iron pushed under the shed. Its life with me hadn't been long, whenever I took it out it always broke down, the exception being, going backwards and forwards to the farm, but you could hardly call that a journey. As I rode along that morning I thought, seeing that I was going to work in a garage, perhaps I could bring it back to life, or go one better and rebuild it to look like new, this was wishful thinking. I hadn't even started working in the garage, what's more to the point I hadn't got there yet.

Before I tell you about my working with Ted Minster, I will try and give you some idea of Westerleigh Village and some of the people who lived there. The village was shaped like a Y with a little three cornered green where the three roads met and around this green were the Church, the New Inn and the General Stores. Starting at the foot of the leg of the Y, this was the road from Yate to Westerleigh, the first house on the outskirts of the village was the Vicarage; a rather large house standing back off the road in a rather large garden. The Reverend Stevens lived here with his Sister and his Niece Dorothy. Dorothy was a widow but I can't remember her married name, not that that makes any difference as she was always called Dorothy by all the villagers old and young. She was a very large woman and wore dresses with lots of frills, scarves and large floppy hats and she always looked as if she was just about to go on the theatre stage and take the part of a Duchess. Visiting around the village and to attend the church services she drove a small pony and governess cart. Other than a small corner at the front on the left hand side where her Uncle sat, she filled the rest of the cart with her own size and the volumes of dress, cloaks and scarf. Her Uncle and Aunt were very old, in their eighties and her Uncle still took the service at the church, but the Reverend Evans and Dorothy will appear again in this story about Westerleigh.

Coming on along the road on the left hand side there was an old disused Quarry, here two brothers by the name of Eamann had a Carpenters' Workshop and a builders' yard. On the other side of the road was an open patch of grass where the people who lived in the bungalows and houses around the edge let their fowls, ducks, and geese run loose. On the corner of this little common was the Pound; this was a little enclosed yard with a high wall and a locked gate, where any stray animals that were found roaming the roads could be put until the owners claimed them and paid the fine according to the number of days they were in the pound.

Next to the quarry was an old Farm House and out buildings where a Mr. and Mrs. Tolman lived; they had one son about my age whose name was Bill. On the other side of the road was a few houses which came out on to the path. Next to the Tolmans was an orchard and then a high wall with a large garden behind, a small space and now we come to the Frickers family, Mr. and Mrs. and their two children Doris and Joe. We have now reached the three cornered green and across the green from the Frickers lived another character, Alex Trilby, the blacksmith. Next to him lived Sargeant Major Tomkins who kept the General Stores with his wife and three daughters Phyllis, Dot, and Vera. In between the Frickers farm and the New Inn lived Sailor Button, passing the New Inn we now enter the left hand road which made up one of the forks of the Y. This is Westerleigh Short Hill, up here were three or four cottages; the first, a very small cottage, I can't remember the person's name, but she was a very old lady and next to her lived Jimmy Minster, his wife Polly, and his two sons Tom and Harry. On up the hill lived a Mr. and Mrs. Barren and their son. In the last house up the hill, this is now in the steep part of the hill, lived a young couple but I can't remember their names.

Coming back to the green, there is a rather nice house on the corner, then we pass the Church to enter the right hand road which made up the other part of the Y. On the right hand side of the road were a few houses starting at the General Stores and with a little space between them and the house and garage where Ted Minster lived with his wife Anne and his daughter Kathleen. Joe Minster, his old father, also lived with them. Across the road and next to the Church Steps was the Old Inn. Its proper name being the Kings Arms, but so as not to get confused, one Pub was known as the Old Inn and the other as the New Inn. Mrs. Reed kept the Old Inn assisted by her daughter and her son; he was also Ted Minster's partner at the garage across the road. On the same side as the Old Inn, on along the road, was another General Store owned by a Mr. and Mrs. White, then there were a few very old houses, a farm, the railway bridge, another farm and, at the top of the road on the bend before going down Kidney Hill was the School and School house, this faced down the road towards the Church. Miss Damlish lived in the School house and she was a very young and glamorous lady with lots of suitors. On the other side of the road and following on from the garage was a row of Council Houses, about ten or twelve of them, next to these was an old gabled house where the Brothers Eamann lived, the two men who kept the Carpenters' Shop in the Quarry. Crossing the railway bridge again there were some farm buildings belonging to the farm across the road and owned by Phillip Tibbs, and from there on up the road to the top of the hill were fields until you came to the School at the top. I hope you can build up a mental picture of this village because this is where I worked and to a certain extent spent most of my time for the next three or four years and very happy years they were too. There were a number of farms and other houses and cottages all around the district, but what I've told you about so far is more or less the part that was known as the village. I've already given you some idea of what the Vicar and his family were like, I will now go round the village and try and do the same with some of the others who have any kind of a story which can be told about them.

Starting off with Mr. Frickers, he was a little man very like a jockey and could well have been one. He farmed a small farm behind the house, but most of his time was spent breaking in horses, getting them ready, either for work, drawing carts, working on farms, or riding and hunting. Joe, the son, was a little younger than me and worked in a garage learning motor engineering at Chipping Sodbury. Later on, but while he was still young, he married a widow much older than himself who set him up in business in a garage of his own. Mr. Frickers' daughter, Doris, was courting a man by the name of Stan Ward and eventually they were married in the Church across the green. There were no carriages, they walked to and from the Church which made a very pretty picture in the centre of the village. It was a very posh affair, top hats and tails and all the village turned out either as guests or just to watch. Whilst they were in the Church at the service the Church gates were tied and bride and groom had to pay to get out.

The Frickers were very well known and had a lot of friends and relations, Stan Ward's father was a retired farmer and Stan was now a commercial traveller and was a very likeable fellow. Neither family were rich, but they both liked a bit of a show and this was what was put on, on this particular day. The Frickers' house was not big enough to hold all the guests so they had a marquee on the lawn at the back of the house. The whole of Westerleigh was a buzz of excitement, not because it was a big wedding, or that it was Doris and Stan who were getting married, all the excitement was because Doris wasn't pregnant. It was said she was the first virgin bride to be married in Westerleigh church in living memory. I don't know if this was true, as there were some very old people living in the village and in their life time there must have been one or two good girls; anyway, it wasn't saying much for the ones that were making these statements. Doris and Stan had the last laugh, as they kept the secret as to whether Doris was a virgin on her wedding day or not to themselves.

The man next door to the Frickers was Sailor Button and he lived with his wife in one of the best kept houses in the village, but according to his wife he wasn't one of the best of men to live with. She often would say, "I've had to come out for a few minutes or I shall go mad, I'm too old to change." As his name implies Mr. Button had been a Sailor. He joined the Navy as a Cabin Boy and served all through his teens on sailing ships in the Royal Navy and I've heard him tell stories of his early days at sea when the last man up the rigging had so many strokes of the rope end across his legs, also that they were not allowed to wear boots or shoes on deck, one reason so as not to get it dirty, but the main reason was to reduce the wear and tear on the wooden decks. That was his early training, he stayed in the Navy and served his time, twenty one years, then he had to do his boy's service because this didn't count as active service. When he left the Navy he went into the Lighthouse service, and retired from that just before the 1914-18 war. He then went back into the Royal Navy as an instructor for the duration of the war. When that was over he then joined the Coast Guards and served in that for a few years. He had only just come home to live, retired, in his house at Westerleigh, when I went there to work.

Can you imagine what it must have been like for Mrs. Button. She had lived by herself and I think with one or two children, while her husband was away in these three services. She had lived her life as she pleased, doing as she liked, having her meals when she wanted and how she liked, she kept some hens in a pen at the bottom of the garden and they did the same as her, they were more often out than in. Then all this had to change, more or less over-night. Sailor Button came home and took charge. His life had been so different, living in a confined space most of his life, having to be tidy. Everything was labelled, a place for everything and everything in its place, everything folded and stowed away, no muddles, all spit and polish, a bell rung to get up and a bell rung again for lights out. I only heard what he was like in the house, all the pots and pans had to be kept in size order, nothing had to be seen that could be put in a cupboard or drawer – everything, including meals, getting up and going to bed had to be done to time. Mrs. Button once said, she had known him whilst he was having a meal look out of the window, notice a flower growing out of line – the time she was talking about it was a daffodil – get up from his dinner, cut a stick, tied the daffodil back in line with the others, returned to the house and continued with his meal. Everything was scrubbed clean and polished, including the big flag stones on the top of his front wall.

What I knew of Sailor Button, was seeing him about the village. On Thursday mornings at eleven o'clock he would walk from his house down to Whites General Stores to get corn for his hens. It wasn't exactly a walk, it was more like a march and the sack he used to get the corn in was folded in exact folds and put over his arm so that the two ends were the same length. Most days he visited the Old Inn for a drink before dinner, he always arrived at the same time and he always left at the same time, even if he was in conversation with anyone it was brought to an abrupt end and off he would go. In his retirement I don't know whose life was the hardest, him trying to get Mrs. Button shipshape, or her trying to get Sailor to live in a muddle.

A Mr. England was the landlord of The New Inn next door. I knew him by seeing him about the village but I never met him or spoke to him, the customers that he encouraged to use his premises weren't the kind of people I liked. They were mostly Farmers, Auctioneers, Butchers and those concerned with livestock.

In the cottage at the foot of Westerleigh Short Hill lived a very old woman who everybody called Gran, other than that I don't know anything.

Next door to her lived the family of Minsters, Jummy was a tall upright man and very smart, always wore a bowler hat even to work and he was a collier. He had a little black and white terrier dog which followed him everywhere and I mean everywhere, wherever Jummy was the dog was at his feet. Jummy was head cook and bottle washer at Westerleigh Church, he was verger, the Church care-taker, the head choir man and the right hand man of the vicar who was, as I said before, very old. But don't think that all this Church business had any influence on Jummy, apparently he had his reasons. After I'd been working in the village for a little while, someone once told me it was a case of; Jummy scratched the vicar's back and the vicar scratched Jummy's.

Jummy sang in the choir and the vestry was by the side of the west door, so there was a procession to and from the vestry and the choir stalls at each service. The boys in front, then two women, a Mrs. Martin and Polly, Jummy's wife, then the men; Jummy and another man. I can't remember his name, being the last, and between these two trotted along the little dog, the vicar bringing up the rear. When they got to the bottom of the chancel steps the procession parted, some going to the seats on one side and some going to the other. The dog would now make a dash through the pews and settle down under Jummy's seat right at the back. Jummy now had to get the vicar to his seat and have his book open on the top of his desk in the right order of service. Jummy's seat in the choir stalls was next to the vicar; as the old man took the service Jummy would prompt him from time to time, also he had a duplicate set of books in which Jummy would find the place and then pass them over to the vicar. In this way the services were kept going at a reasonable pace. If it had been left to the vicar they would have taken hours, because he kept losing his place and he also had difficulty in finding the next prayer or hymn. His sermons were written in exercise books in large letters by Dorothy. The words were written in lines across the two pages and not many lines to a page. In this way he could stand in the pulpit and with his finger on the line read the sermon to the congregation, but if his finger should slip you either heard the same line over again or there was a line missed out altogether. If you stood at the back of the Church when he was reading one of his sermons, where there was such a small amount on each page it looked as if he was idly turning the pages.

Another of Jummy's jobs was to see that after each sermon that exercise book was put at the bottom of a pile in the vestry so that each sermon would be given in strict rotation. This had been going on for so long that Jummy could recite each sermon word for word in front of the vicar; this also helped to keep the vicar's mind on the job. At weddings Jummy had very little to do other than to see that the vicar was standing on the chancel steps to receive the Bride and Groom, that he had the right book and that it was open at the wedding service, also that he had a slip of paper with both their names written very large so that he could see to read them. Jummy now stood beside the organ out of sight, but with all the details of the wedding so that if there was a slip by the vicar, he, in a loud whisper, could put him right. I forgot to mention the dog, he would be keeping Jummy company behind the organ.

Funerals were a different matter; the grave had to be dug and it was Jummy's job to see that it was done on time. There were a number of people he could call upon, but the thing was, who would be the cheapest? – or who would give him the biggest back-hander for giving them the job? If he couldn't get anybody and he had to take into account the time of year, because at certain times there was plenty of casual work and the men in the village could pick and choose, he and his two sons had to dig the grave. At the actual funeral, him being the verger, he had to head the procession from the Church gate and into the Church, saying the responses and the amens, the vicar following next saying the prayers. After the vicar came the bearers and the coffin, then the mourners. This is usual with most funerals anywhere, town or village it makes no difference, except there weren't many vergers that had a faithful dog and also a very old and unsteady vicar. Jummy was concerned that the dog shouldn't trip up the vicar and as he could not walk too far in front or the vicar wouldn't hear his responses and amens, also Jummy had to prompt the vicar from time to time with his prayers. The procession went something like this; starting at the gate Jummy would hurry about getting everybody in order including the vicar, all the time the dog would be about six inches from his heels, then the procession would start and the vicar would say the first prayer and while he was saying this, Jummy would be trying to get the dog out of the vicar's way and send him home. He then would start swearing at him for not doing as he was told, the shooing and the swearing would stop just in time to say an amen, then, when the vicar started the next prayer, the shooing and swearing would start again. This would continue right up to the Church door, then the dog would leave Jummy and dash through the pews to his place under Jummy's seat in the choir stalls.

Jummy's wife Polly cleaned the Church, washed the surplices for the members of the choir and, sang in the choir. She also looked after the old lady who lived next door and in her spare time looked after her own home, Jummy, Tom and Harry. When Jummy and Polly left off looking after the vicar and his family, Tom took over. He was quite different from his Father and Brother; where they were tall and dark, he was short and stocky like his Mother, other than that she had dark brown eyes and almost black hair, while he had brown eyes and flaming red hair. When he was in the distance it looked as if the top of his head was on fire and his temperament matched his hair. His duties at the Church started with bringing the vicar, Dorothy and the vicar's Sister to Church for the service and while Dorothy played the organ he was round at the back of the organ pumping the handle which operated the bellows to give the organ its wind. If he should be neglectful and not watch the gauge which told if there was sufficient wind in the instrument or not, you either had it overfilled and would then get loud snorts and rumblings from inside as if its tummy was out of sorts, or, it would gradually get fainter and stop altogether. There would then be sounds of vigorous pumping from the back of the organ and them back would come the music. Most of Tom's time was taken up working at the vicarage where he was completely in charge, looking after the pony, doing the gardening, acting as the vicar's valet, was the general do-all of everything in the house including being Dorothy's right hand man. The only thing he didn't do officially was the cooking; they had a young woman who did this.

When motor cars became more popular and Dorothy thought that they should have one, Tom was taught to drive and he then became the Chauffeur. Harry, the other son, did not concern himself with the vicarage at all, with the Church only a little, he sang in the choir and his only other activities in this field was to be one of the bell ringers and to wind the clock after the morning service on Sunday mornings. This had to be done after the service so as not to be winding the clock in case anyone should start ringing the bells. It was a job that required more strength than skill and it entailed going up the steps inside the tower, locking the door of the belfry on the way, then going on up and entering the chamber where all the bells were hung. There were six or eight of these, I can't remember which, and they were hung very close together only having enough room for them to swing when they were pulled over by the bell ringers below. The clock was on the opposite wall from the door and to get across to the clock you had to walk along a very narrow plank or cat walk. Once over there you stood on a small platform with a hand rail. This was the only protection you had from the bells if anyone should have started to ring them. This was why the job had to be done after service. Below the clock was a narrow cavity reaching down past the bell chamber and the belfry. In this cavity swung the pendulum and also hung the weights for making the clock go, and also strike. These weights were very heavy and hung on wire ropes, it was these that Harry had to wind up with a handle like a windlass.

Harry was a Blacksmith and had served his apprenticeship at the forge in the village, paid for by an endowment from the Church. This endowment wasn't an annual thing, it was only given when the fund had collected enough interest and then it could be used either to send a boy or girl to a Grammer School or to apprentice them. These lucky children were few and far between and they also had to be the right age at the right time. After I had been working at Westerleigh for a little while, Harry and I became quite good friends.

On up the hill lived Mr. and Mrs. Barren. Mr. Barren was a very sick man, all the time I worked in the village he was ill most of the time, he had been in the army and had caught some tropical disease from which he had never really recovered and I would think that earlier in his life he had had Small Pox bcause his face and hands were very deeply pitted. He spent most of his time either in bed or sitting in a very easy chair by the window and his main hobby – relaxation, interest, call it what you like – was studying horse racing and trying to pick the winners. His little slips of paper recording the horses' names, would come down to the garage most mornings to be phoned through to his bookmaker. Mrs. Barren was a very good looking woman and I would imagine, much younger than her husband, their son worked at Douglas Motor Engineers factory at Kingswood, apprenticed to be a Miller and Turner.

Going back to the three cornered green and along to the houses opposite Tolmans and Frickers, there lived a young man by the name of Jake Cray. He was a few years older than me and worked at Chipping Sodbury Gas Works attending the retorts. This was shovelling coal into the Gas ovens to make the Gas and to come out Coke, so you can tell having to do this kind of work he was very strong, but it wasn't his strength that I'm concerned about in this story. It was his passion for guns, any kind of gun, muzzle loaders, cartridge firing single barrel, double barrelled or rifles, anything that went 'BANG'. It didn't even have to go bang, he was also quite happy with an air gun. At the Gas Works he worked shift work, six in the morning until two o'clock in the afternoon, or, two in the afternoon until ten o'clock at night. Other than his work and playing football on Saturday afternoons when it was his

Saturday off, his relaxation from shovelling tons of coal, was to sit in his living room with the window up, have a row of tins on the wall at the bottom of the garden and with one of his guns shoot them off the top of the wall. Cartridges were expensive, so for this recreation he would use his muzzle loading gun, the cost then was the gun powder, the other ammunition was anything that would go down the barrel and also depended on what he was going to shoot at. For instance, shooting at the tins he used marbles, either ones he bought or some he made from clay and fired in the retorts at work. If he was going out to shoot rabbits or birds and he could afford shot he used it, if on the other hand he was broke and this was a very natural state for him to be in, he would use small nails or bits of wire cut up small with a pair of tin snips or even better still cut up bits of lead.

The villagers didn't like Jake's pastime and tried to persuade him to give it up. These sessions of gun firing kept the village awake, the loud bangs echoed through the village street and could be heard for miles around, it was no good even to go in your house and shut the door. The bangs could still be heard. The worst part was the uncertainty of when the bang would come, or was that the last. It wasn't like an engine's exhaust, even and regular, or the tramping of feet which came past and then went on into the distance. There would be a terrific bang and everybody would jump. They'd say "That's Jake started again," they would also grumble a bit. Minutes would pass, then there would be another bang, you may not get any more that day, or, it could keep on for an hour or two and this was what upset the village.

Then one day there was a tremendous bang; it echoed up and down the village street and round and round the Church tower. People came out to see what on earth it was, thinking it couldn't possibly be Jake's gun – but it was. He had been experimenting with his muzzle loader by sawing off the barrel about half way down, he then put gun powder and chewed up paper down the barrel and rammed it in tight. On top of this he had put nails, broken glass, and anything else he could lay his hands on and rammed this with more paper into the barrel, he then went out into the garden and fired the thing 'OFF'. The barrel split, Jake's face was blackened and pitted by the smoke and explosion and the next door neighbour's cat was never seen again. The neighbour went straight off to Chipping Sodbury and reported Jake to the Police accusing him of being a danger to the community and also of killing her cat. The Police came, had a chat with Jake, and that was the end of Jake's gun practice from the comfort of his own living room.

At the end of the houses where Jake lived was the Forge, Alex Trilby was the blacksmith and farrier and I suppose, because of his business, he would be about the best known man in the village. He shod all the horses for miles around and repaired most of the farm implements. I don't know if he carried on the business from his Father but he had been there many years. When I first knew him he was then past middle age and had taught Harry Minster the trade; apparently he had turned him into a first-class blacksmith but according to Harry, he was a very hard tutor because he had a rather short temper as well. Life for Harry wasn't very pleasant while he was serving his apprenticeship and as soon as he was 'out of his time', he left, and went to work at the Iron Works at Chipping Sodbury. Harry's job first thing in the morning, and this was at seven o'clock, was to open the Forge doors and then with the hammer strike about a dozen blows on the anvil. This would make a ringing sound and then Alex would know that Harry was there and about to light the fire and clean up the workshop, or any other job that Alex had given him to do the night before. Not only did this ringing of the anvil tell Alex he was there, it also let him know it was time for him to get up, he would then have his breakfast and go out into the forge by about eight o'clock, so, if Harry was late, Alex was late and then woe-betide Harry for the rest of the day.

There was another nasty habit Alex had with his Appentices. If he asked for a tool and they didn't give him the right one or gave it to him the wrong way round, he would then throw it at them, they had to jump out of the way, dodge quickly behind anything that was handy and then try again. With all his quick temper and the fact that he liked his drop of ale or cider, he was a first-class blacksmith and his work was looked upon as of the very highest standard. If Alex couldn't make it out of iron, it couldn't be made. I didn't see these articles, because his daughter was about thirty five to forty when I knew them but I was told, and knowing Alex I have no doubt that it was true. When she was about to be born Alex made a rocking cradle out of wrought iron, then, when she was old enough, he made her a wrought iron high chair, the only thing that wasn't iron was the seat and this was a piece of Elm three quarters of an inch thick. It was too heavy for Mrs. Trilby to move about so he made, and put on, some iron wheels. The last thing he made out of iron for his darling daughter – who was the apple of his eye – was a bedstead, a very ornate wrought iron affair, all scrolls and leaves twisting and twining one within the other, but this was all before my time. The Alex Trilby I knew, was an older man, the daughter was married and there were no apprentices at the Forge; he now worked on his own and the main work was the farrier side of the business. In his younger days I think he must have been either ginger or had sandy coloured hair, but now it was grey, his eyebrows were very thick and bushy but because of his work in the smoke and the burning horn of horses hooves when fitting their shoes, they were dark brown. He had a moustache which was straggly and unkempt, burnt in the centre where his cigarette hung while he worked. He wore an Oxford shirt and corduroy trousers and on top of these trousers he wore a leather apron with a slit in the centre. When he was out in the village walking about, one corner of his apron was tucked in the top of his trousers.

Working at the garage I had a good view of the Old Inn, and this was when I would see Alex; he visited this establishment many times during a day. The first time I'd seen him coming for his refreshments I thought there was something wrong, this chap came round the corner just above the garage in a hurry, walking two steps and running one. I found out later that when he was in a great hurry he would run two and walk two, or, run two and walk one. He entered the Old Inn, was in there a few minutes and was out and on his way back up the road again. In the space of two or three hours he did this two or three times. When I enquired what was going on I was told that Alex was shoeing a horse.

The procedure for him to shoe a horse was to remove the old shoes, nip down to the Old Inn for a quick one, go back and make the new shoes and then nip down again, fit and fix the front shoes and have another drink of ale or cider, according to the time of year. Beer in the winter and cider in the summer. After the horse's back shoes were on and they had left the Forge he came down again, but this time not so fast. He was a good customer at the Old Inn, he was such a good customer that the doors were never closed on him, if it wasn't opening time or if the Pub was closed in the afternoon, he went through the stable yard to the back door and revived himself there.

A funny story about Alex went round the village while I was there. One day, when he was shoeing a horse, Alex wasn't feeling too well, it appears that he had a pain in his back, a stiff back, or that he just didn't feel too good. When shoeing a horse's front feet there is a metal stand that farriers use to put the horse's foot upon when he is filing off the horn around the new shoe, but when he is doing the same thing to the hind feet he has to get the horse's leg between his legs and hold the hoof on his knee. This is why farriers have a slit up the centre of their aprons. Horses can stand on three legs quite well and not even put any weight at all on the leg that is held in this way, but on this particular day, the horse must have got bored waiting to have his new shoes put on and also waiting whilst Alex went to the Old Inn so while he was holding the horse's leg in this way and filing away at his hoof, the horse changed his position and put his weight down on Alex's knee. Alex got out from under the horse in a terrible temper and started to hammer the horse with the file he had been using, saying as he did so, "What did you do that for? You knew bloody well that I had a bad back." Who told the horse, or how the horse was supposed to know, the people who were in the Forge at the time didn't know either, but they said it seemed that Alex put a great deal of energy into giving the horse a good hiding for anyone with a bad back.

The population of Westerleigh was made up of farm workers, miners and railway workers. The London Midland and Scottish railway ran through the village going from Bristol to the North. On this line there was a goods yard and Station at Yate, there was also the big Westerleigh sidings at the bottom of Kidney Hill and the mineral line from the sidings to Coalpit Heath Colliery. Just outside the village, and crossing over the Midland line, was the Great Western Railway from London to Bristol and Penzance, with Coalpit Heath Station and goods yard on one side of the village and Sodbury tunnel on the other. Both of these had to be looked after, most of the men that worked on these railways were permanent maintenance labourers. The miners either worked at Coalpit Heath or Parkfield Collieries and the farm workers were many because the village was surrounded by farms.

Ted's Father lived with them amd when I started work there he was an old man, he had been retired from the mines for years. He'd been a collier all his life and Ted, his only son, had followed in his footsteps for a while and had terrible marks on his body to prove that he knew what mining was all about. He had quite a number of blue scars but the worst of all was the marks of what was called, the tugger chain. This chain went around the waist and then through the legs to be fastened to some trucks of coal which you then pulled crawling on your hands and knees because the roof of the workings were not high enough to walk upright. Perspiration, coal dust, and the weight of the loaded trucks caused the chain to chafe and cut into your flesh. When these wounds healed, having the coal dust still in them, the pattern it made was a perfect chain around your waist, this was what Ted had and it was so perfect it could have been tattooed by an artist. Ted and Anne, his first wife, were teetotalers. Ted said his Father had drunk enough for both of them and if what the old man had drunk could be put in one pond, there would be enough to float a battleship. When I knew them, he couldn't afford very much to spend on beer as he only had his pension, Ted said he would see that he had a roof over his head and food to put in his belly, but that he wouldn't give him a penny to spend on drink. The old man would stand at the gate at the side of the house and look across the road very wistfully at the people drinking in the Old Inn and if any should come out and walk a bit unsteady or sway about, he would give a little resentful laugh and say, "I suppose he reckons he's drunk? Well, I think a man is drunk when he's lying on the grass holding on as tight as he can for fear of falling off."

The 1914-1918 war had been over for something like seven or eight years and we were in the middle of the roaring twenties. Roaring was about right, the newspapers reported all-night parties of the wealthy, coming out of the Debutants and young girls and men coming home in the early morning when the milk was being delivered. Jazz bands were all the rage, strict tempo ballroom dancing was on the way out. The Charleston was born and the more steps of your own you could put in, the better. Another section of the people who were roaring were the middle classes, also the upper middle classes. Before the war domestic servants were easy and cheap to get and now they could not understand why girls would not work for the pittance they offered, so they 'roared' that girls shouldn't be allowed to work in offices and factories. But the biggest roar of all came from the workers, the manual workers as distinct from some of the other workers who called themselves 'upper and middle' class. In my view, there are only two classes – the rich who have no need to work to survive, and the remainder of humanity who, unless they work, they die. These workers had been told, that if they went to fight in the war that was to end all wars, the country would be proud of them and they would never be forgotten; they would come back to a land fit for heroes to live in; also, anybody who wanted, could have an acre and a cow. When were these things going to happen? Wages were low and it was proposed to reduce the miners' wages even lower.

The garage where I worked was the meeting place for most of the men in the village and as they were all miners, railwaymen and farm-workers, they were low paid. It was in the garage that they aired their grievances one with another.

Then came the General Strike and Ted immediately shut the garage doors and locked the petrol pump; the only business that was carried on at the garage was supplying paraffin oil and doing any repairs to bicycles that were needed by the strikers and their families. All this was done 'on credit' and in some cases, for free. Ted's father had been a miner all his working life, and Ted, all his early days and into middle age, so although he was now self-employed, he knew what working down a coal mine was like and he had great sympathy with the strikers. I can't remember much about the strike other than the garage was full of men all the time, and the talk was about, 'how long would it last?', 'could they last out longer than the Bosses?' Another thing was, Ted was out by the petrol pump having heated arguments with people who wanted petrol and he wouldn't sell it to them. Some of these people had been regular customers, but they drove away shouting they would never buy any petrol from him in future.

MY CHILDHOOD IN KINGSWOOD BY MARIE ROSSITER

I was a young girl in the 1920's. I lived in Soundwell Road, Kingswood, went to Two Mile Hill day school and Zion Sunday School.

Sunday School was a must for every child in those days. I didn't much care for it so I went for a walk instead sometimes, but felt so wicked after that this rarely happened.

Those mosaic days of magic and fun, scraps and tears, reading and dreaming. I read endlessly and anywhere – in the apple tree in the garden in summer, by a roaring fire in the old black-leaded grate in the winter, by the light of an old oil lamp set in the centre of the kitchen table, which was covered with a crimson damask cloth, or sometimes in the cupboard under the stairs by the light of a torch. This cupboard was always warm as it was at the back of the neighbour's fire.

I was an only child, living with my mother and grandparents in a small terraced house. My grandfather made boots for Pratt's factory in his workshop at the back of the house. He had a little stove there kept alight in winter by shrid or leather off-cuts. My mother was a dressmaker.

The wash house with the boiler was outside, as was the lavatory, Gran used to fill the boiler with water from the cistern which was outside the back door, as was the only tap we had. She used to light a fire under the boiler every Monday to boil the 'whites'. The rest of the washing was done by hand in the wash tub.

We used to boil our Christmas puddings in the boiler, 12 hours at least. It used to be lovely sitting by the fire with the spicy aroma filling the wash house.

At the end of the street at the back of our house were fields that sloped down to Charlton Road. There were a few cottages in these fields where the owners kept pigs. The hedges were full of May Blossom in spring, and in high summer the hay was cut and we played among it.

The magic moments came in the evening when the grown-ups, their day's work done, leaned on the garden gates and gossiped while the children played whip-top or pottle, skipping or higher and higher with the rope, ran up the street with our hoops. There always seemed to be a rosy red glow over the roofs and up as far as Cossham Hospital.

On winter nights we children all gathered round the only street lamp. This was lit by a lamplighter. It had a horizontal bar sticking out from the top and a child would climb the post and hang on it a plaited rope to

Marie Rossiter

make a swing. This rope came from the greengrocer's wooden crates.

Christmas time was sheer delight. A fire was lit in the front room and in the front of this I would sit and eat and read all day long. I read comics; 'The Rainbow', 'Tiger Tim' or 'Playbox' and I always had an Annual. Later my favourite reading became the 'William' books. After tea the grown-ups would sit around the fire, put a row of coloured candles all along the mantelshelf and have serious discussions on money problems. The room had previously been decorated by my mother and I with paper chains which took hours to make.

All through the year we ate by the kitchen fire. The joint was roasted on a spit and had to be turned often. The vegetables were boiled on the fire in two large black saucepans. Gravy was the fat which fell from the joint into the tin underneath it. In the small oven by the side of the fire a rice pudding was cooked. My favourite tea was a buttered crust and a banana.

Every Friday night we had a bath in the tub in front of the fire. I was bathed first and sent straight to bed.

At school we had to sit up straight with our hands behind our backs. The teachers were very strict and we youngsters were terrified of them though we used to whisper and giggle now and again. Some little girls came from a 'home' in Charlton Road. They were distinctive in their dress and always wore spotless white aprons. At Christmas the Hall was decorated and a magician came to entertain us, the whole school sitting cross-legged on the floor.

On Empire Day children from the schools in Bristol were picked to give a display at Aston Gate. We usually formed a Union Jack and felt very proud of our empire. At Whitsun all the Sunday School pupils in Kingswood formed a procession with bands and banners and marched to the Kingsway and back along the main road to the fields which are now Kingswood Park.

The children from Zion Chapel, which I attended, marched back to Soundwell Road, then along it to the large house and gardens belonging to G.B. Britton, the boot and shoe manufacturer who was once Lord Mayor of Bristol. There we played in the spacious gardens until we were sent home to dinner at twelve o'clock. The afternoon fell rather flat after that until three thirty when we went back to Sunday School to tea.

During the evening we had races and games on some fields in Made-For-Ever which are now built on.

At some time in the summer there used to be swings and roundabouts on the corner of Soundwell Road behind the shops where there was some waste land.

Life was not all rosy in those far-off days. There was the tragedy of the boy who was killed by a charabanc in Kennard Road, and there were a few children whose parents were too poor to afford to buy them shoes, so they had to have free ones at school. I can remember a girl fainting because she had no food before coming to school, and it was rumoured that one boy had to stay in bed while his only set of clothes were washed.

When I was eleven I won the Scholarship and went to St.George Secondary School, but that is another story.

Marie Rossiter (seated) and friend at Redcliffe Bay, 1930

TIMES REMEMBERED BY EDNA RICH

As one grows older past years, like an old friend, nostalgically cry out for remembrance. It was in the back streets of Bedminster where my childhood was spent. A time of economic and social injustice, poverty was a way of life, courage and endurance the only antidote to its ills. The people who lived during this period are now a dying race, but from these dire circumstances qualities and virtues evolved and a social consciousness that inspired in a determined way politicans and people of good will to bring about social reform and economic justice.

The milk of human kindness was our "Welfare State", sharing with others what we could ill afford to spare in food or clothing. In sickness one could not afford a doctor, hospitals and dentists symbols of fear and pain. As a child I sensed this in the furtive tones of adults as they discussed the medical ills and cares of the day. Also observed mothers carrying crying children through the streets after the obvious signs of tonsil or adenoid operation. There was the little black van that took one's playmates away, and after a long absence told they had gone to live in the country. The blind, disabled and mentally retarded were kept indoors and were very rarely seen. If one caught a glimpse of them and in greeting called they would hurriedly turn away.

The sick and dying here were succoured with neighbourly care and pain relieved with grandparents' secret formulas or herbs and cheap ointments. The cure? A lot of hope and faith! Babies were brought into the world by a capable but often unqualified nurse at times surrounded by seven or eight children of the same family, who could hardly welcome another mouth to feed.

Most of the homes were overcrowded. The grandparents treated with respect, sharing the homes of their children. Other elderly folk with no family to care for them sometimes occupied a small room; the rent one shilling a week, supplementing the poverty of another family, for the elderly and the children were expected to run errands and do odd jobs voluntarily, never to expect the odd farthing or halfpence one at times received from younger adults for a service of this kind. The church played a prominent part in one's welfare with very small monetary gifts, second-hand clothing and the opportunity to discuss one's problems and fears, giving one hope and sustenance.

There was much unemployment in the street. The local iron foundry 'Capper-Pass' and the 'Tannery' employed a few men. This involved night work, the noise at night often disturbed one, the smell from the 'Tannery' offensive, working conditions unhealthy, laborious and underpaid.

The few allotments available gave some of the men a little dignity. Flowers and vegetables were grown and at times shared with the many needy families. Unemployment benefit was a pittance and insufficient to feed the many large families. To appeal in desperation to the "Parish" for additional help meant perhaps one shilling or a loaf of bread and loss of one's pride. If one could afford to have the occasional luxury of meat it would mean purchasing as the butcher's closed, late Saturday night, in Bedminster. At a confectioners stale cakes, which meant standing in a queue in the early hours of the morning and often when one reached the counter they would be sold out. Sometimes a welcome sound would penetrate the street; a fruiterer's cry: "Pinky fruit!" He would dispose very cheaply of all his damaged fruit. The aprons of mothers held out would be full, the children's pockets too, contributing much to the only vitamin C that we could obtain.

There was an unemployed amateur shoe repairer if one could afford the shoe leather. But more often than not the only alternative was the insertion of cut cardboard to cover the offending hole in a desperate attempt to obtain protection from the inclement weather.

Fortunately there was refuge for the unemployed in the only elevated premise in the street, the 'Windsor Castle', a public house. There they could retreat and over a cheap pint of beer stay for a while commiserating and sharing with other men the problems of living.

The women, overworked and harrassed, were resourceful. They would clean public toilets, offices, anything to obtain a little more money. For a pittance a family's laundry would be laundered in a Victorian, meticulous way, scrubbed, blued, starched and ironed. If mangled (a strenuous chore!) instead of ironed, a smaller rate of payment. Their customers were usually the more prosperous from another district. Also there were seamstresses, rejects of the industrial machine age, their handiwork, particularly the crochet, was beautifully and artistically made. From adults' worn clothing they would produce useful attire for the younger children, woollen knitted garments would be laboriously unpicked then re-knitted into socks, mittens, gloves, scarves, hats. Nothing was wasted or thrown away that could be used.

There was pride too! The local pawnshop an added humiliation to one's poverty. To alleviate some there was a pawnshop runner. For two pence she would take and fetch a bundle, which usually consisted of blankets, clothing, treasured wedding ring or keepsake fully aware, and sadly this often happened, these possessions would never be returned if the time for repayment and collection of goods expired on a specified date. The pawnshop runner was my literary benefactoress, who for six pence a week did early morning cleaning in a bookshop. She developed my literary taste and I am indebted to her for the many books she gave me, mostly children's english classics, that gave me hours of adventure and delight, alienating me from the deprivations of my environment. Conscious of her generosity and fostered by a widow my services as pawnshop runner were easily obtained to fulfill her duties, fetching the bundles when she fell ill.

I was a proud sensitive child deeply conscious of the social stigma of pawnshops. I made my services conditional, a large sheet of brown paper and string to be provided to enable the bundle to be given an air of respectability it most certainly deserved. Always it was a secret

mission! I avoided everyone! As I approached the pawnbroker's shop, the three gold balls would gleam like a 'royal ensign'. Its symbolism to me represented an evil three-eyed monster, mercilessly trading off the backs of the poor, denigrating also my pride.

One entered a long dark narrow passage that led into a large back room; behind a very high protective counter stood the pawnbroker ably assisted by two assistants who obviously enjoyed their power. A ticket to identify the bundle would be tendered and the goods thrown, usually ending on the floor. Giving the bundle the prescribed treatment a trembling heart would accompany me to the door keeping well back into the passage. I would wait anxiously for a passing tram car to enable me to emerge unseen by the people across the road. It was the local pastor who did see me, parcel clasped to my breast, beautifully wrapped. His friendly curiosity made me assert myself and assured him with an air of affluence that I had just collected a new costume for my foster mother from a reputable tailors' shop in Bedminster. Revealing the incident to her when I arrived home, her hands and voice were raised in consternation, fearing that her occasional small monetary gift from the chapel, also the loan of a winter blanket, would be withdrawn. Of course not! He was an intuitive and compassionate man.

Recreation for the children was performed in the street or local park, the first "Ragged School" situated in Stillhouse Lane opened its doors once a week to deprived children. Games and folks songs were performed and encouraged with the help of voluntary workers. On special occasions I was allowed to produce a pantomime 'Cinderella'. The cast I chose from the children in the street where I lived, the costumes we excitedly made from coloured crepe paper, dances imaginatively improvised to the amusement and delight of the audience.

The local picture house was an added attraction, admission two pence, a fortune! And impossible to obtain from one's parents, but there was the initiative of poverty! The possibility of eight jam jars from benevolent neighbours, if one did them a service. The rag and bone merchant would give one farthing each for them if perfect. On tenterhooks, the testing would begin, dull tones often resounded on an eager ear, which would mean the eligibility of a paper windmill attached to a wooden stick in lieu of perhaps three perfects jars. The only consolation; it exhausted one's disappointment, it required running at a very vigorous pace to operate same.

Everyone in the street was acquainted with everyone, with their vices and their virtues, their grandparents, aunts, cousins, the entire lineage and the skeletons in the cupboard! There was a caring, closeness, front doors always opened, problems shared and advised. There were the personalities and characters that I knew, uninhibited by press, radio and television, their natural talents suppressed by lack of money and opportunity, would provide much entertainment and laughter. Comfort, too! – in the knowledge that besides poverty, there was also happiness. Something money cannot buy.

Edna Rich's mother – shortly before her death as a result of a backstreet abortion in 1912

Sometimes the monotony of life would be brightened by a wedding, the atmosphere of preparation shared by all; hats, shoes, clothing, for relatives and guests readily loaned, cash to make the event possible borrowed. The comings and goings of people, the secrecy made one realise that somehow, somewhere all that was necessary to celebrate would be obtained. The celebration in the evening of relatives and guests would be very noisy, raised inebriated conversation, laughter and outbursts of singing. The children in the street, unaccustomed to such revelry would cluster around the door of the house, their faces animated by the sounds, would watch the street come to life, neighbours would sit on their front doorsteps long after dusk, eager to participate and capture the all too brief sounds of happiness that they knew tomorrow, with all its problems, would disperse, bringing everyone back to reality.

The street vendors provided much entertainment, selling or bartering their wares, most of them Dickensian in character and dress. There was the Knife and Scissor Grinder who would arrive on a three-wheeled bicycle servicing, for a small sum of money, all that required attention.

A dignified Umbrellaman garbed in a very worn ancestoral frock-tailed jacket and top hat over his shoulder. He would carry a large canvas bag that contained umbrellas, ivory and bone-handles peeped out, that had obviously known better days. Also black practical ones according to one's need. He would sell, repair, or exchange. The repairs expertly serviced by him on the pavement. Thre was the Fly Catcher Man, also frock-tailed jacket and top hat, the fly paper elegantly draped over his hat and clothing, its poor victims desperately trying to escape, gave him a would-be air of honoury distinction, amid much laughter and ridicule he would appeal to reluctant purchasers to witness the truths of his cries.

The Welsh Cockle Woman, another colourful personality clothed in Welsh costume complete with shawl that enhanced her buxom figure, and hardy face. On her head she wore a black Welsh hat that supported a tub of fresh cockles. In operatic tone, her passionate cries for customers would pervade the street tantalisingly falling on the ears of hungry people who would have loved to indulge, but through penury were deprived. Her presence fascinated the children. Mischievously we would follow her mimicking her competitively, taking a mean advantage of her preoccupation with the balance of her tub of cockles, making it impossible for her to retaliate.

A welcome figure, the lamplighter, and with nothing to pay! He would come as regular as a clock, morning and evening to service the street lamps, a short man with a gentle demeanour. Over his shoulder he would carry a long pole to light the lamps that would create a bright warm comforting glow across the street and into one's room, compensating and alleviating at times the lack and warmth of a fireless grate.

Few people possessed musical instruments in the street, a comb perhaps covered with fine paper produced musical sounds, mouth organ or an inherited accordian. My aptitude for music encouraged me to use as a piano my foster mother's old sewing machine. There my tiny

Edna (left) and brother William Henry and sister Ethel May

fingers would play imaginary rapturous sounds. Hymns too would be played from a treasured "Sankey's" hymn book, my foster mother joining me always in the singing of her favourite hymn "Tell Me The Old Old Story".

The greatest influence on my formative years was the teachings of Philip Street Baptist Chapel. The administrators were comfortably well-off financially, some Bedminster trademens, they and their families were the leaders of the Band of Hope. To become a member one always made a promise and declaration at each meeting, "I promise with God's help, to abstain from all intoxicating liquor." Also 'Christian Endeavour' and others, Sunday School teachers, they were dedicated Christians of the Baptist faith. They knew our families, our problems, guided and helped where they could. We liked their good manners, taste, and mode of dress. At times an invitation to their homes was much enjoyed.

Music was encouraged and played a large part in the life of the Chapel. Hymn singing was joyous and rendering of scriptures fell like poetry on my ears. This was further influenced by a Mr. George Lewis, Superintendant of the Chapel, an accomplished lover of music, and tutor of choral celebration, especially the yearly 'Anniversary Sunday'. This was a great challenge for all Sunday School scholars. For many weeks before the event we all met for rehearsal and under his guidance rigorously trained for perfection, to be worthy of the anthems and choral oratorio from well known composers. On that very special day people came from all over the district, the Chapel packed, chairs in the aisles would be placed, steps leading to the pastor's pulpit occupied. The children were helped and encouraged to wear white, however cheap the material. White sandals, ribbons for the girls' hair. The fragrance from the abundant flowers that decorated the chapel brought from people's back gardens and allotments, mingled with the reverence of the occasion. A brief anticipatory silence before the triumphant chords of the organist's introduction reverberated throughout the chapel. The scholars in the gallery would rise and render to perfection the worthy efforts of Mr. George Lewis.

Another special event was the annual Sunday School outing to Weston-Super-Mare. The parents usually contributed one penny each week during the year for rail fare and a little to spend. Early with great enthusiasm a collection of mothers and children would set off to enjoy the day. Reaching the Esplanade one instinctively felt the magic of this strange new sphere in contrast to the poverty of streets we had left behind. Invitingly it held out its arms, the vast rolling sea, golden sands, sweet fresh salted air, and canopied blue skies intimated; "this too belongs to you! It's your world to be enjoyed!" And we did. We explored the pier, revelled on the beach, paddled with the mothers in the sea, avoided the cruelty of 'Punch and Judy', one ice cream and ride on a donkey or pony cart. The mothers' treat; a plate of Weston cockles, and in the latter part of the day a ride in a horse drawn carriage to see the retired donkeys in a field at Uphill. With persuasion the driver would agree to take four mothers and five children for ninepence on condition that the children at intervals would get out and run behind to alleviate the weight off the horse. This we did and enjoyed. As we cantered along an aura of royal grandeur would possess the mothers, their heads condescendingly would bow from side to side of their carriage, their work-worn hands with acquired grace would acknowledge the imaginary cheering crowds. There was laughter and sentimental songs, it made their day and was their day too!

Before returning home the last meagre refreshment, a back street public house with a garden would be found – for the mothers one half pint of beer, the children would share lemonade and twopennyworth of chips between them, with strict instructions to keep a watchful eye for the pastor or any member of the chapel who might pass by.

HOW I LOST MY FIRST JOB
BY DANNY PRICE

He walked towards the college playing fields to take up his first job since leaving school as an apprentice carpenter. In the first twelve months or so he would perform the duties of tea boy and fetching errands for the craftsmen as was customary in the building trade.

He could see the partly constructed pavilion at the edge of the cricket pitch. He looked curiously at the open windows of the Elizabethan buildings flanking the quadrangle from which he could hear the sound of boyish voices singing a stirring tune which appeared to be the school anthem.

It seemed as though he had been walking through another world since the uniformed porter had admitted him at a wicket gate, alongside a large archway entrance to the college grounds. The grass on the playing fields contrasting startling verdant green to the grey buff stone of the building. Both had stood the test of time, the stone constructed building welded together by the boy's craftmen-ancestors and the cricket pitches cut, mowed and rolled by artists for their betters to play on.

He listened again to the noise emitted by five hundred boys, so resounding, so dominating, so royal. A song which had been sung every school day for two hundred years. He thought of the opening day hymn of his late lamented elementary school at St. Philips, which he had recently left, aged 14. A spirit of impish fun combined with curiosity entered his head and he decided to peep through one of the open windows. He stood transfixed by what he saw.

There in a large hall with huge portraits hung around the walls of what he took to be distinguished 'old boys', were standing five hundred boys loudly and boisterously singing in martial strains the school hymn. At the far end facing him was a platform and a huge wurlitzer organ was being energetically played by one of the masters. The Head, garbed in mortarboard and gown stood at the front of the platform and immediately behind him, similarly garbed, was what the boy took to be forty form-masters. The five hundred boys in the serried ranks were all dressed in the same uniform of stiff starched collars, Eton jacket and pin-striped trousers.

The boy pondered. There before him stood the ranks of future privilege and power. How many past generations had stood there, dressed in the same uniform and singing the same song? These were the heirs of those who had represented the bastions of rule for 250 years in India, Africa and other parts of the British Empire. He contrasted all he had seen, that early morning, with that of his own elementary school of St. Philips.

His school with three others catered for the children born in a valley south of Old Market Street. When Blake wrote of those 'dark satanic mills' he aptly described St. Philips, a place with a saintly name but deathly surroundings. It was six square miles of manure works, gas works, corporation refuse tips, knackers yards, rag and bone works and soap works. It also included a firm making sausages and pork pies and a factory making custard. It was a residential district for 50,000 rats, 100,000 bugs, and in the summer a resort for a million flies attracted there by the Feeder Canal into which spewed all the industrial waste of industry and also the River Avon, a tidal river flowing to and fro like a huge lavatory flush, taking away all the human waste which was deposited on the mud banks until the tide would roll back to collect more effluent for transmission into the sea adjacent to the seaside resorts of Clevedon and Weston Super Mare. Besides the extensive rodent and vermin population there also lived ten thousand humans; men, women and children.

The three elementary schools were of the same type and the boy could not remember or did he ever hear of any child ever advancing to university or college? His school, like the college, catered for the same number of pupils; some five hundred, but there the similarity ended. Instead of a building set within acres of pleasant green parklands and playing fields, it was located in a back street with a corporation tip on one side and a railway marshalling yard on the other. The playground being a small area of cracked tarmac. Every day the opening service would take place with Old Tomlin, the Head, conducting with his cane, which he used as a baton and also as a weapon of offence against any unfortunate child seen picking his nose or otherwise transgressing the rules. The children had no uniforms and were wearing cut-me-downs handed down from the eldest to the youngest. The boy remembered very vividly how on many occasions he had to keep pressing a patch back into the arse of his pants and how many of the children's footwear were heavy boots provided by the Lord Mayor's Christmas fund. The hymn they sang to music given out by an old out of tune piano was appropriate for the children of his school, where education was provided only sufficient enough to guarantee a supply of wage labour for the very people the boy was staring at now, a servile hymn with words "the rich man in his castle, the poor man at his gate, God made them poor and lowly, he made them rich and great."

All this passed through the boy's mind and he was so preoccupied that he forgot his exposure to those inside. One of the boys in the back row happened to look around and spot him. He nudged the boy next to him. There was a titter, whereupon the next row looked round. This was repeated right throughout the ranks with all five hundred completely ignoring the music, their heads turned the other way laughing uproariously at a boy's face (a stranger) with a man's cap and a muffler tied around his neck.

The organist stopped playing, puzzled. The Headmaster, being extremely short-sighted had not seen the boy at the window and his attention was drawn by one of the masters to this rare phenomenon of a grubby urchin, a usurper trespassing in their inner sanctum. He strode borough the centre of the laughing school to the back of the hall, stopped, looked up at the object staring at him and in his most authoritative voice said: "Go away, you have no right to be here."

The boy did not waiver. He stood there, his brow wrinkled with thought. He pictured his Dad who had fought and been wounded in the trenches and was now on the Means Test, his mother who because of constant worry of how to manage was old before her time, and of all those countless children of St. Philips who had never had a chance. He deliberately looked at the awesome figure in front of him and loudly, firmly and slowly said:

"PISS OFF."

That's how I lost my first job.

THE LEARNER
BY MARJORIE GROVE

November of the year 1929 it was. Winter gripped the land, and the night had been bitterly cold. The pale morning light groped its way through the fog, which hung like a pall over the little mill town. Down the street trudged the 'knocker up', a stout old man, raggy mittens covering blue sausage like fingers. Grasping a long wooden pole, wire atop, he rapped on each bedroom window in turn, along the row of grey slated cottages. One by one the gas mantles flickered on, thrusting pale shafts of yellow light into the gloom outside. The mill folk were stirring once again, preparing for another day's slog in the weaving sheds.

It was customary for both parents to work, so poor little babies were shuffled round to the nearest child minders very early in the morning, except Sundays of course. Elder children were used to getting themselves off to school, usually after a meagre breakfast of bread and dripping and cocoa.

At number seven lived the Sugden family, a widowed mother and her three growing children. Lottie (named after some obscure film star) was the eldest. Scarcely fourteen years old, she had been obliged these last few months to go 'learning' in the big black Mill on the edge of town. She was petrified of the place and became more and more reluctant each day to enter the evil smelling, rat infested pandemonium. The hideous clackety clack of the looms was so terrific that the weavers could only communicate by lip reading and gesticulation, at which they were adept. Most of them became at least partially deaf after a few years in the industry.

Lottie awoke with a start, with the rap rap on the window. Lifting a corner of the lace curtain, she could see by the light of the street lamp, the rain slanting down. Sinking back onto the warm, hard palliasse, she was roused by a shrill "cum on tha lazy little bitch, tha'll be getting t'sack before long". Mam it was. Flinging back the bright patchwork quilt and noting that the second bed was empty, she scrambled onto the cold oil cloth, hurriedly dressed, and stumbled down the steep staircase to the room below. Huddled on the sofa, in underpants and petticoat respectively, were her younger brother and sister. No money for nightclothes in this household! Mam, a thin, harassed inquisitive looking woman, a riot of auburn hair in disarray about her shoulders, stood pouring hot water from a hissing kettle into four mugs, a spoonful of cocoa and sugar in each. Lottie crossed the room and warmed her outstretched hands by the glowing fire. The room was sparsely furnished, a home-made rag rug by the hearth, a curved backed horsehair sofa (which prickled your legs when you sat on it), a Windsor armchair which had seen better days, a couple of bentwood chairs and

a well scrubbed wooden topped table. Dominating the room was a big black range, boiler on one side, oven on the other, gleaming like polished jet from many a hard 'blackleading'. The high mantel-shelf above was draped in velvet, once crimson, complete with faded gold tassels. On the opposite wall a large cupboard calendar reigned supreme, several years old, displaying a colourful picture of the Taj Mahal. Behind the door leading to the scullery, where the wallpaper hung down with the damp, hung a fretwork picture of a man shooting at a rabbit. Father had fashioned it whilst ill and unemployed. He'd been clever with his hands had Father, except when he took the big round clock off the wall to repair it; he always had a couple of spare parts left over when he had finished. So the now discarded clock stood silently propped in a corner under the stairs.

This was home, pathetically poor, spotlessly clean. Mam scarcely had a kind word for her girls, but lavished her affections on her only son. She neither knew nor cared about Lottie's hatred and fear of the Mill. One couldn't talk to her, let alone confide in her. Children were to be seen and not heard.

Of course the poor woman, young and attractive still, struggled to bring up three children on a ten shillings a week widow's pension, plus the little that Lottie earned. However, she did a little furtive business in fortune-telling, attracting quite a few gullible people, mostly locals. She read tea-cups, cards, palms, and she even had a crystal ball. She never retired for the night until she'd 'turned up' her own playing cards to foretell the likely outcome of the following day.

"Cum on, get thee clogs on," commanded Mam. Doing as she was bidden, and leaving her cocoa untouched, Lottie pulled her shabby blue coat around her thin shoulders, crossed the room to the back door, and with a quiet 'ta ra' closed it behind her. Down the street she went. She passed a dozen or so dwellings, all the same two up two down, with outside toilets in postage stamp backyards, each with its own large zinc bath on its hook in the rain, ready for the general Friday night ablutions in front of blazing fires. All had open middens, inviting disease, nothing unusual about that. Only the well-to-do business fraternity had dustbins outside their splendid 'semis'. She turned at the end of the street and joined the throng hurrying over the shiny wet cobblestones. White aproned, black shawled women, flat capped mufflered men, plus a handful of 'learners'. A quarter of an hour's walk brought them to the Mill yard, where amid good natured laughter and ribald jibe they shuffled inside the Mill. All, that is, except Lottie. She cowered by the door, afraid to go inside. She couldn't bring herself to enter the place again.

The rough domineering Judd Haye was teaching her to weave. A dour, lean, bean-pole of a man, he swore and bullied the girl mercilessly each day. He chewed tobacco endlessly and spat into a pool of slimy brown spittle between the heaving looms. He was a good shot too – he never missed!

His long suffering wife had recently run off with a spotty faced young postman half her age. No-one was surprised, despite the inevitable gossip.

Marjorie Grove's mother and sister in their back yard

The din of the endless looms, row upon row in the fluff laden atmosphere, the reek of raw cotton and hot machine oil made Lottie feel sick. Several times a day she was expected to carry great laps of cloth to the warehouse below, cringing between madly waving picking sticks and flying shuttles, and huge whirring leather fan belts, which it was said, had ripped the hair from many an unwitting girl's head. She was terrified of the youth whose task it was to sweep beneath the looms. He would have a grimy hand up your drawers before you knew it. He rejoiced in the nick-name of 'Pinch-bum'.

Suddenly she was almost swept off her feet by a big rough hand on her shoulder. "Oh it's thee agen is it?" bawled t'gaffer. "Late agen I see, that's three times thas bin late this week. Get up ta th'office and get thee cards, and bugger off home – there's plenty more as'l be glad of thy job."

Slowly she turned, then fled to the gate and away down the lane to the mill stream. Flinging herself down onto the grass, she sobbed uncontrollably. When it was over, quietly composed, she dried her face on her coat sleeve. Though mortally afraid of facing Mam, she was filled with an exquisite overpowering feeling of relief, and determined never to enter a Mill again.

She reflected awhile on last summer's school holidays. They seemed so distant now. The three children had spent many happy hours by the mill stream. They'd fished for minnows and bullheads. How they'd laughed, as they'd slithered barefoot over the green stepping stones to the opposite bank, where fields and hedgerows stretched beyond. She knew where to find the loveliest primroses and choicest wild strawberries. Many times they had spent the whole day by the sparkling stream, with a packet of jam sandwiches and a big bottle of water between them.

Small brother announced that when he grew up he was 'going to fly to Australia like Bert Hinkler'. On saturday afternoons they were allowed to go to the 'pictures'. Two pence each it was to go in the best seats. They each saved one penny a week from their sixpence pocket money. One could buy four ounces of sweets for a penny – coconut chips, aniseed balls, tiger nuts, love hearts – scrumptious!

Lottie always gave a ha'penny to the Hurdy – Gurdy man who played his music outside the cinema. A plump jolly man, he always had a kind word, a smile, and a pat on the head for Lottie.

Tom Mix and Hoot Gibson were small brother's favourite cowboys. Many's the time the Manager cum Film Operator switched off the film till the kids quietened down, and ceased hurling abuse, orange peel, etc at each other during the cowboy films. They all enjoyed Fatty Arbuckle, Harold Lloyd, the Keystone Cops, Chester Conklin with the funny eyes, dashing Douglas Fairbanks, beautiful Mary Pickford and many more. But oh – the excitement of the serial – last week Pearl White was tied to the railway lines, and a huge express train about to run her over. One had to wait a whole week to find out the fate of the poor lady. 'Coming Shortly' was Doctor Fu Manchu, with Warner Oland. All those mysterious Chinese people, and the fascinating Anna May Wong. Once, with money she had saved, she had been allowed to go with a friend on

Marjorie (left) and her sister at Stanley Park, Blackpool

Sunday evening to see a Mr. Cherry Kearton at the Grand cinema. She thought 'Cherry' a funny name for a man, but he was wonderful. He gave a lecture, with magic lantern slides. They saw pictures of tiny little pygmies who lived in the jungle and shot poisoned arrows to kill wild pigs for food. There were monkeys in trees, crocodiles in green swamps, huge elephants and also giraffe-necked women who had to wear many tight bands around their necks, and were never allowed to take them off – their elongated necks were considered beautiful.

Mam always seemed pleased with a wilting bunch of wild flowers when the children returned home for tea after a long day out by the mill stream. Once they gathered, especially for her, a bunch of fragrant delicate May blossom, for her delight. But Mam was angry and threw it in the midden, saying it would bring bad luck to the home – and it did – for not long afterwards, Father and baby sister both died within weeks of each other.

At length she rose and walked away from the stream and the Mill, along past the weavers' cottages, windows ashine, with bright brass door knockers and clean worn steps, past the fish and chip shop and the 'cloggers'. Last week, as she had sat waiting for her clogs to be re-ironed, the old Clogger had remarked "By gum lass, tha wouldn't half be tall, if tha wasn't turned up sa much on't bottom." Well, she thought wryly, she wouldn't be wearing her size seven clogs much longer now – probably quiet shoes and rough apron in some old kitchen miles away – she'd have to go 'into service' now.

No doubt when she got home Mam would give her a hiding and lock her in the cupboard. It wouldn't be the first time. On she went – the newsagents shop was empty now. No sound except that of her footsteps, the rumble of the Mill in the background, and somewhere near, around the God forsaken streets, a solitary Milkman whistling the morning away.

Reaching the corner of her street she paused momentarily. As she did so, a thin shaft of watery sunlight glanced across her face. She smoothed her hair from her forehead, straightened her shoulders a little, turned – and was gone from sight.

(The child, Lottie, in this true story is, in fact, Marjorie Grove, who has lived in Bristol for the past 50 years.)

MY FATHER: A FAMILY RELATIONSHIP
BY DILYS WALTER

Only now, at the beginning of my seventh decade, and eleven years after his death, am I beginning to understand my father. Time and thought have re-awakened feelings of affection in me, in addition to the enormous respect of which I have always been conscious.

The overriding impression I retain is of a stern, unyielding, Victorian parent; although of a later era. His inability to relax or be light-hearted with me gave the erroneous impression that the affection he did not show, also did not exist. He certainly did not lack a sense a humour, but I do not remember an occasion when I was involved in it. His unwillingness to praise any small achievement, apart from the odd academic success, gave me an overwhelming feeling that he was totally uninterested in my activities. The only exceptions to this were my educational progress, and, on a lighter note, my proficiency in swimming, in which pursuit he was my instructor.

I suppose, in order to understand him, it is necessary to realise that in his age men were not expected to show emotion in the way they now do. They were embarrassed by sentimentality, which was regarded as unmasculine. In addition, the harshness of life for the working man left little time or energy for the refinements of life.

My father was born in 1888, the offspring of an uneducated labourer and illiterate mother. As a child I tried to teach my grandmother the letters of the alphabet, but she was barely able to make a round letter 'O'. In spite of this I cherish the possible illusion that she did not lack intelligence. My father was born into a family of eight children, three of whom died in infancy. The quality of life in their poor country cottage would be unimaginable in England today. A labourer's wage would not support his family above the poverty level; and when a considerable proportion, as in my grandfather's case, was spent on drink, the children's diet was barely adequate. They were sent to school, each with a penny batch cake, their food for the day. It was no wonder that my father succumbed to rheumatic fever, and grew up with a very pronounced pigeon chest; a legacy of rickets.

At the tender age of eleven he obtained a certificate stating that he had attained the required standard of education, which enabled him to leave school. The little money he was able to earn helping on local farms was a welcome supplement to the family income. His only surviving sister went into service, also on a farm, as was the general custom for girls from poor families. She was married when my father was fourteen to a furniture maker in Bristol, where her circumstances improved, although her husband had a reputation for meanness. She bore five children very quickly, one of whom weighed fourteen pounds at birth; an unimaginable experience considering the medical facilities available in those days. She died at the age of forty four, a victim of her hard life.

The eldest son in the family joined the Army. This was an option many young men, unable to obtain a living elsewhere, were glad to take up. He died of enteric fever at the age of twenty two, at Bloemfontein in South Africa, during the Boer War. He is remembered with two other young men who died in that conflict, on a stained glass window of St. Mary's Parish Church at Berkeley.

The second son left home for North Wales, where he found work as a chauffeur to a country squire. He married a local girl in the same year as his sister. They had a large family of seven children, one of whom died of diphtheria at an early age.

My father was next in line. At the time he left school his younger brother was only three, so that, after the death of his eldest brother, and the marriages of his other brother and sister, he was the only one able to supplement his father's low income. He left for a time to live with his brother in North Wales, where he found work at a trout hatchery. It was while he was residing with his brother's family that his small niece died; an event which left an indelible impression on him.

In 1911 his father died at the age of fifty five, after a lifetime spent working on the estates of the Earl of Berkeley. From then onwards his mother relied solely on his financial support. He therefore returned home on his father's death, and became a dock worker. In the years before the First World War there was much unemployment; before the advent of the Welfare State life for the unemployed was harsh. Men wishing to find work on the docks were obliged to attend at five o'clock in the morning. They sometimes waited all day for perhaps an hour's work, or often none at all. Dockers were not registered, or guaranteed a wage as is the case today; and it was left to the whims of the employers whether they found any employment. Some of the men unable to find work would cycle from farm to farm during harvest time. Here, in exchange for their labour, and in addition to a small wage, they would receive bread, cheese, onions and liberal quantities of home made cider. They often ended up by falling off their bicycles, sometimes into the canal, on their way home. I heard the story many times of two of these labourers, who told my father that at the end of a day's harvesting they had each drunk twelve pints of cider. "And dost thee know if we'd wanted we could've had a bellyful."

However, there was a lighter side to life. My father was a keen and active member of the local swimming club. Here there was a great deal of camaraderie and home made fun. In the summer of 1911 he decided to attempt a swim across the River Severn from Sharpness to Lydney. This was a difficult feat necessitating exact timing, owing to the strong tide and treacherous currents in the river; one of the fastest flowing in the world. He was accompanied on the swim by a small boat, the Mary Ann, with a companion, Bertie Goodman, aboard. He, by virtue of being

The local swimming club – Dilys Walter's father is seated, second row, 4th from the right. Bertie Goodman, far left

a dwarf, was a well know local character, and was chosen for his knowledge of the river. My father dived off the pier at Sharpness at half past eight in the morning, and successfully landed on the other side of the river about half an hour later to cheers from his supporters on both banks. This event was later celebrated at a Dance and Social evening, when, during an interval between waltzes, lancers, veletas, two-steps, schottisches and various other entertainments, he was presented with a gold chain and medal commemorating the occasion.

A secondary interest was singing. He was the possessor of a reasonably good tenor voice, singing in the chapel and also entertaining at various local events; he being one of a quartet, consisting besides himself of soprano, contralto and bass voices. When war was declared in 1914 life changed for everyone. My father was a pacifist at heart, but decided to compromise by joining the Royal Army Medical Corps. After training in England he was sent to the trenches in France as a stretcher bearer, where he rose to the rank of Staff Sergeant. Here he spent three awful years. Although in later life the war was an endless topic of conversation for him, he played down the horrors and never mentioned his own heroic part in it. One of his favourite stories was of how he and a party of other soldiers, during a lull in the fighting, had found a cafe where they hoped to get something better to eat than bully beef and the usual army rations. He entered the cafe and spoke to the proprietor. "Avez vous pommes de terre, oeufs, me beaucoup famished. Comrades out in the road just the same." This evidently produced the desired results.

In October 1917 my father was awarded the Military Medal while serving with the 107th Field Ambulance. The citation stated that "This N.C.O. displayed great coolness and gallantry under heavy shell fire in connection with the evacuation of wounded from the aid post near the Forest D'Houthulst to the Advanced Dressing Station. His services throughout the day have been of the greatest assistance to the wounded.

In 1918 a Supplement to the London Gazette dated April 17th read, "His Majesty the King has been pleased to award the D.C.M. to the undermentioned for gallantry and distinguished service in the Field." Here his number, rank and name were followed by "For conspicuous gallantry and devotion to duty during operations. He has been in charge of stretcher bearers for a long period and always displayed great courage and initiative in collecting and evacuating the wounded. He set a magnificent example to all with him."

War brings out the best as well as the worst in us; in my father's case it showed his best qualities of hard work, leadership and integrity. A reference from the Lieut-Colonel under whose command he served could not have been more glowing. It spoke of the great respect he received from both the men who served under him, and the officers who led him, and ended with the words, "He is one of the best N.C.O.s and leaders of men I have had the honour to command." It is doubtful if this was of much use after the war in gaining employment; but throughout his life he received the same respect from everyone who knew him, many of whom were much higher up the social scale. His lack of formal

William Price, Dylis Walter's father

education did not detract from this in any way. It became obvious that he was an intelligent man who endeavoured to educate himself by reading, mainly books of a political or historical nature, and by attending Adult Education classes. Although I was always aware of this side of my father, to me it was largely overshadowed by his hard attitude and quick temper, to which his previous environment must surely have contributed.

My father married at the age of thirty five after a long courtship; a late age dictated by economic circumstances and the necessity of supporting his mother. She lived with him and my mother, apart from a few short holidays spent with a relative, until she died about twelve years later. By this time, I, who was his only child, was eleven years old. I remember my grandmother as an old lady usually dressed in black. One of the few incidents about her which I recall was of my mother offering to make her a pretty white blouse. She turned this down with the words: "Tis too grand for I."

We lived in a small terraced house in the country, where for many years we had no running water. A well was shared with several nearby houses, and we handpumped the water up into buckets. The virtue of this particular well was that, unlike some of the others nearby, it never ran out of water however long there was a drought. Those unfortunates whose wells dried up queued at ours for even their drinking water. Saucepans and boilers were used for heating this precious commodity. Under these conditions a bath was a weekly event before the fire; as I grew older my parents retired upstairs to give me some privacy when bath night arrived.

We relied on gas for lighting the downstairs rooms; the rest of the house being lit only by candles which we carried around in candlesticks to wherever they were required. Needless to say the toilet was outside in the small back yard. Much of the space there was taken up by large barrels used to collect rainwater. This avoided some of the pumping at the well, and the water being soft, was ideal for washing hair. When eventually water pipes were laid to the house, and later electricity arrived, we felt ourselves to be living very luxuriously. In spite of now having the opportunity for a more comfortable life, my parents never had more that one cold tap in the house, and only the minimum of electricity, with one of the three bedrooms still lit by candlelight, until they died. Such was the frugality of my father's earlier life that when in later years he could have afforded a few luxuries, items which we now regard as necessities, he could not bring himself to indulge in them. He gave the impression of meanness, and I resented the hardships my mother unnecessarily endured, especially when her health failed. I think now that it was not that his nature was mean; but of his having a strong feeling of it somehow being wrong to make life easier for oneself, or to spend on the material things of life unless they were absolutely essential. This was well illustrated on an occasion when his granddaughter ate a large quantity of strawberries which would otherwise have been wasted. This caused him to completely lose his temper and she was made to feel that she had certainly committed the sin of gluttony.

During the years I was growing up, my mother, who before her marriage had been employed by the Post Office, became the local sub-postmistress. The office was a conversion from our front rooms. This work supplemented the family income, and although the wage was small, was at least regular. In these years before the Second World War there was a great deal of unemployment on the docks, and it meant much to have a steady job. We therefore had the financial edge over the other dockers' families.

My father had always lived in the country; he walked for miles and sometimes rode his bicycle to follow the Berkeley Hunt. This was a sight not to be missed with the huntsmen in their hunting colours, and the hounds in full cry after a fox. The implications of fox hunting were lost on me in those days, and I never questioned the ethics of it. I was his companion on many of his walks; he taught me the names of the wild flowers, and knew just where to find the different ones as they bloomed. In the spring I came home with bunches of primroses, cowslips, bluebells, periwinkles and even wild daffodils. He read me stories and was proud of my apparent prowess in reading, whereas, in fact, I knew the stories from memory having read them so many times.

We had a good relationship then, before I was old enough to question him or become the recipient of his sharp tongue. He was not physically violent in any way, and never even smacked me; but I was afraid of his quick temper. I shrivelled up at the unkindness of his words, and it became only necessary for him to glance at me to completely subdue me. In spite of this apparent harshness he was not an unfeeling man, and I have more than once seen him near to tears over a distressing item of news. He was unable to show this emotional side in relation to me and seemed compelled to suppress his feelings. My only awareness was of a complete absence of understanding towards me.

In those days, only the comparatively affluent had a telephone, so that as there was one in the Post Office, we were often asked to deliver messages to neighbours. When a communication was received for one whose young daughter had died, my father asked me to relay it to her family. I could not bring myself to go to the house where a dead child lay, not from a fear of death, but from a dread of facing the emotions of the parents. This earned me a stern rebuke but still I could not go. I wonder if his reasons for not wanting to take the message himself were the same as mine. On another occasion a telephone call was expected by a neighbour from a relative in Australia. She was so overawed by the thought of speaking on the telephone, an instrument which many were intimidated by, that she missed the chance of talking to a loved one far away; and could only carry on the conversation through an intermediary, in the person of my mother.

My father had always been interested in politics and the Labour Party, and offered himself for election to the County Council. He became a councillor for Gloucestershire, and was also a Parish councillor and a governor of two local schools. These activities took him out on many evenings. I looked forward to his absence, for it was only then that I felt relaxed and the atmosphere at home lightened.

These and other interests earned him everyone's respect. Ever since his Army days he had been consulted on medical matters by folk unable to afford the doctor's fees. Our kitchen often became a First Aid Post for dressing and bandaging wounds, which were always cleaned with permanganate of potash. On one occasion however, he watched powerless to help his own brother-in-law who, after an accident, bled to death in a few minutes from a severed artery in his neck.

During these years my father still worked as a docker; he never used bad language at home although it must have been commonplace at work. When a friend told me that she knew my father swore, I simply could not equate this with my image of him. I felt compelled to tackle him about it but only obtained a denial. In 1934 family finances were so stretched that he reluctantly decided to give up his County Council work, for attendance at meetings during the day meant the loss of his wages. There was no payment to councillors, and this occupation became a luxury he could not afford. With great regret he did not seek re-election, in spite of many requests he received from fellow councillors for him to continue; (including pleas from those of the opposing political persuasion.)

My father took me with him to the local swimming club where he was instrumental in teaching many people to swim. At this time the swimming pool was an old dock where the depth of water was thirty feet in all parts. Learner swimmers wore a belt around their waists with a hook attached. From this they were suspended on a line at the end of a rod which the instructor held while walking up and down. When a swimmer became more proficient the line was slackened so that eventually, although unaware of it the pupil had no support at all. This ultimately led to swimming unaided, and proved to be a very successful method of instruction. One of my father's pupils, a middle aged lady, learned to swim after only six lessons. She could often be seen lying on her back in the water smoking a cigarette. I was only allowed to attend once a week and then only to remain in the water for half an hour, however warm the weather. As this was an open-air pool my lessons were further limited to the summer weather. One day when I was about nine years old I jumped in the water at the end of my rod and line; the hook pulled out of my waistband, and I went down in the water to what seemed like the bottom. When I surfaced my father was in the water beside me urging me to swim on my own, which from then onwards I was able to do. In this instance I am grateful to him for the pleasure which swimming has since brought me.

My father was a typical countryman, and when visiting a town, would cross the road oblivious of the traffic. He was a keen gardener and grew far too many vegetables for our needs, the surplus being given away. Flowers in a garden he considered to be a waste of good land. He brewed home-made wines, blackberry, dandelion, elderberry, sloe, potato and others, some of which became quite potent, but they were always consumed in moderation. As a child I was sometimes sent into the fields to gather the ingredients for this. It was such a common occupation that the dandelions in particular were left to seed themselves and sometimes became quite hard to find. He clung to old country superstitions such as it being bad luck to bring May blossom into the house. This seemed to be a contradiction of his intelligence, and when a grandchild brought May blossom home it occasioned an unbelievable outburst of temper from him.

In our small village there were no strangers; everyone who died was carried from the church or chapel to the local cemetery, which journeys involved passing our house. When a funeral was due all the curtains were pulled across the windows. The hearse and any cars were followed by a walking procession for about two miles, my father always among the mourners. He seemed drawn to these gloomy events, but no doubt from the best of motives.

One of his great interests was education, mine in particular. He refused to buy a radio considering that it would be a distraction which might adversely affect my progress at school. We must have been almost the only family in the locality without one. He was anxious for me to have the education he lacked, but unlike many fathers today this did not extend to material things. For lack of other interests in a country village I attended a course on Agricultural Economics with my father, a subject which, had there been an alternative one, would have had no interest for me. To a young person today my life then would appear indescribably tedious but it was accepted in the absence of any alternative. However, the fact that I was restricted in my freedom more than my friends were made me inwardly rebellious. I found my parents' overprotectiveness very irksome, although certainly done with the best of intentions.

For a time my father left the dock work to become a Trades Union Officer. The aggravation of this occupation adversely affected his health, causing him eventually to give it up and return to his former employment, from which time his digestion returned to normal.

At the outbreak of the Second World War my father's knowledge of First Aid made him an ideal choice for instructing various local groups such as Special Constables, Fire Watchers, Home Guard and other interested persons. On one particular night these organisations were alerted to the imminent possibility of invasion by the Germans. It seems somewhat unlikely now that Gloucestershire would have been the venue for this, and of course no such event transpired.

During these, my adolescent years, I was kept on a very tight rein. The opportunities for any kind of frivolity were very limited, and any such activity looked upon unfavourably. Sundays were very strictly observed; even when time was at a premium for my father, perhaps when he had been working all day and all night to unload a ship quickly, nothing could be done on a Sunday. A garden could become a wilderness before he would touch it on that day; and he imposed the same restriction on anyone else who would otherwise have worked in his home.

Every year, the Transport and General Workers Union, of which my father was a member, held a Festival at the Colston Hall in Bristol, where, in addition to the speeches, various well known personalities from Workers' Playtime entertained. Attending this gathering was an event to which I looked forward. Ernest Bevin, who had been the General Secretary of this union for many years, and who was now Minister of Labour in the government, was usually present. It was not considered prudent for him to stay overnight in Bristol while the air raids were taking place. He was therefore driven by one of my uncles to a country hotel for the night. On two such occasions I was a passenger in the same car when he chatted with my two younger cousins and myself who were in the back seat; and was not so aware of his own importance that he did not notice us.

Eventually I was drafted into factory work and left home. The freedom was glorious, and in spite of the war I enjoyed myself as never before.

My father and I had always been, in spite of many similarities in our characters, on different wavelengths; our relationship was never close. His inability to show understanding towards me or express his feelings, albeit through no fault of his own, made a gulf between us too wide to bridge. I could not understand his thoughtlessness to my mother who bore unnecessary physical deprivations without complaint. His reluctance to visit her in hospital when she was terminally ill, did not equate with his tears when she died.

The years since his death have, to a certain extent, increased my admiration and understanding of my father, but he still remains a contradiction and an enigma.

TIMES AND PLACES REMEMBERED
BY STEPHEN JAMES RANDY

2 rooms, 18 Weare Street, Bedminster, March 2nd, 1916. Not a very auspicious date and address to start life. Mother a tailoress, Dad an ex-Miner and Carter at Bristol Docks. They said I had strong lungs and good voice. One of my earliest memories when three years old, was standing on a scrubbed deal table in a neighbour's kitchen singing "I'm forever blowing bubbles" and having threepenny bits thrust into my tiny grubby hand.

As the family increased we moved to a cottage in a courtyard in St. Judes, a typical city slum with two outside cold-water taps, and two earth toilets shared between ten homes; washing was boiled in a bucket on top of the fire; meat, when available, was cooked in a Dutch oven hung in front of the fire, which supplied heat, hot water and cooking; lighting was by oil lamps and candles. The living room was stone-flagged and the two bedrooms led direct from it. This was accommodation for two adults and six kids. Pleasures were simple and according to Season; Tops for whipping, Hoops for bowling, and swimming in the Docks during summer, although this was frowned upon by both parents and the River Police, who used to patrol the Harbour, chasing us out of the water when they spotted us in the noddy – we couldn't afford costumes.

As kids we always looked forward to a visit from the barrel-organ man. We would sit on the kerb whilst he ground out the Top Ten of the twenties. His bottler would sometimes do a Charlie Chaplin routine complete with bowler hat and cane and then collect the pences and halfpence from us kids.

It has always been stated that charity was greater and more sincere among the poorer classes of society; I remember a wonderful day during the General Strike when a group of South Wales miners who had been busking in the Castle Street shopping district were invited into the St. Judes back streets for a bite to eat. The local housewives served them steaming mugs of tea with thick hunks of bread with Jam or beef dripping.

After they were replete with the hospitality of the locals, the 18 miners sang "Cwym Rhondda" as only the Welsh can and there wasn't a dry eye to be seen.

Christmas time usually included a visit to an uncle who was a well known local entertainer, who used to demonstrate sheet music of popular songs in 'British Home Stores' and 'Marks and Spencers', his daughter playing the piano. They were the D.J.'s of the 20's and early

30's, so naturally we had a good old ding dong at the party. Father was a good song and dance man and all the kids had to do their piece, whether song or recitation. No telly or wireless to intrude. At the end we were sent to bed, four at the top, four at the bottom.

Around this time, 1923, I was a pupil at St. Pauls School, in an area quite posh, in comparison with our slum district. I made good progress academically, within the confines of a restricted curriculum, and at the age of 11 years I won the "Abraham Birkins Scholarship" and the "City Junior Scholarship" which gained me a Grammar School entrance. After a month my parents were asked for £10 for book fees; as Dad was working two days a week at the docks during the 20's slump they could not even find 10 pence, so I had to go back to my old school at St. Pauls. The Headmaster wanted my parents' permission for me to sing in the Church choir, so one afternoon they drove up to the entrance to our Court and sent a boy to ask my Mother if she would come up to talk with them. Being a very proud person she said they would have to discuss it in the cottage, which they eventually did. Within six months I was Head-boy and earned many a half-crown singing solos at weddings; quite a bonus for Mother.

Having attained the top class at 11½ years, the Headmaster devised extra tasks to keep me occupied. Two mornings a week I was sent out with a leather cash satchel strapped to my wrist to collect the rents from the streets of terraced houses which he owned, with a bar of chocolate as a reward. Another errand was to visit a local herbalist with a wax-sealed envelope containing many £1 notes and strict instructions not to tell anyone where I had been sent. As there were two very attractive female members on the staff the significance of these errands never dawned on me until I started work and had become more worldlywise.

The annual highlight for us as children were outings by Brakes. The horses were supplied by Dockland Companies for whom our father worked. We once went to Weston-Super-Mare, four lusty shires pulling the brake; when we got to Rhodyate Hill on the Weston Road all the kids had to get out and walk up the hill as the load was just too great. Tea was taken in the Salvation Army Hall just off the Front. After games on the Sands and a good paddle in the muddy water, if the tide was in, it was all aboard and singing all the way home until we fell asleep.

I always enjoyed going to the stables on the dockside on Sunday mornings to muck out. The manure would be piled on carts on the quayside ready for the market-gardeners from the St. George, Hanham and Kingswood areas, who after bringing their produce to the Bristol Market in Baldwin Street would go back with a full cartload of maure. Father's horse was "Dobbin", a lovely gentle shire and when grooming with the curry comb I could walk under her belly with ease.

Every summer the workhorses were put out to grass for a week or more to get them in fine fettle for the gruelling year ahead and, one day, to my delight Father announced that I was to help him take six horses to 'Farmer Crane's' at Lulsgate Bottom, more affectionately known as "Lousy Bottom" even today. We set off quietly enough from the Docks at Prince Street with me perched on Dobbin's neck and leading one, with Father handling the other four. All went well until we reached Ashton Gate and they got the smell of grass in their nostrils. With a loud whinny the one I was leading broke loose and galloped around Gores Marsh. When order was restored we moved along the A38, stopping at every pub that had a horse trough outside; "Cross Hands", "King's Head", "Winford Arms", "Fox and Goose". Whilst the horses were drinking so was Father and ginger beer for me. So with the quart of scrumpy at Farmer Crane's, after the horses were let loose in the field, it was the end of a near perfect day for horses, Father and me.

Fry's, the chocolate people, had moved to Keynsham and every summer we were packed into barges and lighters and taken from Bristol Docks to Keynsham, where games were organised and tea was taken in a huge marquee, and we were given bars of chocolate to eat on the journey home.

The halcyon days of childhood were nearly ended. It was early 1930 and having no relatives in the big Bristol factories to speak for me (a recommendation), I was on my own. English and Maths being my strong subjects I applied for a job at "Douglas Motor-Cycles" at Kingswood. I was 14 years of age and for the princely wage of eight shillings and sixpence (42½p) I worked a 48 hour week. Thus began a new education in the "university of life".

Douglas' ran an annual sports meeting which attracted the best riders and runners in Wessex. The great draw after the races was the Beer tent, but fourteen-year olds were excluded, so my mate and I filched bottles of ale from under the canvas. I had ridden my cycle from St. Judes to Kingswood, but by 10 p.m. I was more than a little bit tiddly, so I was put on the last tram-car to return home and just escaped a whacked bottom as my two elder sisters told Dad I had arrived home at 10 p.m.

My hobbies were swimming and boxing and I won a bronze medal for life-saving. I trained and sparred at St. Judes Boxing Club, run by the local Coal Merchant, Bert Budd which was behind "The Crown" Tavern at Lawfords Gate. One night I came home and told Dad I was to have my first fight – a four-rounder – at the local Boxing Hall. He asked how much I would be paid; it was seven-shillings, but the Manager would have half-crown and the seconds two-shillings, leaving my reward a half-crown. Dad told me he would give me a hiding for nothing, so my boxing career never got off the ground.

My eldest sister was a good ballroom dancer and I was her avid pupil. On St. Patrick's Night 1932 we went to a dance at the Co-op Hall in Castle Street; we came second in the Quickstep competition and as they had an Irish song contest I entered as Steve O'Reilly and won; not a bad night out.

In the mid-thirties the slums were being demolished and we moved to the southern edge of the City, surrounded by open country. We had a lovely black and white mongrel, but it was mine really, he was a wonderful ratter, and Sunday mornings, before the local pub opened, we would have about six rats in our traps; the dogs would be held on slip-leases, usually a handkerchief through the collar, and as each rat was released the dogs were slipped and the one that caught and killed first picked up the cash kitty. As my dog, managed four out of six kills it was a fair morning's winnings.

I was becoming more interested in girls and motor-bikes and met my future wife when she was sixteen and I was eighteen. We were married at St. John's Church on December 26th, 1939.

I was now a skilled machinist in the tool-room of the Bristol Tramways Motor Works, but we never went on honeymoon because of war-time emergency orders. We took out a mortgage on a small house in Headley Park, Bishopsworth Village and my mates said I was mad to saddle myself with such a burden in those troubled and insecure times, but we felt happy with ourselves and the family, which became three lusty infants by Novemeber 1945 – a girl and two boys.

During this time Ack-ack manning duties, the Royal Observer Corps and entertaining, took care of my spare time. I entertained mostly in Military and Naval Hospitals such as Winsley at Bradford-upon-Avon, and Barrow Gurney, the last named being only a stone's throw from where we are now living.

Of necessity I was cultivating an allotment plot to augment the family income and feed the five of us. We took the family for a week's holiday every year, the few shillings I earned entertaining helping towards this.

An old 1929 Norton motor-cycle, with sidecar, got us mobile in the early fifties, with many a pleasant trip to Shearwater and longer trips to Lyme Regis, Combe Martin, Weymouth etc. It used to raise a laugh sometimes when we arrived at our destination and began to unload – first the kids were lifted out, then the buckets and spades and picnic. Lord only knows how we crammed it all in and for good reason we only set off when the weather forecast was good.

Approaching my fortieth birthday I reckoned that twenty-three years at Tramway Motor Works was enough, so I joined the Development Tool-room at Patchway – now Rolls Royce, where a better chance of advancement occurred.

As the family had outgrown the old Norton I obtained an old A.35 Austin van, and within a few months I converted it to a Countryman Shooting Brake. My daughter was at Grammar School and had a steady boyfriend, so with the two boys we toured Snowdonia, the Lake District, Pembrokeshire, the Black Mountains and the Brecons, enjoying the pleasure of Fell-walking, swimming, fishing etc. and for summer evenings it would be Priddy Pool on the Mendips or Shearwater (before the Lions) for more swimming or fishing.

At the age of forty-five I had cleared the mortgage on the house and for the first time since our marriage we were able to begin to save some cash.

On 23rd March, 1963, my daughter Stephanie married her schoolboy sweetheart at St. Peter's Church, Bishopsworth. The boys were both working, the eldest at British Aerospace, and the younger in London as a Computer Trainee. A year after finishing his apprenticeship, Roger, the eldest son, told us he was getting married and going to Toronto, using the boat trip as their honeymoon. We gave out blessing and off they went in April 1965.

As we were once more on our own after twenty-six years of married life, we looked for, and found, a cottage with a quarter acre in the village of Dundry, a Mendip outlier, where we have lived for the past twenty years.

Looking back there have been many changes in my 70 years plus. Bristol City Docks, once alive with shipping in the 20's and 30's, is a more sedate area. Hard drinking pubs of yore, such as the "Llandoger", "Hole In The Wall", both on the quayside, are today chic eating houses.

"The Naval Volunteer" in King Street, once a renowned Draught Guinness house, was presided over by "Uncle George", the last of the bare fist pugilists of yesteryear.

The Baltic Wharf, where deal runners unloaded timber from Scandinavia is a prestigious housing project, as is Rownham Mead on the Hotwells side of the Harbour where once stood the cattle pens for the Irish cattle boats to off load. The coffee shop at Cumberland Basin, where once dockers and carters and drovers had mugs of tea and corned-beef sandwiches is now lit by soft candlelight at night, serving French cuisine.

Children are on the whole bigger and healthier than in the twenties. My younger brother died from a mastoid condition which would not be fatal today. Diptheria, Scarlet Fever, T.B. were rife, children wore iron calipers on their legs because of rickets, a malnutrition effect. It was all accepted with a fatalistic philosophy. Families were more closely knit maybe than they are today. I was lucky in having wonderful parents who were hard-working when work was available and although my Father died of an industrial induced cancer when he was 53 years, my Mother lived until she was 85 years. A marvellous matriarch, loved and revered by her six children, twelve grandchildren and thirty great-grandchildren who are all living today.

EARNING MY DAILY BREAD
BY OLIVE KNOWLAND

I left school at the age of fourteen in 1930. My first work was at Frys Chocolate Factory in Pithay. I started in the foiling department, hand wrapping small chocolates in tin foil to go into fancy boxes. I liked this work, but after a while I was sent to work at the new factory in Somerdale. There I worked on a conveyor belt taking bars of chocolate off and putting them into trays. This to me was very boring. I hated it there and after 11 months I left.

Being unemployed for a couple of months I got a place working in a house at Ashton doing housework, cooking and looking after a family of four; this was the man of the house who was a widower, his unmarried sister who worked at Wills cigarette factory, his son of twelve years and his three year old daughter.

My first job on arriving each day at 7.30 am was to cook breakfast for the man and his son. If I wanted it I also cooked for myself, the aunt had already gone to work. The boss and his son left about 8.30 am for work and school, I cleared breakfast and washed up, then it was time to get the little girl up and feed, wash and dress her. I then had housework to do, I also washed and ironed the girl's clothes, the aunt doing the others' clothes. As well as doing this and looking after the girl I had to prepare and cook a midday meal for five of us.

After the family had gone to work and school there was washing up and cleaning to do. Each afternoon I was expected to take the girl to the park for a couple of hours. It was hard work for a girl just fifteen on a wage of six shillings (old money) and food a week, but I enjoyed it there until the man got married again and once more I was looking for work.

This I got at Brights of Bristol (now Dingles). Not a very brilliant job, but then as now we were glad of any work to get a job. I was in the still room where washing up from the restaurant was done. It was all right there because I worked with decent girls and we all worked well together. After a while I was put on a job no one liked doing, washing teapots all the time. It was most monotonous and you got rather wet doing it if they were busy in the restaurant. I asked for a rise in my pay, but the one I got was outside!

I was now about seventeen years old and longing for a permanent place of employment. This I thought I had with my next place, a bakers and confectioners shop. I started there on a holiday Saturday; an extremely busy day, how could they teach me my job on a day like that? So I was taken to a room that was going to be used as a staff room and set to scrub paintwork round a window and clean the windows, also the walls and the floor. The room had been unused for a very long time and it was very dirty. I was told I had made a good job of it and that I was not afraid of work.

After that I started in the shop when the holiday was over. I had a very good tuition and really enjoyed working there. Unfortunately there were no spare workers and if you were ill for more than a week you had to apply for your job again. If you were lucky you got it, but sometimes they had taken someone else on and you were out. This is what happened to me when I had a very bad attack of tonsilitis. This sort of thing happened in lots of places just before the war.

I was given a very good reference from this place and within a week I had another job in the same sort of work. This was at Melhuish's in Peter Street opposite St. Peter's Church, now a wartime runined shell in Castle Park. There was a bread and confectionary counter, cooked meats and cream counter and inside was a cafe. It was also a Commercial Travellers' Hotel. It was a good place to work and I was very happy there.

I worked for a couple of years on bread and confectionary, then I moved to the cooked meats side of the shop. When they were busy in the cafe I would help in there as a waitress. I enjoyed my five years I worked in this shop and cafe which was one of the places destroyed in the bombing of Castle Street and all surrounding places. A great tragedy for all Bristolians at the time.

I was married then and expecting my first child so I did not work again until I was about forty five, when I got a job part-time in a small busy bakery putting the jam in doughnuts, cream in buns and finishing lots of small cakes, like the ones which years before I had sold over the counter.

I had a happy time there until I had trouble with angina and had to give up working. Nowadays the thought of work comes to me again, wondering if my grandchildren will be able to get the jobs they want to make them happy. At present I have a grand-daughter in full-time work and strangely enough it is the same sort of job I enjoyed so much; bread, cakes, cooked meats, cheese, frozen foods and tinned goods. I think she enjoys it as much as I did. I hope my other grandchildren will be as lucky in their employment when their time comes.

ELECTION DAY – OLD STYLE
BY B. PRICE

Only the adults got upset on Election Day; for us, "too young to understand", electioneering was fun, Elections hilarious, and Polling Day was usually a Mini carnival.

There were, of course, the traditions to be upheld, you NEVER, NEVER enquired how someone intended to vote, even when they were festooned with Party Rosettes, had Party posters in their windows, and invariably swore at any conveyance, or speaker, belonging to the rival Party.

In addition to the convention of not enquiring about one's voting intentions, there were certain other rites and traditions, well and truly observed. The vast majority of artisan and manual workers were solid Labour, rock solid old-style Labour. Shopkeepers, schoolteachers, policemen (we didn't know many of them), clerical workers, and STAFF, (Bosses' Narks), were adjudged to be permanent Tories, and not to be acknowledged as a part of our world.

This made life a bit difficult, as it was impossible to boycott the local General Store (rank Tories) because this was the only shop selling ½d. bread rolls, with a scraping of Maggie Ann, which often provided our mid morning, school "lunch". Political principles were sacrificed on the altar of the gurgling gut. Since half the local families were "on tick" till Friday, principles took a further, and substantial, battering, from our parents.

The run-up to an Election was naturally "The Campaign"; not the glossy, televised "imagery" recently served up "ad nauseum". Candidates, with their assistants and party workers, generally took it "turn about" in hiring the local Parish Hall, or other suitable venues. They also took to the streets, with portable collapsible rostrums. These gadgets were extremely practical and their portability was a boon, when the candidate found it expedient to make a rapid retreat, from a hostile audience.

Most of the open air meetings I attended took place on the corner of Kingsland Road, and Sussex Street, right by Cardwell's fish and chip shop, in the Dings. This was handy for sustenance, and the high step up from the pavement was a vantage point, but hungry chip addicts could, when in a hurry be provoked into pushing you off the step, and invariably, you landed on some-one's toe, and the air would be filled with expressions of basic Anglo-Saxon which distracted both the speaker, and the audience.

I often wondered why speakers chose this spot for their meetings. I asked my friend, "Porky Norton", who, with the advantage of wisdom acquired with age, (he was three months older than I was), pointed out that the street lamp, bang on the corner outside the Chippy, was brighter than any other lamp in the Dings. Clever stuff. I always felt that Porky would go far, and he did; North Africa, Sicily, Italy, and eventually, St. Pauls.

Our best remembered candidate was a Labour man called Johnny Allpass, and our greatest delight was to "march", in column, behind a square lantern, illuminated by a centrally placed candle, emblazoned on all four sides of the lantern was the legend "Vote for Allpass". There were great advantages in a name like Allpass, because when we bellowed out the Party ditty, "Vote, vote, vote for Johnny Allpass, Turn old Apsley out the land", it was absolutely astounding the way that hitherto unsuspected poetic gifts, of the local children, could adapt the next few lines, to convey to Lord Apsley, where he might deposit his unwanted manifesto.

Heckling was a form of both Aural and Oral ART; and comprised satire, razor sharp wit and ridicule, all delivered by men who could make "Merry Xmas" sound like an invitation to commit suicide. I well remember an outside candidate, whose entire speech was flattened into nothing, by frequent demands from a bantering audience, to know, "Who pinched the Babby's milk?", a reference to reduction in the entitlement to free school milk, for the under nines. He knew neither his audience nor their challenge and he left the rostrum, defeated. But, strangely enough, had he appealed for "Fair Play", he would have won his audience over; at least to hear him out. In those days an appeal for "Fair Play" was always honoured.

On Voting Day all the parents of our street went to Sussex Street School to cast their opinion on the state of the Country, and its leaders. Husbands and wives went together, usually, he to see how the Missus voted, she to see that the old man didn't get dragged, unwillingly, into the Mason's Arms or Bobbie Alden's for further political indoctrination. The children, if they were of our age range were permitted to join our group, with the admonition to "keep out of trouble, mind". Useless admonition, it was, too. We were staying to watch the fun. Some party workers tried at each election, to get their supporters brought in to vote on any means of transport that they could beg or borrow. This was supposed to be frowned upon as "Corrupt" but as both sides did it no-one complained. It was however, the height of political acumen, to get a lift to the Station, particularly in the late evening, in your opponent's transport. This could well mean that the vote which might negate yours, might never get to the Polling Station on time.

I did realise, even at that early age, that there was a serious side to all of the carnival show. It was the time of the depression, times were hard, and our teachers accepted as a genuine excuse for non attendance at school, that an errant pupil might not have the shoes to come in. I knew that to be unemployed meant children being sent off to live with relatives, with smaller families than their own. I knew that it was possible to justify a World Recession, on Trade Grounds, but as I learned from my father, you can never justify, to any man, why it should be he, who is without a job. He won't accept it.

My Dad had a simple philosophy, he voted as his father and grandfather; and like Archbishop Cranmer, the Medieval Martyr, he feared his right hand would wither and fall off if he should ever put his cross for any other candidate than Labour. But still, he would listen to other views, and respected them, but would never have changed his own.

My mother was not so tolerant; I well remember after the defection of Ramsay MacDonald, the chaos it caused. When this event occurred, she failed to indulge in our usual daily ritual of "Get up, you'll be late for school."

"I'm tired. Five more minutes."

"Get Up. Right Now."

"In a minute," and so it would go for some ten minutes or so, daily.

It didn't happen on this particular day, and for the first time that I could remember, I got up, dressed and went downstairs, unbidden.

Mother sat staring at the newspaper, tears of rage in her eyes, Labour was out, ousted by a National Government, of Ramsay MacDonald. She sat and stared, mesmerised; and totally unaware that I was too late for school.

Gradually the shock began to lessen, sufficiently for her to begin automatically, to prepare breakfast for my sister and me. Since my Dad was in regular employment, even if low paid, we got a good breakfast every day.

With the innate cunning of all boys, I realised that something was up, and that I had to play the cards right. I didn't realise that my political education was about to start, immediately.

I ate my Quaker Oats slowly, piling on the sugar and milk, and hanging it out. I pleaded further hunger and murdered three doorsteps of toast and marmalade, slowly and sadistically. I slurped two more cups of tea, to distract attention from more important things; but then she noticed the clock.

"You are late for school," she accused me.

"But I had to have my breakfast and you were looking at the paper till quarter to nine. Wasn't she?" I sought my sister's support, normally very sparsely given, but I knew, I was dead to rights; brassbound, in fact.

Since I was already too late for morning classes I played up the change of government, not knowing what it meant, except that it could upset the maternal sense of priorities. I was most successful, for this was the only time that I can ever remember getting a note for the teacher, saying that I was too unwell to attend – to take with me **THE NEXT DAY.** Ramsay MacDonald, might have betrayed the workers, but he got me a day off. What is more, my Dad didn't find out for a week and it was too late then, nothing could be done, I had exceeded the Statute of Limitations. I had also had my first real lesson in the exploitation of a political situation.

Elections can teach you useful things, sometimes.

LOOKING BACK
BY ALEC ROBINSON
OF PURDOWN HOSPITAL

Foreword by Leslie Johnson
of the Friends of Purdown Hospital

Alec Robinson was born on the 2nd January 1919 near Wellington in Shropshire. He was found to be lame and mentally backward, and was "put away" as an infant in a local Childrens Home. He has no memory of his mother or father, but recalls a sister visiting him and an older brother in the same Home. He last saw her in 1925. Since then he has neither seen nor heard anything of his family, and has no recorded next of kin.

In other memoirs he describes how well he was cared for at the Home and local school, and later at a boarding school in Bryn in North Wales. From there he was moved to Petton Hall, near Shrewsbury, and then transferred to Stoke Park Colony "to learn a trade". He soon found that it was not quite what he expected. In later years he tried several times to write his memoirs, but found it very difficult, as will be seen from the extracts from his writings. But he has a truly remarkable memory and it was this – and the uniqueness of his story – that led me to offer to ghostwrite for him. He always declared that no-one would believe him. I trust his readers will prove him wrong

STOKE PARK AND PURDOWN IN THE 30'S WHAT IT WAS LIKE

I shall never forget the day I was sent to the old "Stoke Park Colony". I say "old" because Stoke Park and Purdown Hospitals today are very different places from what they were then, with a standard of care and comfort unheard of in those days. My sixteen years in Shropshire were over, and on a dull rainy March Tuesday in 1935, escorted by a man I did not know, I set off by train for Bristol Temple Meads. There we took a taxi to Stoke Park, and upon arrival my companion promptly vanished, leaving me to find someone to report to.

I knocked on the door of what I later learned was the old Dower House, at about 3 pm. I was miserable and pretty hungry, as I had not eaten since breakfast. After a while it was opened by a short lady – in temper as well as height – who asked me what I wanted. I had to take my shoes off before I went in, although they weren't that dirty. I was told that I was too late for tea, and would have to wait until breakfast next morning. While I was waiting I started talking with one of the girls there, and Matron caught me. "I don't allow that sort of thing," she said, and sent me off. I afterwards heard that the girl was sent to bed as punishment.

My bed for the night was in a small bare room with brooms and other odds and ends stored in it. I was given one sheet, one blanket, and an uncovered pillow; and it was cold. I was up at 6.30 am., and went over to "Central Hospital", where it seems I should have gone in the first place. This was the Admission Block, where you had to stay for three weeks, and I did not like it one bit. There were five other new ones with me, and we had to put on nightshirts and stay in bed most of the time. In fact, you got into trouble if you were found out of bed without permission. You were allowed up to go to the toilet, or to go downstairs for meals, and from 3 to 4 pm. each afternoon we went outside into an enclosed play area called "the Cabbage Patch", which had swings and suchlike in it. During the three weeks Doctors came to See us to decide where we should go. A Doctor me and told me he hoped I would enjoy my stay in Stoke Park. I soon found out that this was rather a sick joke.

I was sent down to Purdown, (which was called "West Side" then), and it was hard going compared with what I had been used to at Wellington; and you were in trouble if you put a foot wrong. We got up at 6.30 am., and after washing, dressing, and cleaning shoes, we all lined up and went down to breakfast. This was in a large room with long wooden tables and forms, and we sat six a side. In front of you was a half slice of white bread and margarine, and beside it a half mug of cocoa; and that was it. Four or five staff would be watching you, and if you took too long they took it away.

After breakfast we all went off to our various jobs. Floors and tables – even the legs – had to be scrubbed; also the outside yards and so on. For dinner we often had unpeeled boiled potato with gravy over it; now and again a single slice of meat and a bit of cabbage, or just soup and a roll. Afterwards you'd have a couple of spoonsful of sago or rice, or a slice of rolypoly and a little custard. It wasn't much and we were always hungry. Some staff used to slide the plates down the long tables, and if yours fell off that was just too bad; you didn't get any more.

In the afternoon some finished off the cleaning jobs, and others went to work on the Farm or Market Garden, Boot Shop (where boots were made as well as repaired), Carpenters Shop, Laundry, or Mattress Shop. Here fresh mattress covers were filled with flock from old mattresses: not a pleasant job, as some had been soiled and were very smelly, and there were fleas! At 4.30 a whistle blew and we returned to Towers Ward. In Towers at that time there were about 200, so it was pretty crowded. Before tea we had to go to the bathroom to wash and clean teeth. For tea there was a whole slice of bread and marge, and the usual half mug of cocoa.

All had to be in bed by 7 pm., winter or summer, and the windows were opened wide, whatever the weather. They were sash windows, pulled up or down by two separate cords, each with a metal "Mouse" on the end which would be slipped under the frame at the bottom to keep the window in position. With only two blankets and a sheet you'd get mighty cold sometimes. Then the door was locked, and there had to be silence, or else...!

There were no personal lockers or cupboards, so you had to roll up your clothes in a bundle and put them under your bed. The chances were that in the morning you would find your laces gone, and later on find someone smoking them downstairs. This may sound unbelievable, but it's true. Some chaps would smoke anything; even stuffing from a mattress, or straw from the Farm, or leaves; and when you asked for new laces, they would cut one in two, half for each boot!

We were always on the lookout for more food, and on one occasion we were lucky. The kitchen door – like most others then – was locked again after meals; and one day some fat left in the oven caught fire, and smoke poured out. We broke down the door, and in all the confusion, took the opportunity to raid the larder. I hid bread and stuff in the woods below Heath House, and recovered it next day.

Pinching food when you had the chance was a way of life; you were not ashamed of it.

There were lodges at both entrances to the Hospital in those days, and iron gates that were lockd at 4.30 pm. by one of the "Park Rangers". There were about six of them, and their job was to supervise the grounds, which at that time stretched right up to the Dower House at Stoke Park. There were public footpaths passing through, and the Rangers had to make sure that "outside" people kept to them. I can hear them now, calling out "Keep to the path!" to anyone straying off them. They would also keep a lookout for any wandering patients of course.

Some did try running away at times, and when caught by the police and brought back, were punished; usually by a week or more in the "Red Room" upstairs in Towers; so called because when on punishment you had to wear a red jacket and trousers. You were kept separate and locked in, and strictly supervised while being put to work on meaningless cleaning and other boring tasks. "Towers" in those days was regarded as the Punishment Block (called by some "the Piggery"!) where there were punishments of a more instant and violent kind. Saucing staff or disobeying orders could easily lead to being taken into the bathroom and getting beaten up by staff. It happened to me so I know. Sometimes two or three were dealt with at the same time, and you dare not complain.

Violence and broken windows were quite common, and if a patient went berserk he was put 'out' with an injection. I remember one chap who gave a lot of trouble, and was always running away. One day he got up on the turret roof of Towers Ward and threatened to throw himself off if anyone came near him. Two staff grabbed him in the end, and he was sent back to Rampton, which is a kind of Broadmoor.

Lots of bullying went on, and some staff behaved more like prison warders than nurses. It was a "them or us" set up. Anyone telling tales was done over by the rest.

In those days the staff wore black uniforms with brass buttons, and a peaked cap, and carried big bundles of keys for locking and unlocking doors, and they were pretty rough with us. If you were put to the Doctor and told him that one of the staff hit you with a bunch of keys, watch out afterwards! This was not on one day, but every day. People today would not believe it. It was always the patient's fault of course, or they'd say he had a fit and hurt himself. The staff couldn't do anything wrong, and no-one would believe us. There were exceptions of course, but things were very strict. People today have no idea. For instance, if a patient had visitors, they were put in a separate room, and one of the staff had to be there all the time, and you had to be careful what you said. If the patient was given a gift, it was often taken from him after they had gone. Letters were censored or confiscated, and you had to be very careful what you wrote; but only a very few could read or write anyhow.

We were expected to keep the place clean, and keep ourselves clean too, but what we were given to do it with was very crude. The bathroom was a draughty place. There was a row of about twenty washbasins, and six baths placed end to end. We had a bath once a week, two to a bath, half cold water, and a piece of soap the size of a toffee; and you were watched the whole time, even in the toilet.

You were allowed five minutes to bath, then another pair followed you. The water was changed after six had used it. Inspection followed and if you weren't clean enough you were sent back to go through again. Then you were given a clean vest and shirt of some sort (no pants) and a pair of socks (usually odd). The only other clothing you had was a secondhand jacket and trousers, and an old overcoat in winter. Things like ties, pullovers, gloves, hats or scarves were almost unheard of. You had to be tough to survive, so I suppose I was tough!

Keeping warm was quite a problem. There was nothing like the cosy carpeted Wards we have today, nor were we so well dressed. As I said, most of our clothing was secondhand and well worn, and didn't fit properly.

We really did look like "Charity Boys" when we were out on our "crocodile" walks. Nowadays, we can go out shopping and choose our own clothes, and pay for them with our own money, but then we had to put on what we were given whether we liked it or not. What a change! So few of the present Purdown folk know what it was like, or realise just how much better off they are. Only us older ones remember, and are thankful.

The buildings then were heated by coke-fired boilers in the cellar, and each Block had its own. The coke was brought up by lorries three or four times a week. It was unloaded beside coalholes outside each Block. It had to be shovelled down the hole by one of the "Boys", and shovelled away by another down below. It was a regular job for some of us and it took hours to do. The boilers were banked up at night and kept the chill off rooms I suppose, but not like today; and in wintertime the dormitories with their open windows were perishing sometimes. There was a boilerman named Jim Nash who used to make a round of all the boilers every morning and afternoon, and George Downe used to help him, and Teddy Stiles helped Mr. O'Donnell up at Heath.

The kitchen ranges used anthracite, and on Towers the kitchen was at the back, and here all the food for the Block was cooked. The anthracite was loaded into the stoves with long tapered scuttles; and all the hot plates had to be cleaned with wirewool every day. Jack Frost used to do that; and at the weekend the fire was let out for cleaning out, and relit with a shovelful of coke from the boiler in the cellar. That was cleaned out weekly too.

The Day Room on Towers was where the Dining Room is now, and there was an open fireplace on the right hand wall in which a good coke fire was stoked up on Saturday afternoons, which we had off. We used to sit around it, and when it got really warm, some would take their jackets off and put them over the backs of their chairs. If they went to sleep this was a signal for someone to tie a knot in their sleeves, tie bootlaces together or pour cold water in the pockets! The staff always put that fire out at 5 pm with a bucket of water, and we had to clear up the mess and take out the ashes etc. New "Boys" went through it of course, and would get "French Kip" (apple-pie) beds, or a back trouser button repair sewn through to shirt and vest and so on.

The ovens of the Bakehouse, where bread for all the Blocks was baked, were heated by coke too. I worked there, and one of my weekly jobs was to clear out clinker, and put back the firebars, which were still hot I remember. The Bakehouse was roughly where the Staff Dining Room is now. Nowadays there's no Bakehouse; the bread is bought in; and all cooking done by gas in one big kitchen by paid staff, with just two or three patients helping in washing up pans, etc.

A lot of people don't realise how much work was done by the patients at that time and for just a few pence a week. We made a lot of the things used by the Hospital, such as scrubbing brushes, toothbrushes, floor cloths, mattresses, doormats, brooms and candles. Also tables, chairs, cushions, tablecloths, garden tools, and even leather footballs. The various workshops were over where the M32 fence is now, and most of the more able ones – and there were many more then – worked there. Over the years I worked in many of them, such as the Carpenter's, Mattress, Brush, and Mat Shops, and in candle and football making. I also worked as the Glazier's mate for a long time. Windows were always getting broken then, and it was a whole-time job replacing them.

Apart from that and the Bakery job, I worked as lathering boy in the Barber's Shop. A barber, Mr. Morgan, came in daily from outside to shave people, and I had to lather them up first. He used to use a cut throat razor and used to jokingly threaten to use it that way on anyone who did not behave!

In Towers about this time there was a boy named Peter. He was 20 or 30 years old, and his father worked on the railway in Bristol. He loved reading books and things, and there wasn't much about on the Ward. One day he told me he wanted to go and see his father to see if he would give him some. I told him to be a good boy, and I would try and get permission to take him to see his father. But he would not wait, and one night he got out of bed and through a downstairs window, and walked up the hill past Heath, and over the railway line, where he was knocked down by a train and killed; and he was still in his nightshirt.

"LIKE A LITTLE FACTORY?"

On Sunday mornings when it was fine, all able-bodied "Boys" assembled outside their Blocks after breakfast, and set off crocodile style on a long walk escorted by 4 or 5 staff. I said "walk" but it was more like an army route march really, for you had to keep in line and walk in step, and got told off if you didn't! If the weather was really bad we in Towers were locked in the Day Room until dinnertime. There were never enough chairs to go round, and people sat on window ledges and on the floor. There was nothing to do; just sit or wander around and wait.

In the afternoon we had to go to a church service in the old Chapel/Gym., (burnt down several years ago; the new Hydrotherapy Pool and Physio Room is there now). You had no choice, just did what you were told. You had to clean your boots with blacking and put on "best clothes", which was a brown corduroy jacket (without pockets) and trousers. The suit you got was not your own; they all came out of a cupboard. You had whatever more or less fitted, and after use you had to roll them up, tie with a bit of string and put back in the cupboard again. Shirts were of thick material in various colours. There was no tie, and as likely as not you would finish up with odd socks. There was quite a good brass band in those days, when there were far more really able "Boys". It was led by Mr. Calloway, and accompanied the hymn singing, while staff were lined up at the back.

Then back to the Block and after tea a bedside roll call at 7 pm. and so to bed. One of the staff would be stationed outside the dormitory, and woe betide if you were caught talking! On Sundays though, the door was left ajar for you to hear "Sunday Half Hour" from the radio outside. Another thing was that we always said the Lord's Prayer before and after every meal, and on Sundays stood at table to sing hymns before and after tea. Old John Gedney used to lead them. John loved his chapel and later became a Server. It never really interested me.

In those days there were hundreds more living in Purdown than there are today. All were men or boys, but all referred to as "Boys". There were far more "high grade" patients then, capable of making and doing things well; so that many of the things the Colony needed were made in the Workshops or produced within the grounds, and in this way we helped to support ourselves. Others did portering and labouring jobs.

There was the Farm, which had over 100 cows, milked morning and evening; two or three bulls, 20 or 30 sheep, a lot of pigs, and several horses. It was run by a head Farmer, who had a house in the grounds. He had a "2nd Chargehand" and five or six "landsmen". They supervised gangs of the Boys doing various jobs such as milking (by hand of course), working in the fields, cleaning out the stalls and so on; all the usual farming work. There was even a slaughterhouse up near Stoke that some Boys worked in; and the meat and milk and so on was used in the Colony. At one time I looked after the horses and cleaned out the stables. There was a black horse called Sam, who pulled a cart, and two others named Violet and Diamond. Two Boys looked after the pigs, and seven or eight milked the cows.

The Market Garden was on what is now the football field, where we grew cabbages, swedes, sprouts, carrots, and suchlike, and also rhubarb. There were some fruit trees and raspberry canes; and just over the hill in Lockleaze there was a big potato field where twenty or thirty of us worked. We used to dig them up, put them in buckets, and then into sacks which were taken away by the horse and cart. Sometimes vegetables were entered in local Shows outside.

The Bakery was where the kitchen is now, and supplied the hospital – and Hanham Hall too – with all its bread and stuff. There were two bakers and four cooks; and apart from bread they made things like Harvest Loaves and pastry. Sacks of flour, a bucket of yeast, and some water were put in a dough machine turned by hand, and it was hard work. Everything was baked in a coke-fired oven. I remember baking started at 5 a.m. so you had to be up very early. One of our jobs was to wash the floor afterwards, and I soon found that it paid to make a good job of the edges and corners and not worry much about the middle, for they seldom inspected there!

In the Carpenter's Shop they did all the hospital repairs, and made furniture and toys for Christmas too. The Boot Shop not only repaired our boots, but made new ones as well. Boys in the Tailor's Shop made shirts and suits and did repairs. Coconut matting came from the Mat shop, and brushes of all sorts – even toothbrushes – from the Brush Shop.

The Laundry did all the washing of course, and always "ponged" because of all the mucky sheets and clothing there.

It was like a little factory, and quite a few staff and scores of Boys were employed in this way for next to nothing. In some ways it was a good idea but we were marched about like prisoners, with staff collecting us from Wards and escorting us back afterwards and watching us all the time. Many of us resented it, but there was nothing we could do. I remember a jingle that one of the Boys made up; it went like this:-

They say the Colony's a nice place,
But I don't think it's true;
For once you get inside of it
There's lots of work to do.
Up and down the dormitories
With dustpan in your hand
As long as you're in Stoke Park
You'll never make a man!

SOME COMPENSATIONS

But there was a lighter side too. Even though things were rough, there was always some joker to make you laugh. Sometimes we would cheer ourselves up by singing one of the jingles that used to around, such as:-

We are but little children weak,
We only get ten bob a week.
The more we do the more we may,
It makes no difference to your pay.

– or the one we used to sing in the Dining Hall sometimes:-

Every morning at half past six
Our daily work begins.
Cocoa, porridge, and a dork, (hunk of bread)
And we're not allowed to talk.
Blimey, what a life!

We had a good football team, and a really good brass band, that used to play on Open Days, and at Stoke Park and Hanham Hall and other places too. I remember them playing once at the Clevedon Flower Show. They wore a smart black uniform and peaked cap. It was formed in the 1930's, and the first Bandmaster was Mr. Calloway, who was here for five or six years. Then there was Mr. Mott, who was middle aged and rather stout. He had dark hair and shiny eyes; and after him Mr. Pryor, who was tall and thin. There were a lot of good players in the Hospital then. Most have left over the years, and some died; and the Band today is only a shadow of what it was.

Things were better at Christmas too. Staff would decorate the Ward a bit and there was a Christmas dinner; also simple gifts made in the workshops. I remember having a Ring Board one year, and a Yo-yo on another. Some had building bricks made in the Carpenter's Shop, but nothing like we have today. Just a few would get parcels from home, which they would hang on to of course. I remember too, a jolly Head Cook named Mr. Perrett, who used to go round the Wards playing his piano accordion; and he got up a concert in the old Gym. on Christmas night.

But those were certainly not "The Good Old Days", and it was years before things began to look up. It was only after the League of Friends came (1954) that things really began to improve; and now we have so much that patients today don't realise how well off they are.

PURDOWN AT WAR

When the War started in 1939, the first thing that happened at Purdown was that blackouts were made for all the windows, and Ward lighting was cut down. We were also each given a gas mask ('nose bags' we called them) in a small cardboard box, which we carried around with us at first, but gave up later on when nothing happened.

Heath Ward, up on the hill, had a basement which was used as an air-raid shelter by the folk up there; Beech House, down on the main site, had one too, but they had to share theirs with Cypress, Cedars, and Cherry 'Boys', because they had no basements. There were no women patients in those days of course. Towers Ward had no basement either, and there the top floor was left empty, and when there was a raid, everyone crowded into a ground floor room which was sandbagged up. Bucket latrines were put in the corners, and in a long raid overflowed sometimes, I remember!

Right on top of the hill, where the Post Office Tower is now, there were three anti-aircraft guns in separate concrete bunkers. Two were close together but the other was a bit further away, and was nicknamed 'Purdown Percy'. There were also guns in Eastville Park; and when they were all going there was a terrific racket. Towers used to shake with it. The danger outside wasn't from the bombs (as far as I remember none fell on Purdown except a few incendiaries which were put out without damage) but from shrapnel from bursting shells overhead. Bits whistled about all over the place, and sometimes were too hot to pick up afterwards. I never heard of anyone getting hurt.

The first warning of a raid we got was a loud whistle from the hill where the guns were, and soon after that the sirens went. By that time the Cypress, Cedars and Cherry boys were all down in Beech basement. We in Towers would troop down to the ground floor with any blankets and so on we grabbed on the way, and stayed there, sometimes for hours, until the all-clear sirens went. As I said, no bombs fell on us, but we could see the fires all over Bristol, for we are high up here. I especially remember a heavy raid on Good Friday 1942. Despite the noise, most Boys took it calmly; anyone who got really upset was quietened down with a 'jab'. Some staff did firewatching, and we also had A.R.P. Wardens and troops up here. We could hear the German planes flying over, and the bombs going off: and once we were told that a German pilot had parachuted into a tree in Eastville Park. I don't know if it was true.

We got on very well with the Ack-Ack men on the hill. On the first Christmas morning of the War, some of us got out of Towers through a window, and went up to see them. They did us proud; with things to eat and cigarettes. We didn't get back until 11.30 am and the Charge Nurse was waiting for us. We were told off, but let off punishment, as it was Christmas. Most Saturdays they would come down and play us at football. Once their air-raid warning whistle went while they were here, and they had to drop everything and chase back up. Yes, we got on really well with them.

Some staff were called up, and young chaps without experience came in their place. They just did what they were told. Because we produced a lot of our own food, we didn't notice rationing much. Incidentally, in those days we only had a spoon to eat our food with, except on Christmas Day, when we had knives and forks as well. I think they were afraid some patients might use them as weapons, and injure themselves or other people.

No, the War didn't make much difference really; except that for the first time they started issuing Parole Cards, so that you could go out on your own in pairs. You had to be back by 4.30 pm in winter and 5 pm in summer. That was quite something, believe me.

WORKING OUT

After the War, I went out to work as a porter in Colston's Boys' School, just across the road from the Hospital, and I really enjoyed it. I got on well with the staff, who respected me and treated me very well. I worked Monday to Friday from 1.15 pm to 8.30 pm, had Saturday off, then worked 7 am to 2.30 pm on Sundays. I was pretty fit and active then, despite my "gammy" leg, and used to do various cleaning jobs, take messages, help unload supplies, and generally make myself useful. The boys were little demons and were up to all sorts of tricks, but I was young once and used to cope with it alright. It reminded me of my school days in Wellington, when I can recall rigging up a can of water to drop on someone when they opened a door, and putting drawing pins on the teacher's chair, and potting with peashooters and so on. Oh! I was no angel, believe me! I lived for sport and playing about. In later years I bitterly regretted not having paid more attention to my lessons. The teacher warned me about it at the time, but I knew better of course. It is one of the big mistakes I have had to live with since: I made my bed and have had to lie on it. However, to get back to Colston's School: there was a Headmistress there then named Mrs. Thomas, who was strict but fair. There used to be a big school party at Christmas and I was invited too. The Headmistress agreed and I would wash and change and then come back to join in the party. Some of the boys used to go home at weekends I remember. I worked there for about 12 years, and they were good days.

Then I was given the chance of living and working outside, at a Convalescent Home at Clevedon. People used to come to it from the B.R.I. and all over. It was explained to me that I would be on trial for six months, and if considered satisfactory I could leave Purdown and live there. What a laugh! I had to get up at 4.30 am each morning and work until late at night; scrubbing, cleaning windows, helping with meals, washing up, and anything else that needed doing. There were only 10 minute breaks for meals, and very little time off. I got tired out, and after a week or so I gave up. I told the Matron that she didn't need me; she needed a couple of donkeys! So back I came to Towers again.

Then in the 1950's I went into lodgings in Washington Avenue, Eastville, and did a kitchen job at the Hawthorns Hotel in Clifton, cleaning floors and tables and washing up. Later they gave me a room there. I remember the mountains of plates and cups and cutlery. There seemed to be no end to it, and you just had to carry on until it was all done. It was run by a family then, a Mr. and Mrs. Mackison, and my boss was the chef; and they all treated me with respect. Friday was my day off, and I was usually only too glad to sit down and have a rest! I used to get two weeks holiday a year; one week in the Spring, and one in September, and usually went away then, perhaps to Porthcawl or Barry. I worked there for about six years, but by then my leg was giving me a lot of trouble, and the time came when I had to give up.

I returned to Elms Ward at Purdown, and from then on lived at the Hospital. There was far more freedom in Elms than in Towers. You could go out whenever you liked, and sometimes go to say, Weston or even Weymouth. Most of the Boys there went out to work, perhaps in the Fruit Market, or the B.A.C. or roadsweeping for the Corporation. Others worked in the Colony: on the Farm, Market Garden, or Workshops. There were a lot of very able Boys in Purdown then. Most have long since left for places outside. Others-like-me have got too old or infirm to want to go.

When the League of Friends first came to the Hospital in 1954 they brought sweets, chocolates, and cigarettes with them. Later they used to bring up really good secondhand clothing, far better than we were ever given, and they were marked up with the Ward name. That was when we first saw things like pullovers, gloves, and – believe it or not – handkerchiefs. Until then we usually used our coat sleeves!

VISITORS: THEN AND NOW

As I said previously, I don't remember my mother or father, for I was put away as an infant; but I know I had at least two older brothers, Wally and Bill, and two sisters, Edith and Agnes. I always understood I was the youngest. Bill was with me in Wellington Childrens Home, and sister Edith used to visit us there sometimes. She was married to a man called Bennet. The last time I saw Edith was in 1925, when I was about 7, and she came to the Home to take away Bill, who was 15. You couldn't stay there after that. From then on, I never saw or heard anything of her or any of the family. It was as if they had "written me off". I would dearly love to meet Edith again, and find out what happened to her and the rest of the family.

She lived in Birmingham then, and I still clearly remember the address. I wrote once or twice but had no reply. Then I got the hospital Social Worker to try, but the letter came back marked "not known".

The only other visitors I can remember having until the League of

Friends came was the Board of Governors in Mrs. Burden's day. Around a dozen of them would call about twice a year. She used to meet and talk with them in the old Dower House at Stoke Park. They would interview a few selected patients; some from Stoke Park on their first visit, and from Purdown on the second. I went up two or three times over the years. After waiting for perhaps an hour, I would be called in for a few minutes and asked questions, such as when and where I was born, and how I liked it at Purdown. But you had to be careful what you said, for there was always a member of staff present, and if you said a word out of place nothing was said at the time, but you were in trouble when you got back. In those days some of the staff were really vicious. I remember one in particular by name, who was really what you'd call sadistic: a shifty type who would never look you straight in the eye, but was quite happy to give you a real bashing in the bathroom.

Some of the questions the Guardians used to ask me were quite silly, as if I'd got no sense at all, such as "What colour is cabbage?" or "What's the last thing you do before you go to bed?" But if I asked how long I'd got to stay in Purdown, they would say "until you have improved yourself". Then, when I'd gone they'd decide how many more years it was going to be. There was nothing you could do about it; you were helpless; they'd believe staff rather than you, and nobody outside seemed to care.

In those days, Open Day was for "Boys" and relatives only; no outside people were allowed in, so people like me had no visitors at all. Still, it made a change, and the staff were on their best behaviour. It's so different today; people would never believe; but us older ones remember those days as if they were yesterday. Present day patients don't know how lucky they are.

Many times I've thought "I'm all alone in the world and no one really likes me; and I wonder whether anyone will miss me when I've gone?"; then I tell myself not to be silly, and put on a smile instead.

Life is worth living here now. I am well looked after, and have my own "den" where I can please myself, and make cups of tea for some of the other chaps; and I keep it clean and tidy. Last year I had a marvellous holiday in a hotel at Teignmouth with some of the others from the Ward. We paid for it ourselves and were taken down by one of the staff in the minibus. He took us around and gave us a wonderful time, and we could please ourselves what we did. What a change from the old Colony days!

I have had a wonderful year: people have been coming to talk with me, instead of me going to them.

Mr. Johnson (of the League of Friends) says it's important that people outside should know what did go on before it's too late, and I must say I've enjoyed our sessions together over a mug of tea, down in the little room they've let me have. Just lately I have been asked if I would like to leave Purdown and have a room of my own in a house outside; but I think I'm better off where I am. I have worked outside before, but am too old for it now, and who would I have to talk to, and who would look after me if I was ill? No thanks!

EXTRACTS FROM AN EARLIER ACCOUNT WRITTEN BY ALEC ROBINSON

"This story is true. In my beging when I first came into hospital, there are still a few here now like can tell the same story as I can. Times were very hard then. All in the past I had a great super time in my younger days during my school career, until I was told I was coming to Stoke Park Colony but not as it is now. It was named Old Stoke Park then and Purdown was named Westside Stapleton. All the times year after year day after day it was a hard time. All the way round to me it was like a prison Camp, plenty of hard work and no play, not like it is today. Whenever you had an order by one of the staff you had to obey it straight away not later or tomorrow.

I know there are some boys older than me but not so crafty as I am. To be crafty you must well know the less you say the more you get thought of which I think is a good thing. 'Ear all see all and say nothing. It is easy to learn this, once you learn it you will know it. If you can only read my mind what I don't know this story is true right from start to finish. I only wish people could read my mind. People don't know how this place was supervised in them days. How our life was spend in this hospital (? I they?) last to kept it up I don't know but it did. So in time it all came to a word stop. Then the (life) of this hospital got easier. The patients started got out in toos by themselfs. Go for trips and go away somewhere for a weeks holiday the first time. It was great for something to (look) forward for, and today our life is worth living now. The people who made have it is now the League of Friends and they are still making it greater. They can only do so much and no more. Of this cruelty, if any of the patients went out (ran away?) they would no where to go. If a patient fell ill during the day or night they would tell him to see the Doctor in the morning. So when the Doctor arrive you were took in to see him. What ever he ordered for you to take they would send upstairs for you to take it. If you did not come you were for the high jump, there was no marse (mercy) in them days. They where always ready to hit somebody. Life in them days were not worth living. It was not one day it was every day of the year, day and night. It went on until one day some of the boys ran away. When they were caught they would be taken in the Bathroom with 4 or 5 staff. You could never tell what is going to happen from one day to the other. You would be lucky to have a day as you please. Its either one thing or the other. If we were talking to one another they would stand behind you and listen then after they would send for you to go upstairs in the Office to find out what you were on about. If it was about them down in the Bathroom they would take you, with doors locked and into Action. They would say you had a fit or fallen down. It was all Tommy Rot. In the end they were a found out sooner or later so I did it not to please them. I did it to please myself. When they heard about doing things to please myself I was for the high jump. I would be took in the Bathroom and one would start then the rest would join in. By the time they all stop hitting me I could not move. I was in a bad way, there was blood all over me. They did not care, after that they put me to bed, until next morning they put me to the Doctor. So by the time the Doctor came I had to wait in the Dining Room. I did tell him how it happened so he told me how many hit me. I told him 4, not only me but other patients as well. They (staff) told the Doctor I had a fit. Then the Doctor asked for my Case Paper. He open it to see if I did have any fits. So he replied to the staff this boy don't have fits he has never had one at all. So he replied after who is telling a lie you or him? So I came out and left them in there with the Doctor. If they had children of their own would they treat them as they did us. During that time the word is no. Not only in Towers (ward) but all the way round you would hear of somebody getting slaughtered until one day it come to stop and those staff pack up their bags and left because they could not have their own way. It was just like going to bed having a dream and it come true and this one did all the way round. Nobody would think so but it was, and many thanks to the people who as made it like home for us all as it is today, especially the League of Friends of Purdown and the Doctors, also the Nurses who are doing a great job in the hospital. I have always said it is not how you come but what you can do that helps. Don't come half-way, come right in and make yourself welcome. Make your mind up and come and have a look at the work that some of the patients are doing. All different jobs, it is more like home now, not like it was before. It make life happier for all of us. It goes a long way .....

....I am thinking of giving a Demistion (?demonstration?) how I used to act when I lived in old Towers when it was then. It would surprise all of you. You had to look after No. 1 to stay alive. If ever I got caught I would get the Bath Towel tied round my neck and put in bed for a while until they think of telling (?setting?) you free again. Then they would get you up. You would have to wear a Red Coat and Trousers to walk about in the Block until your time was up. Then they would find you a job around the hospital to see if you can improve yourself. If not you would go back and start all over again. It is all true thanks to people who have made it as it is now. It is Going to bed and having a Dream and it came true ... some people think they know it all but they don't. There would be no Fried Eggs for Breakfast or Bacon. You had to to eat what was given to you. If you did not fancy that, you would have it for your Dinner, until you made up your mind to eat it. There was no how your Father in those days or telling them Your an old Soldier, it didn't work then. (Once) in the summer we went for a half day trip to Severn Beach from 2pm to 4pm. It was alright going but not coming back. When you arrived back we had to change into our working clothes, then lined up out in the Back yard (to) go in for our tea, which was not much. Some boys used to give their grub away for a smoke. A cup of tea once a week, also a cup of coffee, for the rest of the week we had cocoa which we called Purdown Mud with no sugar and very little milk. There was no supper in them days. If you were caught eating after that certain time you would be for the high jump. One Sunday night the kitchen caught fire. I shouted come on Boys the cook-house is on fire, so over we went. But not to put the fire out. We all made a raid for the larder. We took what we could find. Then we hopped it and went somewhere safe and had a good feed to make up what we did not have in them days. My Motto was and his still: I'm alright Jack. Number one comes first. What's left Number 2 carries on. It pays to look after yourself in them days. Nobody would not care for you. It is all true from Start to Finish.

So that is why I am still about today at the age of 66 (1985).

(End of extracts)

REMEMBERING YESTERDAY
BY JAN WEBBER

My memories go back quite a long way being in my 66th year. I remember my very early days living in Bedminster – the youngest of three girls and I think spoiled by the whole family as I didn't enjoy good health as a child.

We were very poor – my father had been a time-serving man in the Royal Navy but came out after the First World War wanting to spend more time with my mother and us children. Work was scarce and after walking around seeking a stoker's job (he'd been a Chief Stoker Petty Officer in the Navy) he became a docker.

Sometimes he only managed to get 2 or 3 days' work a month, but could not draw unemployment benefit or get keep from the 'Guardians' as dockers were classed as 'casual workers' and not permanently unemployed. But we were looked after.

Mum took in washing – bless her, she always seemed to be at the scrubbing board in our dark, dingy kitchen or ironing other peoples' clothes! But she didn't mind just as long as she could see us well-fed and clothed. 'Clothing checks' were a boon of course – a shilling a week and a shilling poundage on a £1 'check', but then a good pair of shoes could be bought for 8s 11d!

I remember starting school at Boot Lane School (real name Bedminster Bridge School!) and Mum coming down from Old Charlotte Street where we lived, with a bottle of tea, cups and cold toast and giving it to us through the railings – how lovely it was to see her waiting there. On cold snowy days my Dad would meet me from school and carry me through Bedminster on his shoulders. I felt so proud to be carried on those broad shoulders. How I loved him! I was lucky!

My sisters had progressed to St. Mary Redcliffe School as I continued to attend 'Boot Lane', but I followed on there when I was eight years old. My father loved us going there as he'd gone there himself and had been a champion swimmer in Mr. Francombe's day. His name was Mike Norman – everyone in Redcliffe and Bedminster knew my Dad – he was an amateur boxer and when he was older he helped train young boys to box.

Both my sisters left school at 14. The eldest to work in a box factory, and my middle sister (who, sadly, died at 27 during the last war) went to work in Wills' factory. I passed the scholarship, as it was then known, and got a place at Merrywood Secondary School. My sister helped with books and uniform and because of the family's poor circumstances I was able to have a grant of £7 a year to keep. This was a lot of money to us and paid in three lots, £3 and £2 and a final £2 through the year. I was able to stay until I was 16 so the family made a lot of sacrifices for which I shall always be grateful.

We lived in Bedminster until December 1940 when we were bombed and re-housed, eventually, at Knowle in which district I still live. But Bedminster is where all our roots were. Twopennyworth of jam in a cup from Minterns, faggots and peas from Haynes' shop on Redcliffe Hill, when times were good!

Memories come flooding back!

BOTTOM OF THE HEAP
BY E. L. L. SHADDICK

My story started when Insulin was still a teenager, blood transfusions were in their infancy, Penicillin had not been born, and Prontisil was the new wonder drug of the day.

Dewy eyed budding Florence Nightingales were pitchforked straight on to hospital wards without benefit of preliminary training, and, within the first week, had to produce Matron's essay, "Why I want to become a nurse".

If I'd told the truth, I should have been thrown out on my ear.

I believe in Destiny. That small, seemingly unrelated incidents can channel us into paths we had no intention of taking.

King Richard lost his horse, kingdom, and life for the want of a nail. For the want of a bicycle lamp battery, the nursing profession got me.

Go back fifty years, to a small country town where nothing ever happened. Rather Victorian parents, and a teenage girl so naive and innocent as to be ignorant to the point of stupidity. That was me.

Visiting my girl friend some three miles away, I started for home just before dusk, to discover to my horror, that my cycle lamp battery had packed up. Being law abiding, I walked home. It must have been all of ten o'clock, and the house was ominously silent.

My mother, older sister and two brothers, reading the gathering storm, had pushed off to bed out of the way.

I was welcomed home, if it could be called that, by my father. He might have said, "I love you. I was worried about you", but he didn't, and I was too immature to understand the reason for his anger.

So it was, still filled with righteous indignation and a deep sense of injustice, I knew it was time to stand on my own feet. Clutching a small suitcase holding all my worldly goods, fifteen shillings and a one way railway ticket in my pocket, I set out to seek my fortune.

I chose the East coast, because it was as far away from Devon as I could afford to go, and far enough away to prevent me from running home with my tail between my legs.

I decided on psychiatric nursing because the pay was so much better. £2 a week, less 23/4d for board and lodgings, and 2/4d for superannuation. I hadn't reached the income tax bracket. That left me 14/4d a week pocket money, it was a fortune.

Severalls Mental Hospital seemed like Colditz to me. Surrounded by a high brick wall, inside which, a sunken ditch and railings divided into exercise areas for the wards. At least it was green grass, probably not so humane as a modern zoo.

Signed in through the lodge gates, first priority was a thorough medical. They obviously were not going to waste time on lame ducks. It was just as well I passed, I had no money for another adventure.

Second priority, the issue of some faded, ill fitting uniform, very second hand. Something else they had no intention of wasting money on until they were sure that (a) they would keep me, and (b) I would stay.

Everything issued to me had the same number marked on it. Uniform, towels, sheets, pillow slips, even my bunch of keys, were personal to me. For the whole of my time at Severalls, I kept number 147.

Third priority, was to sign a form promising to obey all instructions, whether considered to be nursing duties or not. That should have aroused my suspicions, but I've already told you I was, probably still am, as thick as a plank.

I can't remember what I did with all my newly acquired possessions, I suppose I was allowed to dump them in my room, but it was rather a long time ago. I do remember being hurried along long corridors interspaced with locked doors, until a double door was unlocked, I was shoved through, and the door locked behind me.

I had arrived on my first ward.

I knew nothing. I had been told nothing. It dawned upon me that perhaps I should make my presence known.

I needn't have bothered.

A voice bawled from somewhere.

"Give that girl something to do. Don't let her stand there doing nothing."

I had indeed arrived.

Charge Nurse Davidson.

We took an instant dislike to each other, and she made my life Hell. Looking back, she probably made everybody's life Hell, but I had all my way to go, coping with my own misery.

Because of the work strain, we were supposed to have a straight working day from 7am to 8pm and then have two days off each week, but often, staff shortages meant cancelled days and a day's pay in lieu. Thank God I had different time off duty than my friend Miss Davidson, so some glorious weeks, we only met for three days.

Not only property, Staff also had numbers, except the Charge nurse. The second nurse was Second, and right hand maiden. Third, worked in the dormitory, Fifth in the dormitory helping Third, Fourth supervised the day room, and so on, depending on the number of staff on each ward. Thus, transferred always knew their duties by the number they were given.

I didn't rate a number. I was the Last nurse. And didn't I know it.

Ward E, my first six months stretch, housed eighty four souls who suffered with varying severity, forms of epilepsy. The beds were only a few inches off the floor in case someone fell out of bed during a fit. Guaranteed to cripple spines for life, we really did have to use a yard stick to ensure all blankets were folded to the same inch.

Mabel told me my duties, nobody else bothered. Mabel must have been one of the oldest inhabitants, and was in charge of the ward trolley. That trolley every single day, collected an enormous extremely heavy, and securely locked dispensary hamper, overflowing with gallons of paraldehyde. It took massive bundles of washing to the laundry, after Mabel and I had sorted it into descending categories of delight.... at least I didn't have to wash it.... We brought back clean supplies, bags of repaired shoes, household stores, and the food container for every meal.

We walked miles every day, but it kept me off the ward and out of Miss Davidson's way for quite a lot of the day. It also developed muscles I never knew I had. I should think it would be ideal for discus, hammer and shot putters.

I was beginning to wonder when my training was going to start. I didn't realise it, but it already had.

I'm a compulsive counter. Stripes on the wallpaper, chips on my plate, and I'm a compulsive picker upper as well. See a bunch of keys, and they're in my pocket in a flash.

On Ward E, after every meal, crockery and cutlery had to be collected, washed, counted and locked before patients were permitted to leave the table. Every bed-time, it was my duty to collect eighty four hair ribbons and eighty four pairs of garters. Broken crockery had to be fitted together like a jigsaw puzzle in case a piece was missing.

My chief duty came after each meal. Tables cleared, paraldehyde dished out by the bucketful, Grace was said.

"For-what-we-have-received-may-the-Lord-make-us-truely-thankful-Amen-down-the-Backs."

Down the Backs, was the lavatory area. I was supposed to know, the Good Lord alone knows how, which of the patients were incapable of attending to their own needs, plonk them on the throne and make encouraging noises to them. Well, I did not know, but I learned the hard way, as usual. The number of wet and dirty drawers rose alarmingly, and Charge Nurse Davidson was not amused.

It was also my duty to clean the Backs. I paid a high price for the failure of that cycle battery.

I cried myself to sleep every night for the first six months.

Things could only get better, they certainly could get no worse. Lectures started, and I went on night duty. From the ridiculous to the sublime. Miss D. and I exchanged no tearful farewells.

I was put on a pleasant villa housing about thirty five private patients, in single or four bedded rooms. The hardest job was trying to stay awake, but I used the time for studying. There was no supper break, and patrol came through every two hours, pegging in at a time clock at every visit.

The Night Sister was a sneaky individual. She used to creep around without making a sound as she unlocked and locked doors, hoping to catch some poor unfortunate napping. The penalty was instant dismissal.

One night, I was ready. Was it MY fault, that just as she crept around the corner, I just happened to be coming from the opposite direction, and just happened to open out a bed sheet in front of me prior to changing a wet bed?

I reckon she was lucky it was the sheet going on the bed not the one I was about to take off.

Funny thing. I always heard her coming, after that.

Night duty made no difference to lectures. Whatever time of the day, we simply got up for them, then went back to bed. Quite early on, we were told, "Mortuary. 11am. Post-morten." Not knowing what to expect, freezing in our cotton uniforms, (the male student nurses were luckier, they had white coats over their suits,) we waited. We tried not to look at the white sheet draped over...what?

A crusty looking little man came in, and totally ignoring us, walked the length of the table, taking the sheet with him.

It revealed a female form, with long, jet black hair down to her waist on either side...slit from thyroid to pubis and retracted back like a carcase in a butcher's shop, prepared for our instruction.

I shall never forget the shock of that awful sight. Perhaps I was luckier than most. At fourteen, I had worked as cashier in a butcher's shop, quite used to the errand boys rolling bullocks' eyes down the desk into my lap.

One nurse fainted. The specimen had been a patient on her ward. None of us, at that stage, had any experience of surgery or theatre work, so it seemed an unnecessarily brutal way of introducing young people to anatomy.

Beau Geste would have considered the Foreign Legion a rest compared with the discipline we endured.

Matron had instructed the Lodge porters not to allow off duty female nurses out of the gate unless wearing hats. Only a few intrepid hardies ventured out, except on a full day off, we were much too tired.

We cleaned our own rooms, which were inspected by the Home Sister at random times. Regimental S.M.s couldn't hold a candle to this breed. They didn't bawl, but left notes. Like,

"Nurse, wash your lamp shade" or "Nurse, dust around the cracks of your door" or "Nurse, you have more than five items on your dressing-table" or "Nurse, you did not open your window far enough." One thing is certain. No Home Sister was ever young, tired, or broke.

During the Croydon typhoid epidemic, the entire hospital staff was jabbed with T.A.B. injections in one day, and remained on duty. During the war, even soldiers were given twenty four hours compassionate leave, but not us.

I was on night duty at the time, and had a fairly severe reaction. Feeling ill, I did sleep on duty that night. Mercifully, a patient, bless her, was awake. She saved my skin.

"Nurse, The Patrol's coming. Wake up."

Not all night wards were easy, I was lucky on that occasion.

On day duty, it was a different story.

Not having wardmaids, the nurses did all the housework, with some patients helping. There were huge open coal fires behind strong locked fire guards.

There were floors to be scrubbed with wax, on hands and knees, then polished with bumpers not much smaller than a Sherman Tank.

There were lots and lots of windows to be cleaned. Cleaning windows was the Last Nurse's duty. In January 1937, I crawled back on duty after a dose of 'flu'. My friend Davidson-Squeers was waiting. "Go and clean the window...OUTSIDE." She probably hoped I would catch pneumonia, for which there was no such thing as antibiotics in those days, and victims frequently died. I shouldn't have cared if I had. I was still only in my teens.

You may be wondering how patients fared, when staff were treated like cattle.

Gone were the days when mental patients were put on show or used for sport like bear baiting. Neither were they thrown into a snake pit in the belief that it would shock them back to sanity.

In fact, they were well fed, well clad, well shod, and weighed every week as a quick way of checking up on them.

There were shopping trips, outings, entertainment, dances, occupational therapy, and other activities. Most reasonable freedom. Locked doors were essential in some circumstances.

If patients were in seclusion, they had to be visited regularly and seen by a doctor. If in a padded room for their own protection, the door had to be unlocked every half hour. The rules did not say the door must be opened, only unlocked. Usually a potentially dangerous situation, four staff at least would be on hand to keep the door closed until the key could be turned again.

Streakers were not allowed. They wore 'Bunnysuits'; all in one white suits complete with feet and mitts, and fastened down the back. 'Strongs' were indestructible blue and white check dresses.

People talk about straight jackets. I never saw one during the whole of my training, much less one in use.

Most wards had at least half a dozen potential suicides. All staff coming on duty had to identify these special record patients and sign the S.R. book. There was no excuse for ignorance or negligence from the Charge Nurse to the Last Nurse.

To be on Red Card was the most soul destroying duty of all, and not for juniors. Imagine the routine.

Report for duty 7am. Proceed to side ward.

There you would find, one bed, one chair, and one patient. The patient had to be checked, and 'Red Card' signed. You would then keep observation on that patient for the rest of the day. The chair was a concession, you would actually be allowed to sit, but not allowed to do anything to distract attention from your charge. Total vigilance was the name of the game, because Red Card, meant actively suicidal. Your only escape was to be relieved for meals, making a very long day of doing nothing for the best part of eleven hours.

Such is human nature, we would willingly have scrubbed and waxed floors instead of that duty.

All these things pass. In two years and eight months, I took my finals and became a fully fledged Royal Medico Psychological Nurse. Predictably, a qualification now obsolete. I had to stay on to finish my three years, but was actually working my resignation to take general nursing, when war was declared.

There was I, a fully trained nurse, facing the enemy on the East Coast. I couldn't cut and run, my Country needed me. I cancelled my general, cancelled my resignation, and waited for Hitler...and waited...and waited. The phoney war dragged on.

The blow fell when I was put back on Ward E. True, I was now a Third nurse, acting Second, and Hitler I could take.

But not Charge Nurse Davidson.

I re-applied, re-resigned, and took myself off to Reading. A few weeks after I had left my old hospital, it was bombed.

During my three years, I'd saved the magnificent sum of £50, and stockpiled enough clothing to see me through general training. My small suitcase had grown into a trunk.

I was at the bottom of the heap again, but that is the beginning of another story.

JUST A COUNTRY GIRL
BY JOYCE GUMBLETON

"Tis time to get up, Joy," whispered my nine years old brother, Jim, shaking me by the shoulder. "Tis ha'f pass six, we'd best get started or we won't be finished by breakfast time." Silently we crept down the uncarpeted stairs to start our Saturday chores, we didn't want to waken Mum or my other two brothers and sisters who were still in bed asleep.

I was third in a family of seven children, who, with Mum and Dad lived in the little village of Chilcompton in Somerset, in the 1920's with its surrounding coalmines, quarries, sawmills and farms. There were a couple of village stores and a few pubs, where the men went for their pint of beer or cider, and a game of darts or shove-ha'penny. Granfer Albert Padfield (Dad's father) also lived with us for many years after he retired, until he died at the ripe old age of ninety-four.

The little village is situated between Bath and Wells, with many very old farms and houses, one being the Manor House, which I believe is mentioned in the Domesday Book. The farmer who lived in the Manor House was also a local magistrate, he owned quite a lot of land in the village and around it.

Nearby, in a kind of vale stands the lovely old Church of St. John's in the quiet Churchyard amidst the tall trees, so peaceful and dignified. We were all christened there when we were just a few weeks old. A short walk along the lane brings you to the little village school with its small garden, which the boys were encouraged to cultivate.

A focal point of the village was the gentle stream which runs down from the many springs up in the picturesque valley. It flows along beside the main street, tumbling over the miniature waterfalls on its way down through the village.

Although we were all christened at St. John's Church, we attended regularly at the little Chapel on the hill opposite the cenotaph, which was at the other end of the village. Our Sunday-school was a wooden building adjoining the chapel, where we spent many happy hours, not least of all at our 'bunfights'. The working class people worked very long hours for pay which was a mere pittance, with just the odd one day Bank holiday.

Dad, who was a miner, had been gone to work a couple of hours since, as he had to walk to work to the colliery at Moorewood, about three miles away. They started work very early in the morning as they often had to walk many miles underground, to get to their places of work. Eddie, my eldest brother had also gone to work at Farmer Grey's farm down the lane, where he helped out after school and at weekends to earn a little money. His pay, though small was a big help to Mum, where every penny counted.

The fire which Dad had lit in the open grate to boil the kettle for his tea, before he went to work, had burnt very low by the time we came downstairs, so Jim raked it out and shovelled on some more coal. He picked up the ashes into the bucket, then he blackleaded the grate and whitened the hearth as we had seen Mum do so many times before. When he had finished he fastened the big wire fireguard each side of the fire place, for safety. In the meantime, I had scrubbed the kitchen table and swept and scrubbed the stone-flagged kitchen floor.

Mum came down the stairs carrying baby Jackie, just as I was going out of the back-door to empty the bucket of dirty water, and rinse out the floor cloth under the water tap in the back yard.

"You'm about early this mornin' bent'e," she said.

"Well, Jim's helpin' me with my jobs indoors, then I shall help him do his jobs outside when we had our breakfast," I replied. I hated housework anyway, and preferred to be outdoors with my brother, but we all had our chores to do on Saturdays.

Mum put the cloth on the kitchen table and, taking the bread-knife out of the table drawer, she sliced the cottage loaf on the bread board, "Here" she said, "Make the toast while I dress Jackie." I put the bread on the long wire toasting fork and toasted it, slice after slice, in front of the fire, then down the stairs came my elder sister, Rose, with Tom and Mary, my younger brother and sister.

"You'm just in time" I said, as I spread the beef dripping on each piece of toast. "Eat it up, before 'tis cold." Mum poured out the tea and we all sat round the table eating our breakfast and making our plans for the day. They sold the beef dripping in the kitchens of the near-by public school for boys, called "Downside College". Eddie used to get a basinful for twopence, it was very tasty and made a cheap and nourishing meal.

Downside College is quite well known, it is in the little village of Stratton-on-the-Fosse. Sometimes they opened their cinema to the public and occasionally, as a treat, Mum would let us go when she could afford it. We paid our twopence at the door and took our seats on the hard wooden chairs to watch the black and white film and be transported into another world for a little while. Of course it was frequently interrupted by breakdowns and the inevitable reel changes.

My sister Rose was two years older than me, she seemed so wise in understanding the ways of life, much beyond her years. She had suffered from heart trouble since birth, so Mum had always taken extra care with her, and we were always told to look after her. She was always full of life and looked a picture of health, with her lovely auburn hair and her much too rosy cheeks. Once, when she was quite small, she woke up one night to find Mum had been taken ill, she was in a coma. Instead of waking Dad, Rose rushed downstairs to the sideboard in the kitchen, where Mum always kept a small medicine bottle with a drop of brandy in it, for medicinal purposes. When Dad woke up, Rose was tipping some brandy down Mum's throat, she thought it would make Mum better. Of course, in those days you could take a small bottle to the pub and buy half a noggin of brandy – (about half a gill) you didn't have to have a bottlefull. Rose lived a normal life until she was thirty years old, defying doctors who had announced at her birth that she would only live for about six months. Needless to say, she was always

Mum's favourite.

After breakfast, Jim and I washed up the dishes for Mum, then decided to clean out the chicken's house first, it was one of Jim's Saturday jobs. So, armed with Dad's spade and shovel, we walked down the cinder path to the chicken-house at the bottom of the garden. We had to drive all the chickens into the big wire pen first, then we set to work to clean out the wooden hut. It was a messy job but we enjoyed it, and after spreading around some fresh straw, we fed them. Mum always saved the potato peelings for the chickens. She cooked them in an old iron saucepan she kept for that purpose, so we mixed them up with some bran and any other scraps she had, in an old enamel bowl, and fed them to the chickens with a few cabbage stalks and leaves, which they seemed to enjoy. When we had finished, we put away the spade and shovel in the corner of the toilet in the garden, where Dad always kept his garden tools. Mum bred two kinds of chickens, Rhode Island Reds with their rich reddish brown feathers, and the Light Sussex, which were white with black feathers round their necks and tails, they were both very good laying and table birds.

"Le's go to the wood now an' get some firewood," said Jim – it was another of our Saturday jobs. "An' on the way back we'll look fer some bird's nests."

"Tha's a good idea," I replied, as we washed our hands under the water tap in the yard.

"Mum, we'm goin' a get the firewood now," Jim called to Mum, wiping his hands on the towel hanging behind the kitchen door.

"Alright," replied Mum, "but don't be gone too long."

Off we went, jumping over the stone stile into the field in front of our house, and keeping to the footpath, we walked the length of the field. We went across the small paddock and into the dark shady wood which was on a slope. We often went there to pick blackberries, hazelnuts and flowers in their season, and of course, firewood all the year round.

The farmer who owned the wood, Farmer Golledge, lived in the farm down the valley and he must have heard us chattering away as we wandered around in the wood. Sometimes he would shout at us "Get out of my wood, you faggots," and we would scarper away as fast as we could go, but he rarely came after us. On one occasion he did, and we scrambled up a tree. We just sat there up in the branches, terrified, as he walked around under the tree looking for us. After a while, he gave up and walked back down the valley, muttering to himself.

This day, we had gone only a short distance into the wood, which was quite dense in places, and I was more interested in looking for birds' nests than looking where I was stepping, when Jim shouted – "Look where you'm goin' you nearly stepped on that adder." I nearly jumped out of my skin. There, curled up on a tree stump right by my feet, was a small snake asleep. Jim said "Don't worry, he won't hurt 'e if you don't tormet 'en." So we wandered on and soon forgot the sleeping snake, with so many other things to attract our attention.

There were the little squirrels with their long bushy tails, scampering up the trees, quick as a flash – the occasional rabbit as it scuttled back to its burrow. As we wandered on through the bushes and brambles, we could hear the twittering of the birds as they searched around for their food.

We picked up pieces of firewood as we walked on over the rough narrow tracks, till we spotted a little robin on a twig. As we moved nearer and peered into the bushes, the little robin flew off and there in a dear little nest of leavs and feathers, were five tiny white eggs with brown spots on them.

"Le's hold one," I said to Jim, holding out my hand. He took one of the eggs out of the nest and placed it in my hand and as I looked at it, I said, "Tis so tiny." It didn't seem possible that a little bird would finally emerge from so small an egg. I reached up to put it back in the nest and as I did so I scratched my hand on the brambles and let go of the egg. It dropped to the ground and smashed.

"Oh, damn it," I said.

"Now your fingers 'll grow crooked, our Joy," cried Jim, with all the wisdom of Solomon, and every day after, I used to look at my fingers to see if they were still straight.

It was all so quiet and almost eerie as we stood there in the wood looking around for nests, then we wandered about for quite a while, having no luck at all.

"Le's go different ways," said Jim, "I'll go this way," he said pointing in one direction, "an' you go that way." So off he went and soon he was out of sight and the only sound was the dry bracken underfoot, as I walked around, looking in all the bushes and brambles.

Suddenly, Jim shouted from the other side of the wood.

"Come an' see Joy, here's a nest." I ran to where he was standing pointing into the green thorny bush.

"Tis a thrush's nest, I think," he said. I leaned forward to take a look into the green foliage, and there, on a small branch was a much bigger nest than the little robin's . This one was lined with hard smooth mud and inside were four bright blue eggs with a few dark spots on them. I just stood there and looked, not daring to touch them as I couldn't face breaking another bird's egg that day.

Next, we decided to concentrate on getting the firewood, so we tramped around picking up all the dry bits of wood we could see, until we both had as much as we could carry, then we decided to go home.

As we were making our way back across the paddock Jim said,

"Le's have a climb up that tree," pointing to a big old hollow tree in the corner of the field.

"Alright," I replied, "We'll have a go." I wasn't sure I would make it but I was always ready to have a go.

We put our bundles of firewood on the grass under the trees.

"You go first," I said, wondering if I had bitten off more than I could chew. In no time at all, Jim had climbed up into the branches looking down at me, as I wondered where to start.

"Come on then, catch hold there an' put yer foot here," he called, pointing to a small dent in the tree trunk, "You'll get a better grip there." I did as he told me and surprised myself by making it at the first attempt. We sat there for quite a while, after finding a comfortable branch to sit on, and I had a wonderful feeling of freedom as I sat there high up in the tree with the breeze blowing through the branches fanning the trembling green leaves. It was just great, and what a grand view.

We could see for miles around – the cottages and farms were dotted around amongst the fields, woods and lanes, many hidden from our view by the tall trees swaying in the breeze. A train was puffing away at a steady pace along the railway line, we watched it until it disappeared into the tunnel, out of sight, leaving a trail of smoke on the skyline.

We stayed there a while, chattering away when suddenly Jim said "I'm hungry, le's go home." He climbed down the tree and I started to follow him, I got so far then I lost my footing. I kept trying, but each time my foot slipped, I just couldn't get a grip at all – I was stuck halfway.

"Tis no good," I said, "I can't get down." I was beginning to get all hot and bothered.

"Go back and come down on the branch," Jim shouted, "Tis easier that way." So, back I went and, slowly turning round, I started to come down backwards on a branch. I edged my way slowly along it and thought I was doing nicely when all at once, the branch snapped under my weight and down I went, still clutching the branch in my hand.

"You should 'ave let go the branch and jumped," called Jim, running towards me, "Be you alright?" "Yes," I replied, brushing myself down, "I'm alright, just a few scratches."

"Look at your frock," cried Jim as I turned round, "Tis all broke' down the back." "Oh my gosh," I replied, "I shall cop it this time." I was always in trouble for tearing my clothes. Almost every other day, Mum swore she would make my dresses out of sackbags.

We talked things over and decided that Jim should go in the house first when we got home, and, when no-one was looking, he would get the needle and cotton from Mum's workbox – it was a cardboard shoebox really – and bring them out to me, in the toilet in the garden. I made my way to the toilet and sat on the long wooden seat and waited impatiently for him to come – I didn't have long to wait. "Here tis," he said, taking the needle and cotton out of his trouser pocket and handing them to me. "Here's the little scissors too. I'll keep watch outside 'till you've mended it." I took off my dress and, turning it inside out, I stitched it up as neatly as I could then, turning it right side out again, I put it on. I had always been good at sewing, even as a child, it was one of my few achievements. We went into the house then and sat down at the kitchen table to wait for our dinner, not daring to look at one another or we should have burst out laughing and Mum would have wanted to know what was going on. I never heard any more about the dress, I think Mum musn't have noticed it, or maybe she forgot to mention it as she was always very busy. Even when she sat down in the evenings, there was always a pile of mending to be done, especially with our socks and stockings. If they were very holey in the feet she would cut it right out and stitch in a new piece of material, which she had cut to the shape of the foot

Dad always repaired our shoes and boots, we used to buy the pieces of leather and a couple of ounces of small nails at the shoe-makers' who lived at the bottom of our lane. Dad had a cast-iron foot which he used. It had two different sizes of feet on it. He would put the shoe on it, then roughly cut a piece of leather the size of the sole and, holding it on to the shoe, he made small holes in the leather with a bradawl, where he wanted to put in the nails. After hammering on the piece of leather of the boot, he would shape it round the sole and then wax round the edges.

Jim liked to go catching butterflies on the siding opposite the railway station. We would set off across the field, taking our hats and jamjars. Sometimes we had to chase them a long way before we caught them. When they pitched on the grass we would throw our hats over them, then slowly lift off our hat, a little at a time, then put them into our jamjars with some wild flowers and grasses. They looked so beautiful, all pretty colours and different sizes, I liked the soldier butterflies, they were red and black, there was a little blue one too, which was very pretty. when we got home, we covered the top of the jars, and put little holes in it. We usually kept them a few days, then we let them go.

We also went catching minnows in our jamjars, we tied a piece of string around the rim of the jar to make it easier to carry and off we would go down to the stream. We'd stay there for ages watching them swimming away, and stepping on the big stones in the stream, we'd put our jars down in the water to catch them. We nearly always went home with wet feet and we got a telling off, but we did enjoy it.

During the long winter evenings at home, we passed the time playing dominoes, writing games or dressing up in old clothes to act in little sketches we made up ourselves. Sometimes we recited poems or monologues, Dad often played his accordion. 'Nellie Dean' and 'Two little girls in blue, love', all the old songs – we got to know them all off by heart.

If Mum was making a rug, which she often did, we would help her. She always had a bag full of odd pieces of cloth, they were all different colours. We would cut the material into strips about six inches long and Mum would thread them into a big new piece of sacking, with a rug hook, then she would tie each piece in a knot, until all the sacking was covered. When the rug was finished she would back it with some very strong material. It was a long process but it made a very lasting rug.

Dad, who was a quiet and vey patient man, would tell us about his childhood. He had lived in a thatched cottage in the middle of a large wood, called Harridge Wood, which at that time belonged to Squire Strachey who employed Granfer Albert as a game-keeper. Granfer always had a great respect for the Squire who lived up at the big house.

Granfer looked rather like Father Christmas, with his white hair and beard. He always wore thick brown corduroy trousers and waistcoat both summer and winter, with black leather leggings and boots, and a wide black leather belt with a large brass buckle. He was never without his walking stick with the bone handle, he treasured it because the Squire had given it to him. Every Friday morning he would walk to the gardener's cottage about four miles away, to get his weekly pension of five shillings, which the Squire paid him for his long service with him.

Dad was the youngest of thirteen children, his mother died when he was a baby and his elder sisters had to bring him up. He never went to school so of course, he never learnt to read and write, he could only write his name. Mum said she could never understand why Granfer was never reported for not sending Dad to school as there was a school officer checking up on them, although they had to pay twopence a week for their schooling. After much thought, Mum said "Maybe Granfer bribed him with a couple of pheasants occasionally."

Joyce's family

Dad was very shy as a boy, and when people came walking through the woods, he would run away and hide behind the trees. He loved the wild life there and one of his favourite pastimes was catching the trout in the stream which ran through the wood and alongside their thatched cottage. He said "Tis easy to catch 'em, you just put your hand in the water and tickle 'em under their belly." Then he would take them indoors and cook them for his dinner.

Dad worked in the coalmines for over thirty years, the conditions were very bad then, his back was covered with the ugly blue marks from the coal, which no amount of washing could remove. The men had to pull the tubs of coal along the tracks underground, crawling on their hands and knees because the ceilings were so low they could not stand up. They had ropes and chains around their waist, which were attached to the coal-tubs. They used small carbide lamps to see their way about underground, these were fastened to the front of their caps. There were no pithead baths, so they had to walk home black with coaldust, to bathe in the big bath in front of the kitchen fire. If we children were at home we had to go in the front room, or out to play while Dad had his bath. The coaldust and terrible working conditions were the cause of many a miner's death, my own Dad's included.

I remember as a child, some of the terrible times during the miner's strike in 1926, it was a very bad time for everyone. We used to go to the Church Hall carrying Dad's large enamel tea-can in which he used to take his tea to work, to get some soup, which the local ladies dished out to us. I also remember wearing the ugly, heavy, hobnailed boots which were issued to poor families. We had the choice of wearing them or going barefoot, as Mum had no money to buy any, it was a constant worry just to keep us fed.

Dad and his mate, George, would go picking up coal on the black coal-batch. Dad on his old bike and George on his three-wheeled trike. They put the sacks of coal across the handle-bars of their bikes and pushed them the four miles home. Some of the men would go poaching for rabbits or hares, anything that would make a meal for their families. People who were really ill often could not afford to see their doctors; we were lucky to have a good doctor, his name was Dr. Bradley. Mum had her own remedies as most women had, but when it was necessary to call him, usually for my sister with her heart attacks, he was always very patient until Mum could afford to pay the bill. He always used to describe my sister as 'a rosy apple with a rotten core' because she always had such a healthy appearance, but a very bad heart condition.

Mum's Dad, (Granfer Jim Stock) was very different from Granfer Albert, he was a wily little man, he had a horse and cart. The cart was more like a trap, he used it for his fresh-fish round in the nearby villages. Each morning he would go off to Shepton Mallet market to purchase his fish, perched up on his seat and puffing away at his old clay pipe. I have only a vague memory of Grannie, sitting in her basket-chair by the fire, with a khaki coloured woollen shawl round her shoulders. I remember Mum lifting each of us up in turn, to kiss her when she died. I was very young when she died, and later, Granfer Jim married again and for that Mum never forgave him, putting someone else in her mother's place.

Mum would tell us about the hard times she had as a child, often she could not go to school because she had no boots. When her brother came home from work, she would put on his boots to go out and get the shopping when Grannie was ill. She said Granfer could never settle anywhere for long so they were always on the move.

Saturday night was always bath-night at our house, no sooner had we washed up the tea-dishes and put them away when Mum would fill the big iron saucepan with water and put it on the open fire to boil. Dad would bring in the large galvanised bath from the wash-house and put it in front of the kitchen fire. He'd put on his jacket and cap and, lighting up his pipe, he would call out "Cheerio, I shan't be long." Off he would stroll across the fields, down the railway siding and up under the railway bridge towards the pub called 'The Railway Inn', since re-named 'The Sword and Castle', for his weekly pint and a game of shove-ha'penny with his mates.

We were usually bathed and sitting in the high-backed wooden settle in our night-clothes, eating our supper, when Dad came home. He was never late, always about nine o'clock as, being an early riser, he was never late going to bed. Nearly always he would bring home a small bottle of stout for Mum, he knew she would enjoy it with her supper. After cutting himself a thick slice of bread from the cottage loaf on the table and a chunk of Cheddar cheese, he would sit in his old arm-chair and toast it in front of the fire. As he was eating it he told her about the people he had met at the pub and all the local gossip about who had got married or who had died, etc. After supper they would empty the big bath together and, taking our candlesticks and lighting our candles, we said our goodnights and all went up to bed, leaving Dad to blow out the oil-lamp and follow us up the stairs.

We were never allowed to play with balls, hoops, tops or any other games on Sundays, so after breakfast, Mum would say, "You'd better get washed and changed, 'tis time for Chapel." So we went and washed and put on our Sunday best clothes, then we made our way down the lane, across the field we called 'front ground' and up the main village street to the Chapel on the hill. On the way we met some of our friends, we were a little early, so we sat in our pews whispering to each other until the service started. I loved singing the hymns, it always gave me such a wonderful feeling. I could never explain, but I soon got bored with the long sermons which seemed to go on forever. Afternoon Sunday school was more enjoyable, teacher would read us a bible story and then ask us questions about it afterwards. She also gave us little Scripture pictures to stick in our Sunday school books.

Some weeks Mum gave us a sixpence or a shilling to give the teacher towards our yearly outing to the seaside, it was a highspot in our lives. I remember one Sunday, as we walked up the village street to Sunday school we stopped to watch the minnows in the stream. We started to throw little stones at them in the water and I accidently threw in my sixpence instead of a stone. The water was too deep for me to get it out, so of course, I got into trouble when I got home. Mum never went to Church, somehow she never seemed to find the time. She only went when the babies were christened, or for weddings or funerals, but every morning and evening as long as I can remember, she knelt down beside the big brass bedstead to thank God for all his blessings.

Monday morning and off to school we'd go. "Did you put on yer clean pinnies you girls?" said Mum as we kissed her goodbye. "Yes Mum," we replied as we buttoned up our coats. We always wore white cotton pinafores over our dresses at school, they usually had a bit of lace on the yokes and over the tops of the sleeves. Mine never stayed white for long as I was always up to some mischief or other. "Oh, here's yer milk money," shouted Mum, as we were walking out of the door. We went back to get the twopence each which we paid every week for the small bottle of milk we had at school each day, at lunchtime.

Down the lane we went, meeting up with some friends on the way. At the bottom of the lane was the little sweet shop where we sometimes bought our ha'penny gobstoppers, mint dumps or aniseed balls. It was owned by old Mr. Perkins and his daughter. We walked on down the narrow lane called the 'Pitching' to school. The village school seemed quite big to us children, but really it was rather small, with its separate entrances for boys and girls. We all lined up in the playgrounds and marched into the hall to start the day with prayers, then we went to the classrooms with our teachers.

The headmaster and three lady teachers were all elderly and just seemed to concentrate on the few brainy pupils in each class, of which I was not one. I liked history, sewing and physical exercise, or drill, as we called it then. I never could get the hang of algebra, and maths was always a boring subject to me.

"Mum, we gotta see the school doctor on Wednesday," I said, when we arrived home from school. "Teacher gave us this note to bring home fer you, can you come down to school, 'tis Wednesday morning?" Mum took the note and read it, she always tried to be there when the school doctor paid his yearly visit to our school. "I 'spect so," she replied, "but you'll all have to have a bath Tuesday night." So we all had to go through the usual bath night ritual on Tuesday night. "Is your mother coming?" asked the district nurse at school Wednesday morning, as we undressed for our medical examination, she was always in attendance when the doctor came to school. "Yes" I replied. "Well you had better wait out there until she comes," she said.
So we sat there, half-dressed, shivering in the cold until Mum arrived with the two babies in the pram, as it was always in the winter time when the doctor came. We took our turn to see him, Mum explaining little ailments we had, then we dressed and went back to our class-room and Mum went off home, pushing the pram back up the lane.

The dentist also came once a year, but Mum never came with us. He would set up a surgery in someone's house, usually with an old lady called Mrs. Bence. She lived in an old house called Somer House with her dwarf brother, Billy Hamblin, who was a tailor by trade. The house was in Britannia Yard, which is off the main village street and quite a distance from the school, many pupils went home when they were sent to the dentist, as he was often very rough in his manner, and careless.

One day at school there was a bit of commotion, all the teachers were huddled together talking in whispers, and we knew there was something in the air, then, in the afternoon the headmaster gathered us all together in the hall. He told us that, owing to the increasing numbers of pupils in the village, our school was to become an Infant school only and all children over eleven years of age would have to go to Midsomer Norton Senior school which was about two and a half miles away. After school we hurried home to tell Mum all about it.

"How be'ee goin' get all down Norton in time fer school?" she said. "They'm goin'a take us down in a charabanc, but we gotta walk home after school." We didn't like the idea at all and most of the parents protested but all to no avail, we had to go. Of course it was a much bigger school with more amenities and we soon got used to the long walk home. The headmaster asked us all to wear school uniform, which was navy-blue gymslips and white blouses, which of course, Mum could not afford, so I made my own in sewing class at school; we were allowed to pay a little money each week, towards the material.

"Tis my turn to stay home today," I said to Mum, I was always looking for an excuse to stay home from school, it was Tuesday, Mum's washing day. Our house was one in a block of three, we lived one end, but the wash-house ways at the other end of the block. During the summer-time Mum always put my youngest brother and sister in the pram and took them with her out in the wash-house when she did her washing, but in winter, it was much too cold, so either my sister Rose or I stayed home from school to look after them, and help with the housework. It was alright staying home but when we had to explain to the headmaster why we were home, we always said we were ill, I was embarrassed. It was a standing joke with him, "It's queer," he would say, "one of you is always ill on a Tuesday."

"Just dust round the front-room if you get a chance when the baby's asleep," Mum would say. "Alright," I'd answer, I hated dusting, still do. On the big chest of drawers just inside the door, were the pair of china lions, one each end. We were allowed to play with them only when we were ill. There was also the silver teapot, the only silver item Mum possessed, the large glass cruet Dad had given Mum when they were engaged, and the family bible where all the births, marriages and deaths in the family were recorded.

We had a sideboard with a couple of vases, a cheese-dish and a few more trinkets on it, and a large oval gilt-edged mirror at the back of it. Under the window was the long horse-hair sofa with Mum's basket chair and Dad's arm-chair each side of the fireplace. A few best chairs and a table covered with a thick, dark old-fashioned tablecloth and lots and lots of old photographs. That was our front-room, as long as I can remember.

"There's a magic-lantern show on in the Hall tonight," said Len, one of our friends, as we walked home from school one day.
"What time?" asked Jim. "About ha'f pas' six," replied Len, "You goin'?"
"We'll have to ask our Mum," said Jim so we hurried off home to see if we could get round Mum to let us go.

"Yes" she said, "you can go, but give me a hand first to get this coal in." Being a miner, Dad was allowed two hundred weight of coal a week, so the coal man came once a fortnight to deliver it in his horse and cart. Of course, it was never in bags, he just tipped it by the roadside outside our gate, so it had to be carried into the coalhouse in buckets. Of course we were only too eager to help so that she would let us go to the show, and as we shovelled up the coal, Jim and I couldn't help laughing as we joked about the person who had just delivered the coal.

"She is a queer'un," I said, "wonder if she is a woman or a man?" There was always a bit of mystery about her in the village. She was called Georgina, and she always dressed as a woman, with her big striped coarse apron. She drove her big horse and cart all over the village delivering the coal, and she was as good as any man at shovelling up the coal from the coal-waggons.

We ate our tea in record time after getting in the coal, then we got ourselves ready. "Don't forget now, come straight home," Mum shouted after us as we walked out the door and made our way down the lane to the village hall. We met some friends on the way and played around until it was time to go in, them we all made a dash for the door.

"Let's sit up the front," said Jim, as we got inside te hall, "we'll see more up there." We pushed our way to the front row of chairs to get a good seat, as we didn't want to miss anything, then we sat down and waited eagerly for the show to start.

A large screen was erected at the front of the stage and a projector was set up at the back by the door. The hall soon filled with people all chattering away to each other, all the seats were filled. Suddenly, all the lights went out and everyone stopped talking, you could hear a pin drop. The silent film started, it was all in black and white. One of the ladies gave a running commentary as we all sat spellbound, our eyes glued to the screen. The film was all about the missionaries in South Africa. The tribesmen looked fierce with their spears and painted bodies, and beautiful feathered head-dresses. It was so exciting, watching them dancing to the rhythm of their many drums and horns, in the African bush. It was a wonderful sight and very interesting to watch, we had never seen anything like it before, it was another world to us. We put our penny in the collection bag as we came out of the hall and talked of nothing else, until we went to bed to dream that we were still in South Africa with the natives.

With the coming of Spring, Mum would set about the spring-cleaning, painting and decorating, even to varnishing the chairs and the kitchen table legs, which always got a bit of a bashing from all of us. We used to trim the rolls of wallpaper ready for Mum to do the wallpapering and help in our childish way, mixing up the paste etc. The wallpaper cost twopence or threepence a roll and the ceilings were always white-washed, Mum bought the packets of whitening and mixed it with water until it was quite a thick liquid, then brushed it over the ceilings.

Dad would sort out his seed potatoes and put them in tomato boxes, in the bedrooms under the beds, then dig up the garden and the allotment ready for planting. We always had fresh vegetables all through the year, Mum never had to buy any. At the beginning of April Dad usually began planting his potatoes, Eddie and I often helped him. He would dig small drills in the ground, then giving us a strip of wood about eighteen inches long, we had to put the potatoes in the drills one at a time, measuring the distance between them with the strip of wood. Then Dad would come along behind us covering in each drill. We liked helping him because he always gave us a penny each.

Joyce, left, on an outing to Burnham On Sea

I think he must have been musical because he always enjoyed playing his accordion, sometimes he would sit my little brother of sister on his knee and sing old country songs. One I remember quite clearly was about pancake day.

"Ash Wednesday, Shrove Tuesday, poor Jack went to plough,
His mother made pancakes, she didn't know how,
She poked 'em and daked 'em, an' made 'em so black,
She put too much pepper and poisoned poor Jack."

After the bitter, cold winters we looked forward to the lovely walks along the narrow, winding country lanes and across the green fields and into the woods.

"Le's go down in the valley," I'd say to Jim, "maybe we can find primroses fer Grannie's grave." It was exciting in the Spring, looking for the first flowers to appear in the hedgerows. Off we'd go, across the field in front of our house, and down through the valley where the trees would meet in the middle above our heads and cast dark shadows all the way down. Then we'd make our way along the lane, which was more like a cart-track, stopping a while to watch the old water-wheel going round and round, taking the water with it. We walked on alongside the watercress beds, where Uncle Jim worked for many years up to his knees in water during the freezing winters. The first wild violets and primroses we picked, we used to put in a jam-jar with some water and take to the Church-yard, to put on Grannie's grave.

We looked forward to Easter, it was a busy time for our teachers at Chapel, as we always sang an anthem on Easter morning, so we had to go to practice until we could sing it properly. As it was a special occasion, Mum always tried to get us new dresses.

"We'll go down the market an' get some cloth," she would say, so off she would go on a Saturday morning to Radstock market, taking two or three of us with her. It was a big treat for us to go to the market in the train, we enjoyed walking round, looking at the busy stalls where you could buy anything from medicines to new and second-hand clothes. Mum would look all around to see which was the best bargain in the materials she could afford. It was usually a strong cotton material costing about four-pence three-farthings a yard, (always referred to as 'four-three'). Then she would look over some second-hand over-coats, which she would wash and unpick the seams, and make up into trousers for the boys, and sometimes coats for us girls. If we were lucky, Mum would buy us a new straw hat, as females were not allowed in Church or Chapel without one in those days, but, if she could not afford it, she would brighten up our old ones with an extra bow, or artificial flower. We walked on past the stalls with their beautiful china ornaments, tea-sets, clocks and jewellery, rugs, furniture and clothes, etc. At the top end of the market were a few butcher's stalls where Mum sometimes bought pig's trotters, or pig's heads to make brawn. Further along was the grocery stall where they sold all kinds of cold meats and ham, 'off the bone'. Next to it was a little cubicle which was curtained off, there you could buy a cup of tea and a home-made cake, or sandwiches. On round the corner was the fish-stall, Mum often bought some fresh fish, mackerel or sprats, or a bit of cod which she knew Dad always enjoyed for his tea.

When Mum had finished her shopping, we would make our way to the railway station which was close by, our bags were always full of goods, as we struggled along, trying to keep pace with Mum. It was usually beginning to get dark by the time we got out of the train at our village station on the way home, and as we made our way back, across the field, carrying our shopping bags, it was a welcoming sight to see the light of the oil-lamp shining from the kitchen window.

Dad always had the kettle boiling on the hob when we got indoors, and a lovely fire burning away in the open grate. "I 'spect you could do wi' a cup o' tea," he would say, as he picked up the tea-pot and poured in the boiling water. We took off our coats and sat down beside the warm fire to drink our tea. Mum unpacked the shopping, telling Dad about the goods she had bought, and all the bargains at the market, which we needed, but could not afford to buy. Then she would cook the fish and we all sat down to tea.

For the next few weeks, Mum would be very busy, making our little dresses and the trousers for the boys, on the little Singer sewing machine which Grannie had bought on credit, and as she could not afford to keep up the payments, Mum had paid them off.

The little Chapel was always packed with people on Easter Sunday morning, all wearing their best clothes, and we felt so important sitting in the choir seats, wearing our new dresses. It was a very moving service, with beautiful hymns, and as the sun shone through the stained glass windows onto the lovely golden daffodils which decorated the Chapel, it really was a breath of spring. One of the older boys sat behind the organ to pump it for the organist, it was considered a privilege, so there was never any shortage of volunteers, and for once I didn't mind the long sermon.

After Easter the annual fairs made their rounds of the surrounding villages, and after much persuasion, Mum usually agreed to let us go. "Here's a shilling between you," she'd say, "an' don't forget to be home by tea-time." "We'll get a free ride if we get there before one o'clock," said Jim. So we put on our hats and coats and, after saying 'cheerio' to Mum, we set off to walk the two miles to the fair. We could hear the loud music of the big organs playing, long before we got there, it just seemed to hurry us along and in our excitement we didn't know where to go first, when we eventually arrived at the fair. We decided to go to the roundabouts, to make sure of our free ride, then we stopped a while at the Noah's Ark, watching the people as they jumped on and off the animals. There were swings, Aunt Sallys, coco-nut shies, the rifle range, the cake-walk and lots of candy-stalls.

"Le's go on the helter-skelter," I said, "tis only a penny a go," so we paid our penny and took a mat and climbed up inside the wooden tower. We could look down on all the crowds of people jostling around, enjoying themselves, and listening to the screams of delight as the amusements went round faster and faster. We sat on our mat and whizzed off down the chute. We saw the gypsies in their gaily painted horse-drawn caravans selling their wares and lucky charms, the lovely shire-horses with their plaited manes and tails, their brass trimmed harnesses and colourful rosettes. We walked on past the caravan of Gypsy Rose Lee who was telling fortunes, the fat lady's tent, the Fire-eaters and the wrestlers. At the far end, there was a crowd of people surrounding a man with a beard, he was selling bottles of his herbal medicine which he guaranteed would cure all their ailments, he was very convincing and doing a roaring trade. We wandered round and round, not wanting to leave the excitement and thrills of the fair, until, tired and hungry, we decided it was time to go.

During the school holidays, we loved playing in the hay-fields and helping to rake the hay into piles with the large wooden rakes, which were almost as big as us.

"Wonder if we'll get a ride in the haycart today?" Jim would say, it was a big thrill to ride in the high hay-wagon pulled along by the heavy cart-horses, they were always so docile and friendly. We would hang around for hours sometimes, hoping for a ride. The farmer's wife always brought along a very large basket of food and big stone jars of cider for the farmer and farm labourers at meal-times. They worked long hours in the hot sun, as they had to do everything by hand. Sometimes we were lucky, if there was any food left over, the farmer's wife would give us a bit of bread and cheese to eat.

My eldest brother, Eddie, who worked on the farm, often went to market with the farmer. It was just for livestock trading, at Farrington. Once they were driving some cows to market and the cows got into someone's garden and it took them hours to get them out, after they had trampled down everything in sight.

When the General Election came round, Mum, who was usually a placid person unless aroused, would suddenly break out and give vent to her feelings. Being a miner's wife, she was a staunch member of the Labour Party. She always nailed up a big poster of the local Labour candidiate, on the side of the house which faced the road, for everyone to see.

"They blasted Tories are no good fer the working man, they look after thur own kind, the rich get richer an' the poor get poorer," she would say. "Once they get your vote they ferget thur promises, but they won't get my vote, that's fer sure."

On voting day, we children wore our rosettes proudly, pinned to the front of our 'pinnies'. We joined in singing a song about the Labour candidate, a Mr. Fred Gould. Dad said he was a good man who helped the miners.

We sang "Vote, vote, vote for Mr. Gould, drive 'old Peto' out the land." I can't remember the Tory candidate's name. Dad said Mum always got on her soap-box at election time.

One day, Eddie came running in from the garden, obviously very upset. "Who let me hedgehog go?" he cried, looking accusingly at Jim and me.

"We don't know what you'm talking about," I replied.

"Yes, you do," said Eddie. "No we don't," said Jim.

"Whatever's the matter," asked Mum as she stood by the table doing the ironing. "Somebody let me hedgehog go," cried Eddie, "I had 'en tied up to the post." "I let 'em go," said Mum as she took another hot flat-iron from the trippet which held it on to the front of the open fire, then she replaced it with the colder iron which she had been using. "You know 'tis cruel to keep 'em tied up, don't do it again."

Eddie was always getting new pets, you never knew what to expect when you looked in his hutches and pens down in the garden. One day it was ferrets, next day it could be rabbits, bantams, pigeons or even pigs, there was no end to his menagerie. We never knew how he acquired them, they just appeared. I think he used to swap one for the other, when he grew tired of them, with his friends.

When we got home from school one day, Mum was out in the garden talking to Mrs. Brown, our next door neighbour. They were deep in conversation, nodding to each other as they chatted away, so we gathered it was something serious.

"Well," said Mrs. Brown, "I saw 'er when I looked out our bedroom window, last night, an' that must 'ave bin ha'f pas' ten, she's a gadabout, always after the men, she's asking for trouble."

"Yes," replied Mum, "She da want her behind smacked wi' a bunch a' stingin' nettles." (one of Mum's old sayings), "She'll end up in the workhouse, tha' fer sure."

"Who's that Mum," I asked, "who'll end up in the workhouse?"

"Never you min'," said Mum, "You go on an' play."

It appeared they were talking about a person who lived down the lane. In those days, young girls who got into trouble were automatically put into the workhouse for many years, if their parents would not support them. Babies were always born at home, neighbours always helped each other and there was always a woman in the street who would help out at births, and do the laying out when someone died, if you paid her a small fee. If a nurse was desperately needed, you had to get a conveyance to fetch her, a horse and trap. Our nearest nurse lived at Midsomer Norton two miles away, then later, we had a nurse in the village, Nurse Bird, who worked there for many years.

"Mum, our Tom's got a fester on his knee," said Eddie one day, "it do look bad."

"Come 'ere, le's 'ave a look at it," replied Mum, bending down, "What 'ave 'ee done?"

"Tis nothing," said Tom, sticking his foot up on the stool for Mum to see. "I fell down last week an' grazed it a bit, now 'tis festered."

"Jus' stay there a minute," she said, as she went off down the garden path. A few minutes later she came back carrying a small leaf which she had picked from a small cabbage plant. First she bathed Tom's knee with hot water to which she had added some boracic powder, then wiping the knee dry, she put the small leaf over the fester, then a pad of cotton wool, then she bandaged it up.

"That'll draw it all out," she said. Mum always had her own remedies for all our ailments. Bread poultices for boils, senna tea for constipation, warm vinegar and butter for sore throats, and rubbing in a bit of butter on a bruise, she would say (to bring it out).

Jim and I often stopped to watch the village blacksmith as he hammered away on his anvil, making the horse-shoes beside the roaring fire, which from time to time he revived with a huge pair of belolws, it was very interesting to us. We used to think it was very cruel when he hammered the hot horse-shoes on to the horse's hoof. Then he explained to us that the horse couldn't feel it, and as the horse never whinnied when we watched it being done, we had to believe him. He looked so big and strong in his large leather as he hammered the horse-shoes in to shape. His workshop was a store of farming implements, some old and rusty, others waiting to be repaired.

My elder sister, Rose, was a girl guide and I was in the brownies, then I too joined the guides. Rose worked very hard to win the row of badges she proudly wore on the sleeve of her guide uniform, while I didn't have any, but I didn't mind a bit. I just went along to enjoy myself, which I always did. I loved the parades and going camping, singing our camp-songs around the camp-fire, it was all good fun to me. When we went to our meetings once a week, our guide leader always inspected our hands, finger-nails and teeth, for cleanliness. Of course, Mum couldn't afford to buy us tooth-brushes or tooth-paste to use, so we had small pieces of clean white rag, and made it damp, then lightly rubbed it on the bar of cooking salt, or on the soot from the chimney breast. We rubbed it over our teeth and then well rinsed out our mouths, it made our teeth lovely and white.

Every year when Armistice day came around, we had to parade with the boy scouts and ex-service men up through the main village street to the cenotaph on the hill. When they read out all the names of the men which were written on the cenotaph, men who had died in the first World War, we were so proud to hear them call out 'Walter Stock' (Mum's brother) who was killed while on active service at the age of eighteen. We always picked lots of laurel leaves from Granfer Jim's garden hedge for Mum to make a large wreath for Uncle Walter, she made one every year. She would bind the leaves on to a wire frame and decorate it with poppies. We had to put it on the cenotaph beside Uncle's name, the day before the service. Mum was very proud of her brother, the Uncle we had never known.

Now, on Armistice days, I remember also, a childhood playmate, Cyril, who was not so lucky as my own two brothers, Jim and Tom, who returned safely after World War Two. Cyril was killed while on active service and lies buried in the corner of a cornfield, somewhere in France.

Young lives wasted in the name of Peace.
Will men never learn, there are no winners in wars,
Only a wicked waster of human life.
For our tomorrow, they gave their today.

OLD CHARLIE
BY B. PRICE

It is a well know fact; reluctantly admitted by some, that horses are preferable to human beings – simply because they are so much more humane than Homo Sapiens, they don't make bombs, or other weapons.

It follows therefore, that men and women who have an affinity with horses are different from ordinary people, because horses understand them.

My Father drove horses, and he was so attached to them that whilst practising, with the utmost severity, a refusal to accept overtime as a normal part of his job, he would take his turn – one weekend in four – at Sunday Stables. This meant mucking out, watering, feeding and exercise round the yard, for several horses.

The only other occasion that he could be persuaded to enter a place of paid employment, out of normal hours, was to visit Old Charlie when he was in the Horse Hospital, or when someone was working on the weekend, whom he suspected might be apt to neglect Charlie.

But that old horse wasn't always the docile character he appeared to be, some of his habits could be embarrassing; whilst waiting outside of our terraced house for my father to finish his dinner – not lunch –, Charlie nibbled, contentedly at the contents of his nosebag, until a crowd of excited schoolchildren gathered around him, and when the crowd was of sufficient proportions, Charlie invariably relieved himself and a comparison with a tidal wave was inescapable The school boys were always delighted, at the feigned embarrassment of the girls, but the horse ignored them all, he had had his moment.

On one glorious occasion, he had performed his usual act, but my father was too busy to go out to him, to assure him that he was still the only horse in the world. Charlie felt neglected; and unmindful of the fact that he was still attached to a half loaded cart, decided to join my Father at dinner. He crossed the pavement, and tried to get into the house, jamming himself in the passage way.

Our house had a long passage way from the living room to the front step, which went straight on to the pavement, and there was a large quantity of horse, irritable horse, with cart attached stuck right in it. This passage had a suspended floor, which had never been designed for man's best friend, or his weight. My father began to worry about the thin boards, and the 4″ x 2″ timbers beneath.

To reverse Charlie out meant that he had to be backed down a couple of steps, and horses aren't fond of steps, particularly in reverse. We couldn't get alongside of him to unhitch, there was no room, he filled the place; and with the cart on, it was just a matter of time before he

began to get annoyed, and either kick out, or stomp the floor, till it collapsed. The kids outside were enjoying the performance, my Dad's language and temper were not completely under control, and the friendship between him and Charlie, was getting to a definite estrangement situation.

By climbing over the neighbours' fence, and in a delicate operation of almost superhuman self control, my Father got the cart unhitched, by approaching from the outside, and whilst working at the harness, he talked to Charlie to pacify him, and save the house.

Neighbours and the kids helped to move the cart back out into the street, and Charlie, tiring of this game backed himself out, did his relieving act, and went, like a lamb, back into the shafts. The kids went off to school disappointed that our house was still standing.

He hadn't however finished; after he calmed down, and had been fed apples and brown bread, he'd sell his Equine soul for an apple, my Father got back on to the cart and Charlie plodded off. During the afternoon, he brushed his cart lightly, against two parked cars, and to round off, when stabled that night, kicked the stall to pieces. Charlie had definitely had a right Sods Day, and let us know it.

I remember the day came when he had to be put down, – old age – it is still difficult to write it down. He was the first horse that I had ever been in contact with and in spite of his moods and whims, a right character.

My Father transferred next day to the mechanical transport. He never handled another horse.

Father and Old Charlie

ANNETTA
BY LEONARD F PORTCH

It was in the late Spring of 1926 and I was just eighteen when I first set my eyes upon her. She was four months younger than I and was still seventeen. She worked as an assistant in a grocers shop at the Ashton end of Coronation Road and I worked on the bus route which passed, or more often stopped outside. From then onwards through that Summer I occasionally glanced towards the shop if we happened to be setting passengers down there and on several occasions upon seeing me looking across if she was in the window she would give me a smile and a little wave. The first time that she did this I must have replied with an indifferent sort of wave and she probably thought, 'what a misery he is'. In fact, she later told me it was true and she did think I was miserable on that occasion. Anyhow, it went along all right after that.

On one occasion the bus broke down before reaching her stop. I was lounging inside the bus waiting for the 'breakdown gang', when I saw her swinging along towards us walking quite briskly, her arm holding her handbag and her left arm swinging freely at a slight angle away from her body. That was the way I had seen her careering along before, on her way home for dinner, lunch or whatever you may call it. This was the first opportunity I'd had of chatting her up, and so I got off the bus and onto the pavement. I can't remember what exactly I said after saying "Hello you", but I know that she stopped and said "Hello yourself". After the first greeting we had a few words and I tried to date her. She hesitated for a bit and then said, "Look, I haven't much time now to get home and back. If you want to, meet me outside the shop when we close unless you don't want to hang about that long." Well, as we'd been chatting, it was the first time that I'd had a chance to study her close up, and I liked what I saw. Her hair was very fair and she had nice blue eyes and a fresh (I could say school-girlish) complexion. I'm not going to give the impression 'beautiful' as an artist would the Mona Lisa, but she was pretty and attractive. That was the honest way to describe her. From then on we occasionally went out together.

My late shifts and her long hours didn't allow us to get out together too often. She was nice to be with though. As you see us today you'd never believe that saying about the 'attractions of the opposites' but whereas she was fair, my hair was black and I was brown skinned. She was never the 'gushing' sort. It took a while to feel that I had her complete confidence. She wasn't a prude or anything like that but she was honest and practical. Being outwardly practical though, gave me a suspicion that she was repressing inward sentiment and emotion, that she didn't want to reveal, not yet at least. One cold evening towards the end of 1926 I had met her as usual outside the shop at seven o'clock and I asked her if she had been home to tea that evening, but she said that the other assistant had had a day off or something and that she had not been able to go home to lunch as usual. I said, "You must be starving", but she replied that she had had a cup of tea and some biscuits at the shop. It was a very cold evening and I suggested going for a drink, but she didn't want that, and so I said that we both needed something warm (besides ourselves) and so I took her up to Mother Haynes Faggot Shoppe on Redcliffe Hill. We sat down at a little table for two and I ordered the usual faggots and peas – twice. It was warm in there with exotic food, soft lights and sweet music, but if you'd ever tasted their faggots and peas then you would know that they easily surpassed exotic. The lighting was brilliant and our 'soft music' was the yell of the waitress through the hatch shouting, "Faggots and peas for two". It was cosy in there anyway and we both enjoyed that 'exotic' dish and when we had finished (me with a slight belch and a pardon) then we had a cup of tea each over a chat and sitting there for a while. On television these days the fellow usually reaches for his wallet when the bill is presented, giving the impression of being a 'money bags', but not in Mother Haynes' though. You paid 'on the nail' when they brought you the dish, and when you ordered your tea it was money please and no messing about. It had cost me one shilling and four pence that night for the two of us, which was about one eighth of my weekly pocket money and that wasn't too bad now was it.

Gosh, it was cold coming out of that warm cafe and so we cuddled up close with her arm in mine as we made our way back to her home via the narrow towpath that ran parallel to the rail tracks in Cumberland Road. We got to her house by ten o'clock and we had only been talking for a minute or so at her door and the time must only have been a couple of minutes after ten o'clock when I was a bit startled by a call from inside of her house. "Come on Netta, it's time you were in."

It was her mother's voice and she must have been told by Nett that we were going out together. I didn't expect Nett to ask me in any evening when I had taken her home, it was a bit premature after all, and I didn't particularly want to.

However, after our engagement I had to call in to see her parents and her mother was quite affable and congratulated us on the engagement and also said that she liked the ring. I told her that Nett had chosen it. Nett's father was out in the pigeon house. I looked through the window and he beckoned me in. He was a dour sort of man whose family went back to Calne for generations. He congratulated me and said, "You ever kept pigeons?" to which I replied that I had not. "Have you ever tasted pigeon pie then?" he continued. I again shook my head. He had a pigeon in his hand and was doing something with it "I'm glad it was you," he said, nodding towards the house obviously referring to Nett. "You got a good un there, and a worker too." He wasn't looking at me and it was as though he was talking to the pigeons. He then went on, "I don't know what we'd 'ave done without 'er when our young 'un was born. She looked after us all and she was only about twelve. She had to stay home from school and I'd give 'er the 'ousekeeping money and she'd se'ed to everything. She got the two young 'uns off to school after their breakfast and she'd do the shopping, keep the place like a palace and me dinner was cooked, hot and ready on the table when I came

'ome from work for me dinner every day. She was just like a little mother, but she always was like that and she always will be. Look after 'er 'ont ee, but then I think that you will." He still seemed to be addressing the pigeons as though he was reminding me. "I'm thankful for that," I said and he knew that I meant it. He finally said, "Tis a pity that you don't like pigeons or pigeon pie." I noticed that in the following years the number of pigeons gradually got less and less, so I think that a lot of 'em went into his pies.

Archibald George Brewer, or George as everybody called him, was a rough and ready sort of man who was just concerned with his home, his family and his attempts at a crude bit of D.I.Y.. He had a tough job at Thomas Ware and Sons, the tannery, and had no interest at all in politics or current affairs. I don't think he knew where Timbuctoo was and probably didn't care a damn either. He was happy in his own tin pot way. Oh, he had Nett's mother's relations who lived at Newport, Worcester and Birmingham (Bernigun was his pronunciation) and beyond that he just wasn't interested. Nett seemed to be closer to him than her mother.

Of course, Nett showed little emotion to me. She loved me and I her but I must make it clear that her willpower was far stronger than mine.

In 1929 we had our first holiday together in the first week in September and we had good weather and a grand time but rotten digs. We didn't let that spoil things though. During the early Spring of 1930 I got my transfer to the tram. It was at Brislington Depot not Bedminster as I had hoped for but it was a case of taking it or waiting until a vacancy cropped up at Bedminster. I was impatient to get married and so I opted for Brislington. There was an increase in wages to about £2.12s.0d instead of £1.12s.0d. I saved all that I could, and Nett did the same from her meagre pay at the shop. I had a week's holiday due to start on Sunday 27th September 1931. We bought our bedroom furniture at a workshop and furniture store combined, namely Lenthall Bros. of Redcliffe Hill. Mum had let two rooms at our house and since then my bedroom had been an attic with a view over Bristol from the skylight. It was a sort of den to me with pin-ups of sporting figures, racehorses and things like that. In those days there was no 'Sun' newspaper with its Page 3 pin-ups. We had therefore to find somewhere to live and unfurnished rooms were almost unobtainable. Nett's mother offered us two rooms downstairs. Neither of us to be truthful was keen, but we accepted her offer in the spirit it was given. Nett was as busy as a bee during the time leading up to the wedding. Her mother turned up trumps offering to make the wedding dress and so Nett chose the material for the three bridesmaids that she wanted to have. We saved as much as we could during the next eighteen months, but during that summer of 1931 we found that we had time to have a day trip from Aston Gate; the fare being only sixpence each return. There was a little cove towards Redcliffe Bay where the tide was always in and so we just relaxed in the sun watching the shipping pass by. Sometimes I'd hire a boat for a row in the lake, but on only one occasion did I take Nett out in a skiff because they had a rudder control and she had no idea of steering. In fact, her navigation was such that we either went ashore on

Archibald George Brewer

the little island or travelled in ever decreasing circles until she got so mad with herself and me that I had to move to the stern and remove the rudder making her more panicky in doing so as naturally, I rocked the boat. She was much happier when I hired the 'tub type'. These were heavier and, whilst I sweated at pulling on the oars, she was quite content to lean back at the stern and let her fingers trail through the water, smirking at me quite openly. Oh yes, she could take the mickey when she felt like it. The charge for the hire of those tubs was sixpence an hour and if I lasted the hour it would only be on rare occasions. Those tubs got as heavy as tramp steamers by then. We usually sat at a little table outside the little kiosk besides the lake with a pot of tea for two.

A few months after I'd transferred to Brislington depot, several vacancies occurred at Bedminster, but I had now settled at Brislington and didn't worry very much. One of the vacancies was given to Tommy Tucker who lived near to us at Mendip Road and whom I'd known from my school days. He was one of those who always fell on his feet no matter what. He was likeable, was Tommy, and talked with a sort of lisp and was always very fond of the girls, even when he was at school and despite his odd way of talking, the girls fell for his charms, lock, stock and barrel. Just after he left school he started courting a little girl who lived with her parents over a corner shop. She would open the side door leading to the loft quite frequently after the shop had closed and her parents were out and Tommy would be waiting to step in at her invitation. When little Tommy Tucker emerged later he always seemed to look at us with a knowing smirk on his face. She couldn't really be described as pretty or attractive and she always seemed to have a lot of pimples on her face. Perhaps they were the cause of her depressing gaze which she always seemed to have. I must say however that after those visits from Tommy she looked so much brighter with a smile all over her face. Tommy managed to keep that smile on her face for quite some time. I'd been on the Cassel Road, Fishponds bus route at the same time as he was and he never altered as he got into his teens and eventually married. The women, young or old seemed attracted to him like a needle to a magnet.

There now, I've gone miles away from the story, so let's get back to the plans that we had made for the wedding. Our draw-leaf dining table and four oak high-backed dining chairs with removable leather seats was also made at Lenthail Bros. together with our bed and I think the lot all cost under £9. We bought a three piece suite in cowhide with thick velvet cushions at Smarts which was then in Broadmead, for about £12.10s.0d. which was somewhat dearer than many. It was the best suite that we'd ever had. Nett wanted a pale blue colour scheme for her bedroom, so her dad papered it in pale blue and gold and made quite a good job of it. As far as I remember, I managed to save about sixty odd pounds from the time I moved to the trams to the time that we got married and there wasn't much of it left when it was all finished up. Nett decided on the pattern and material for the bridesmaids and paid for that and her mother made them up. They usually say that a bride must have something old, something new, something borrowed and something blue. Mrs. Marsh, who lived with my mum, lent her her headdress, her dress was new but I was intrigued to know what was going to be blue. She wouldn't tell me, she said nobody would see it and added that it wasn't what I thought it would be.

I fixed myself up with a brown suit and shoes. Elsie was engaged to Fred Sheather and I asked him to be my best man. Elsie was asked by Nett to be one of her bridesmaids; the other two were Nett's cousins. I believe that we invited about fifty or so guests from her family and mine and also friends. I ordered two Daimler cars from Hodges of East Street, who specialised in weddings or funerals and were very reliable. The hire fee was £2.10s.0d and I arranged for them to pick me up first from home in Mendip Road. We had paid a visit to the Vicar of St. Francis Parish Church and by giving my address as 69 Gathorne Road, it saved the banns being called at St. John's Bedminster Parish Church. The wedding was to be at 2.30 pm and the day came along and everything went off O.K., the organ struck up 'Here Comes The Bride' and it seemed an eternity just standing there waiting for her to reach my side. I glanced sideways at her, she pushed her veil back and gave me a little smile. When it was over we came back down the aisle to the Wedding March, and I'm afraid I started to hurry a little. I then felt pressure on my arm from Nett and she whispered, "Steady boy, there's no need to hurry." The church had been pretty well filled, for Nett had so many people who knew her at the shop and after there were the usual showers of confetti, and we were thankful to move away in the car. A couple of Nett's uncles had used their cars to help out the two Daimlers and some guests simply strolled back to the house as it was less than five minutes walk away.

The cake had been made by Needhams the bakers and was a two-tiered one. Everybody sat down to a cold spread which was laid out on trestle tables in our living room. The French doors leading to the rather large conservatory were open and some more small tables had been placed together out there as well. There were plenty of drinks available; her father had seen to that.

We had some snaps taken afterwards by several people who had cameras but, of course, these were in black and white. I wish that they could have been in colour for I think the colour of the bridesmaids' dresses would have really come out well, revealing Nett's taste. Win and Kath had pale lemon dresses, pale crinoline hats and they carried bunches of large bronze chrysanths, whilst Elsie wore a russet and green flowered dress with a lemon crinoline hat. Elsie carried a bouquet of yellow chrysanths. They all looked pretty, but to me the bride looked prettier. Afterwards, Nett had changed, she came down wearing a fawn tweed costume with tan slip-on shoes with a nice little hat. Her uncle Bill took us to the station and we, of course, had another sprinkle of confetti as we left. A porter, on seeing a few touches of confetti still on us, gave a knowing grin and opened a first class compartment with a key and gave us the come on. So we travelled to Weston in style. I had booked a sitting room and a bedroom at a Mrs. Tanners in Alfred Street for a period of three nights. We left our weekend case and she asked us if we wanted supper, but we didn't need any. It was a balmy evening and so we had a stroll along the sea front, had a drink in a hotel and then went back to our rooms. When I went upstairs Nett was sitting at the dressing table brushing her hair, having already changed into a white silk nightdress. I said, "Here, I've forgotton to ask you about the 'something blue' that you said you would wear." I was glancing across to where she had placed her underclothes but everything was white. She saw my glance in the mirror and said over her shoulder, "I told you that you'd never guess," so I asked her what it was. She replied, "Come over here and you can see for yourself," and there was a frilly garter lying on the dressing table. "It wasn't what you thought it was was it?"

The advice that everybody gave you in those days was 'have a couple of years of freedom before you start a family'. Well, we did, but could not 'go to town' or anything like that, but we had a lot of friends to visit and in return they also visited us. We had an occasional evening at the Bristol Hippodrome which was a variety theatre andd sometimes we went to the Theatre Royal or the Old Gaff as it was called, which was in King Street. Nowadays it is called the Old Vic. There, every week they had comic revues and you could have a good laugh for about two hours or more for a mere fourpence each.

When we did start a family Nett's confinement began, or rather her labour, two days before the baby was born. The sister called because her pains had started and continued all through to the early hours of that morning when the sister called the doctor. Nett's dad and I stayed up all night making pot after pot of tea and smoking just like factory chimneys. At about 5.30 am the squalling of a baby could be plainly heard and Nett's dad said, "It sounds as though that 'un gotta good pair of lungs." About an hour before, young Dr. Sampson had brought down a tray with some instruments on it and asked me to make sure that they had a good boiling.

When the doctor came down a little while after the first squalling he said to me, "Well dad, your wife has just given birth to a baby boy; he must be well over 10 pounds." He then promised to call back later in the day. After a little while more, sister came down and told me that I could go upstairs to see Nett and the baby if I wanted to. I asked the sister how Nett was and she told me that she was a strong girl and would get well in no time at all. I went upstairs and upon entering the bedroom I was aware of Dettol, and since that day the smell of that disinfectant has always reminded me of that morning.

Netta was propped up against the pillow with a bundle cuddled to her breast. She looked well and so happy when I leaned over and kissed her. She pulled away the covering and said, "Sister reckons that he's like you, what do you think, Len?" I looked at the chubby little fellow and his puffy eyes and flat nose and then looked at myself in the mirror. "I don't look like that, do I? The sister must be crazy." She looked down at the baby and then started to whisper baby talk to it. I then told Nett that I did not want to go through another night like that again in a hurry. Netta opened her eyes wide and said, "You don't want to, how about ME? I'll never mind really, in fact you'll probably have to go through more, he'll not be our only one I hope. I wouldn't want it to be just that." Then she told me, though she hadn't mentioned it to me before, that she had bought some wooden clothes pegs at the front door from a gypsy. It had been a couple of years before she'd had a miscarriage. The gypsy was so pleased at getting a sale that she said to Nett, "Have you any children?" Nett replied that she hadn't, to which the gypsy stated that she was going to get pregnant six times before she was finished. I said to Nett, "You don't believe that rubbish do you?" "Don't be daft, of course I don't, but I'd like more than one," she said. We'd heard all those stories about what the gypsies foretold and like other people we thought stories like that were just hearsay. There are, however, many things that people call 'old wives' tales' born of superstition, but just like Max Bygraves says – "I wanna tell you a story".

When Nett was in her pregnancy for this first baby, I always warned her not to stand on a chair to reach for anything on the top shelf of our glass china cupboard. One day however, she ignored my warning and stood on a chair to reach the top shelf. Next thing, she screamed, and if I hadn't caught her as I rushed into the room, she would simply have crashed to the floor. She was as white as a sheet and was holding her side towards her back. Although I was mad at her for what she had done I was also worried about her and straight away got her to rest on the settee for a while. Afterwards I asked her if she was all right and whether she was hurt in any place. She told me that when she had reached for the shelf she had put her hand upon a mouse. We thought no more of it although, at the time, she and I were a bit worried, especially as she had had a previous miscarriage. Anyhow, on the second day after the birth, the sister came downstairs and asked me to come on up to the bedroom, and I immediately asked her if something was wrong. She said that nothing was wrong but just wanted to show me something. I followed her upstairs and when I went into our bedroom, Nett and the sister just grinned at me. I naturally wondered what the joke was all about at first, until Nett said "Come over here." I did as she asked and the sister then turned the baby over and asked me if I could see anything peculiar on the baby's back. I knew that he'd had a few red marks on his forehead where the instruments had been used, but there apparently was something other than that. The sister then told me to look closely where there was a small patch much lighter than the baby's skin. I looked at it closely for a minute or so and was aware of both the sister and Netta watching me intensely. I eventually said that I could make out the shape of a mouse, even to its tail. They were all grinning at me like chimpanzees and I asked what was the reason for it. The sister said, "Your wife has been telling me that during her pregnancy she had placed her hand upon a mouse in your cupboard." I said that she had and had in fact twisted her back. "Did she grab her back?" asked the sister, and I replied that she had, but why did it show on the baby? She shrugged her shoulders and said that stories of these happenings had always been considered as 'old wives' tales' from years back but she had in fact seen nothing like it in her career, but your mother, your wife and both you and me can clearly trace the outline of a mouse. "I can't give any explanations if that's what you want, but facts are facts." That mark stayed on his back even when he was a toddler, sometimes being clear and sometimes not easily recognisable.

Well, Nett and the baby got on quickly, but my mother wouldn't let her out of bed for a fortnight. She continued to breast-feed for quite some time and eventually, when he did turn to the bottle Nett would always give him pasteurised cow's milk. There always seemed to be Robinson's Barley Water around the house and there were baby foods on sale such as Glaxo and Virol but I don't think that she used much of that. Nett used to spend a little while each day when he was about five months or so just brushing his hair, which was very silky and fair, into a 'cock's combe'. We had to decide on his name and I would have chosen William like my grandfather, but her choice was Colin, and that's what it had to be. After all, I think that it's a woman's prerogative anyway. She compromised with me however by saying, "Let's give him William as his second name." As she had said she would, she had put her wedding veil away for her first baby's christening. Colin was christened at St. Francis, the church where we were married. Phyllis Ward, who was engaged to Nett's brother Cyril, was his godmother and she acted just like a real godmother towards him, until eventually she married Cyril and had children of her own. She showed as much affection to Colin as if it were her very own. We bought a shiny black 'Marmet' pram that Nett had picked out and I remember it clearly. It had a white curved design on each panel, was lined cream and had chromium plated handles with a white rubber grip.

We had a straight three wireless set until a couple of years before this and Bob Sheather put it together from a blueprint. I had made a cabinet of plywood for it and bought a 'blue spot' speaker. I had an 'Oldham' low tension battery which had to be charged up periodically, and a high tension battery of 120 volts which I had bought from Woolworths for about 3/6d. They would last, according to use, up to three months, but it wasn't a real success and I had to replace it with a 'Cosser Melody Maker' which was just grand to listen to. We enjoyed all the big bands like Jack Payne, Henry Hall, Roy Fox and Geraldo and Charlie Kunz and Billy Mayeral with their individual style on the piano. It was all swing and sentiment.

We went together to the cinema and Phyllis would come down and look after Colin. On evenings in we would often tune the wireless in to the rantings and ravings of Adolf Hitler and the roars of 'Sieg Heil' from his German audiences, which alarmed some, whilst others casually scoffed. We were cosy and happy with each other and after all, that was far away. However, government propaganda and warnings grew greater and greater despite Mr. Chamberlain's agreement at Munich and his return waving that piece of paper in his hand telling us it was 'peace in our time'. There were continual government exhortations on the news reels and the wireless for volunteers for the services to train (not because war was imminent, they said, but we must be prepared). I had seen all this once before during the First World War on posters with Lord Kitchener's bristling moustache, glaring eyes and his pointing finger, with the caption, 'Your Country Needs You'. It was as though 'this is where I came in'. There had been the Spanish Civil War, where the Germans had backed Franco and his 'falangists or fascists' and Russia had backed the legitimate socialist government. In our ignorance we had never realised that the German Luftwaffe were gaining experience and learning lessons from this Civil War. So we just went along with the 'it couldn't happen here' attitude. But I'm running too far ahead, let's come back a bit in time.

Nett's mother had come home from hospital and the first thing that she wanted to do was to nurse the baby. He was her first grandchild and she doted on him from then onwards. He was always her favourite grandchild out of all those who came later. She soon got back into her stride, getting around with the Liberal Association and she and I had many arguments politically. It couldn't have been avoided because I had always had socialist ideals. Nett's father wasn't interested in politics or current affairs, and Nett was the same. He was earning good money at the tannery and had done so throughout the 1914-1918 war and since. I think that he was exempted from call-up because of his job being necessary for the war effort as far as I know. There was still that 'distant' feeling between us and Nett's mother. We kept to our rooms and lived quite independently. On occasions when they had visitors, Nett would sit alone with the baby in our room and would never be asked to join them. She must have felt an awful feeling of isolation at times, but she wouldn't show it. Admittedly, Phyl would come in and have a chat with Nett, probably realising how things were and to have a look at the baby. It was always that way as long as we lived there.

Elsie and Bob Sheather had married in 1932 and they were living in two rooms at Weston after their first daughter, Diane was born. Bob was doing well on the Post Office and had a gang of his own and earning quite good money. They moved then to a house off the Locking Road which they rented for about £1 weekly. I think that he must have been quite comfortably off because he had now taken out a mortgage on a house in Shaftsbury Road which was quite a nice place.

On Thursday evenings, when I was on early shift, I usually had an hour of boxing tuition in a room above the Albert Hotel on the corner of Sheene Road and West Street, Bedminster. Don Ash, who had been a good amateur boxer and knew a bit about the fighting game, used to put me through the 'ropes' so to speak. I enjoyed it at first until he brought in a lad whom he was hoping to make into a real fighter because he really showed potential and was hot at it. We eventually found ourselves being relegated to sparring partners to him and eventually into 'punchbags' and so I got out of that lark quick. I then did one of the stupidest things that I'd ever done and for the first time I felt that I had let Nett down eventually. All around me blokes that I knew were joining the 'naval volunteers', army territorial units and others such as searchlight and ack-ack units. A bus conductor named Ted Joyce was on duty as my conductor one week in May 1939 and we were chatting about various pals and acquaintances who were rushing to join up and he asked me if I had given it any thought. I replied that I had not seriously given it any thought and added that I had heard about the P.B.I. (poor bloody infantry) of the First World War from my father, who had been a territorial and had also seen the results. I wasn't going to undergo that and as far as the naval volunteers were concerned, I couldn't swim very much and hated the thought of getting a wetting there. Ted mentioned that he had enrolled with the R.A.F. auxiliaries and I was quite surprised. I asked him what he intended to do in that mob. He said that he was going to try to get in eventually as a cook for a trade and I laughed and said that I'd really hate something like that. He invited me to come with him to R.A.F. drill in a hall in Victoria Street. He put in a drill each week and had a good evening on most occasions, so I went there one evening with him. Evidently he got paid for putting in a certain number of drills and that the cash came in useful. Anyway, before I knew what was happening I'd received the 'King's Shilling' and had signed up. Nett didn't reproach me in any way, she knew that I had packed in the boxing and said that it would be somewhere for me to go occasionally to replace it.

I persuaded her and myself that there wasn't going to be any war, until one day in August my calling up papers arrived and it was a shock to her when I told her that I had to report to Victoria Street the very next morning. Her dream of having a house at Headley Park was shattered and she had been saving so hard for the deposit of £25 too and it was all due to my 'thickheadedness'. I thought back to her father's words when we got engaged. "Look after her 'ont ee", and that didn't let me down lightly.

Anyway, I was on guard duty at the main gate on September 2nd 1939 which was a Saturday, from 2 pm until 2 pm on the Sunday. This was a 24 hour guard of 2 hours and 4 hours off and that Sunday night was a wicked one with torrential rain and thunder and lightning. My last 2 hours were from 10 am until 12 noon and at 11 o'clock I heard Neville Chamberlain on a wireless in a cottage opposite announcing that we were in a state of war with Germany.

* * * * *

V.E. Day was celebrated whilst I was out in Egypt and Japan packed up when I was on my way home to be demobbed. I came home, or rather back to Mendip Road about the end of August 1945, or near the beginning of September and our next baby boy was born at 24 Mendip Road on 28th September 1945. He was another one over ten pounds and again it seemed that Nett was never happier than when she had a baby in her arms.

I had my name on the Council housing list for a couple of years, and had written reminding them by air-mail when I was abroad. We were issued with a certain number of free ones each month, and they offered Nett a Council house at 37 Kingshill Road, Knowle, a month or so before I got home. Neither of us were keen on Knowle, always having lived at Bedminster or Ashton, but a house was what we needed and we felt that we would go anywhere. We named the baby David, because the young nurse suggested it. She was Welsh and so kind to Nett, and so I went to the Registry Office without thought of a second name for him, but Nett said that it was my choice this time, so I called him Frederick after my dad. I had seventy pounds gratuity pay for the six years I had been in the RAF and six weeks service pay and allowances to cover my demob leave. It seemed a fortune, but we had to spend it on another bed, bedding, lino, curtains etc., and the one hundred and one things that were needed. I needed spades, garden fork, hoes and shears for the hedging and grass and after six years service life I felt like many others; out of depth now in civilian life. We had lived through six years of life which had seen people change completely in their way of life. They lived with fear, and through that had crowded together causing strangers to talk to each other who would have passed each other by previously. There had been no thought of tomorrow – let's get over today sort of feeling. Women had been directed into munitions or the auxiliary services. The country had been overcrowded with Yanks who had the money to chuck about on the girls. In fact, life for some had been good with the help of the black market, whilst others couldn't get enough to get by on, foodwise. I'd seen a few mates who had received "Dear John" letters as they were nicknamed, to tell them that their wives had gone off with some Yank or other, and seen the hell they went through not being home to see what was going on. Marriages had been broken up which seemed so secure before the war, and I thanked God that I'd had one who had more devotion and strength of character. I suppose to look at it in a humorous way, Nett had been too busy presenting me with babies in any case. She'd had a rough time getting by during the first three or four years, but as my service pay increased and her allowance had increased as well, although it wasn't easy, at least she was better off moneywise during 1944 and 1945. But what had she got out of those six long years? Dug-outs; bombing; losing a baby; occasional hand-outs from the NAAFI of bundles containing articles of clothing etc. Pushing her pram all the way up to Park Street where the NAAFI gift stores were (Navy, Army and Airforce Inst.). A pretty drab life it had been hadn't it? But she'd faced up to it without a grumble, and found happiness in her family – and that to her was everything. Her hair was almost still as fair as when I'd met her, but she looked a little tired; what else could be expected?

And myself? I lived in a sort of cloud cuckooland, never having to worry about where the next meal came from, or the next pair of boots. Having my clothing provided for me, and sometimes not having to think for myself, but let others think for me, as regards the future. I went to, and saw places I would probably never have seen otherwise. I'd seen the beauty of Edinburgh, with its famous Princes Street Castle, Holyrood, and Arthur's seat. I discovered I could sleep anywhere – on bare grass, wooden planks, billiard table tops, or even standing up. I'd looked up at the fantastic height of the giant steel structure of the Forth Bridge; I'd seen the filth of the Glasgow Gorbals – and the elegant parts also, like Kelvinside and Bearsden. I'd been drunk in Sauchiehall Street on a Saturday night – where it was out of place not to be, everybody else seemed to be also. I'd had drinks in the Tower Bar and the Swan at Blackpool, danced to Richard Dixon's Wurlitzer organ in the massive ballroom. Selfish? I've thought about it since, but it seemed to take my mind off home – which I missed very much, and worried about them.

And so I looked upon Ben Lomond and Loch Lomond, afterwards steaming down the Firth of Clyde I took in the breathtaking sight of the purple mountains of Argyle, not knowing where I was going, or when I should be returning. So I went on a "Cook's Tour", and saw the Rock of Gibraltar, and the Moroccan shore on the opposite side, backed by the distant Atlas Mountains. I saw that beautiful bay of Algiers, with its white buildings, topped by a blue dome of a mosque above it. Then there was Malta with its Grand Harbour busy with naval shipping, and the high steep streets of Valetta, and on, still not knowing our destination, except that before leaving Blackpool we had been issued with a "Deep sea kit bag" filled with tropical kit.

But we finished up at Port Said, or rather Port Fouad on the opposite side of the entrance to Suez Canal. I dangled my feet on the edge of the Canal (I hadn't the confidence to swim, it is about 90 feet deep). I'd swum in the Red Sea, and sampled a nose around Suez, where it was risky unless you were with a small gang of mates. I'd camped in the land of Goshen, through which Moses was supposed to have lead the Israelites during the Exodus. I'd seen Cairo, the great pyramids of Cheops and Sphinx, Alexandria with its beautiful cornich, or sea front, and also the colour and the stench of the Mouski Market, "La Rue des

Sears", or famous "Street of the Sisters", where prostitutes hung out from every window. I'd slept on a groundsheet on the desert, where the stars were so many, and so bright, they lit up the sand in the darkness to a colour of whiteness. And one of the most fantastic memories – sunset over the desert sinking quickly in to a rosy halo, finally allowing the darkness to fall with very short notice.

I'd been lucky in that sense, whilst Nett was on the "punishing end", but I think I knew her well enough to know that none of it would have impressed her, and the fact that I was home again with them was the greatest thing of all. Even in her condition she had arranged the removal of our furniture from 69 Gathorne Road to 37 Kingshill Road, and whilst awaiting her baby was staying with dear old mum and at the same time saving having to pay two lots of rent.

When we were lying in bed that night, I looked at her, and from the light of the street lamp her hair seemed just as fair as I'd first known her, though she was now in her late thirties. Like myself, she was awake. The events of the last six long years were passing through my mind. They had seemed endless. At times we had thought that we were living on just hope. Perhaps I could best describe it as travelling through a neverending tunnel and suddenly bursting into light, drawing a deep breath of fresh air and trying to adjust to that light, but finding it difficult. I'd been lucky, there were many names missing from those mates I knew before the war. I said to Nett, "I can't believe that we're back together again and it's all over, it's like a dream come true isn't it?" I put my arm around her and she started to cry quietly. I said, "What is it? Is it this?" and I placed my hand on her tummy. After a short while she said, "You talking about this baby?" I nodded. She said, "You must be daft to think that, you should know me better. I've wanted these babies, and having them don't scare me. I suppose it was silly to give way like that, it was just that during these months I've been more worried about you not being home in time to be with me when he or she arrives." I should by now have known her better. I felt a bit shamefaced. She hadn't pushed my hand from her tummy, and in the silence that followed I felt a tiny jump now and then. She said, still staring at the ceiling, "Understand now?" and we fell asleep.

For the first few years it was hard going. The women were still kept on the buses and as men returned, so the service was increased. The wages were among the poorest now, instead of over average as they'd been before. The winter of 1947 was a bitter one, the coal delivery uncertain. I queued at Bedminster Railway Station yard with the pram for a hundred weight of coal and pushed it up to Knowle. I'm sure Nett had her priorities in what she considered the right order: Firstly she made sure that her kids had full bellies (her thick beef, onion and carrot stews were delicious). Secondly she wanted 'em kept warm and made sure they had dry feet. I had to see to that with my hammer, nails and leather knife.

We didn't feel strange at Knowle, even though we'd lived at Ashton and Bedminster for so long. I think she fell in love with Knowle and, as you know, we put our roots down in Kingshill Road (woodwind, cooch grass and all despite). To help out with their bedding I'd managed to

The Portch family in 1953

scrounge a couple of army blankets that Davey McKie said had "fell off the back of a lorry" when we were at Avonmouth Docks during the war. We also used my tweed overcoat, anything for warmth as it was cold in those bedrooms in the winter. We had a stone and rubber hot water containers which Nett insisted on placing in their beds. Work bucked up a bit and I put in every hour of overtime I could, sometimes doing two days in one. We were then so busy on the buses that I "made" myself a few bob each day, owing to the fact that it was impossible to collect all short journey passengers' fares, and I would often come down from the top deck to find pennies had been thrown onto the shelf on the platform by the conscientious ones. I'm afraid I did a little bit of fiddling myself with regulars as well. "Needs must." They deserved it for paying near starvation wages to keep the fares low, and their profits were good. Anyway, I never mentioned that to Nett, she would probably have had a "betsy". She was straight and detested anything dishonest. I had guilty qualms about it and inwardly hated to do it, but with the overtime etc. we managed to get on a holiday in a caravan at Burnham-on-Sea.

We went by train. I pushed the pram with "Pip" in it to Temple Meads, and Nett brought the others down on the bus. The pram went in the luggage van and at Highbridge we travelled to the caravan site in a cab with the pram strapped on the top with the large cardboard suitcase, and by jimminy we had a glorious week, with blue skies.

Happy, sometimes grim, but oh how wonderful those years are to look back on.

We paid our way though, and never owed anybody anything. There was a day when I was compelled to visit a pawnshop, during a period of sickness just before Christmas one year. Nett always had a saying, like Mr. Macawber, "something will turn up", and by God's grace it usually did, but on that occasion I thought I would give Him some help in my own way. It was a Maltese cross, a family heirloom from Aunt Nell (Helen Flook), and I didn't want to part with it. Nett never knew, and I told myself I'd retrieve it after three months. Still there it is, food and clothing and odds and ends for the kids at Christmas had to come first.

FIRST JOB
BY B. PRICE

"Schooldays are the best days of your life!" That was a statement – in fact – a parental edict, which allowed no amendment, or question. In most cases, it is true, but, unfortunately, it takes sometimes, half a lifetime to realise it.

I could not leave school soon enough. I intended, between the ages of fourteen and eighteen, to completely change the world, and create a Utopia, with Old Market Street as the centre of the Universe. Poverty would be abolished, wealth nationalised, legislation would be enacted to allow Bristol City to be a privileged, permanent contender for the F.A. Cup, tram fares would be limited to one old penny per day.

After this cleansing of the Augean Stables, I would beat the record of William Pitt – and become Prime Minister on my 21st Birthday. Unfortunately for the rest of Britain, something went wrong, and I found myself working for a firm of tarpaulin makers, at 10 shillings (50 pence) per 48 hour week.

This firm (H.Luffman) was in old Frogmore Street, between The Leopard and The Hatchet. It was a marvellous old street, with the majority of its 17th, 18th and 19th century buildings intact; truely – another, happier world, in March 1937.

On my second day at work, I was given the task of delivering a flag pole (bunting supply was our second line) to a house in Shadwell Road, well up the Gloucester Road. The flag pole was intended to be the central piece of a display for the forthcoming Jubilee of King George V. (May 1937). The pole was 18 feet long, with a heavy butt end and a lighter end capped by a lead covered mushroom the size of a dinner plate. I, personally, estimated its weight to be too much for the shop transport, a porter's barrow, but Sid, backed by May the machinist, (they were the only other employees) agreed, that a big lad of 14 could carry such a little pole a few yards up the road, and anyway, Sid needed the trolley.

I was outnumbered; deferring to my elders, as was the custom, quashed any idea of resistance. My displeasure must have been apparent, because Sid relented and said, "Yer's 1½d; when thee's got the receipt signed, come back on the tram – but no hanging about, mind."

Now there are problems, and techniques for solving problems, but I was not quite into the art of balancing an 18 foot pole on my shoulder, and carrying it through the ranks of the unsuspecting citizenry of a busy city. So I informed Sid; he drew a deep breath, puffed up to his full 5 ft. 3 ins., and said, "Let I show thee summat."

Taking a piece of chalk from behind his ear, he marked an X at a point, 8 ft. 6 ins. from one end (the butt), and obviously 9 ft. 6 ins. from the other end. He pointed and said, "See that, dead cen'ner. Pole's pointed, butt's thick, top's thin, but cap is weighty, so ther's the bleedin' middle. Balance ee' ther, an' keep the 'X' 6 inches behin' thee 'ead; wrap thee arm over the top, with the weight slightly at the back end, an' thee's got ee' balance. As'n't?" I could not contest his obvious expertise, so he continued, "Now bugger off, and don't be all ******* day." But, exactly how I was to observe the 'X' six inches behind my head he didn't say; and I felt it unwise to ask further.

My destination, Shadwell Road, was towards the Bristol North Baths area. Sid tacked the delivery documents to the pole, on the 'X', where it was difficult to read them, gave me a lift up with the pole, and off I went.

Walking up Frogmore Street, towards Trenchard Street, I entertained some wild ideas about the French Foreign Legion, but 1½d (old money) wasn't going to get me to France, so I trudged on up the hill, till I got to the brow, or just over, and when I felt I was out of sight I set the pole against the wall of the Countess of Huntingdon's Chapel, like a ladder, and decided to have a crafty puff at the well used end of a Wild Woodbine, nicked from my Dad's daily ration whilst he was arguing about football, and the Adult School (Monkeytown). I always kept these Woodbines, singly of course, in a cut off peashooter tube; it prevented them from getting damaged.

Suitably refreshed, I decided to fulfil my industrial duty, and continue with the Delivery. I was immediately confronted with a problem; picking up the pole on my own. The chalk 'X' to go behind my head I could not manage; but there I stood in a street, approximately the equal in width to the dimensions of my flagpole, I could close off the whole street whilst trying to lift it – and I did.

My main object was to manoeuvre the thing into a position where it could be handled without much damage to innocent citizens; or cause a traffic accident, or demolish the chapel. I hit the chapel wall twice, but under the protection of St. Christopher (Patron Saint of Travellers) and with a fortuitous accident, the pole slid off the chapel wall, and landed gently on my shoulder, right at the point of balance. I took the weight, turned my face towards Colston Street swinging the pole through 90 degrees, hit the wall of the chapel with the butt again and moved off slowly towards the Three Kings of Cologne Chapel. It was about this point that I realised that the technique I was using left the carrier blind on one side.

Reaching Colston Street I turned up the hill towards the junction of Park Row, and Maudlin Street. I managed Lower Park Row without incident, apart from a skidding car which missed me, and getting my heel stuck in the tramlines which led into the old Colston Street Depot (now opposite the Post Office). I lost neither heel, nor shoe, nor even pole, so that was my first Bonus.

I made it safely to the junction of Colston Street, Park Row and Maudlin Street. I had just to cross the road towards the King David Hotel. I could hear a tram clanking up Colston Street, and just as I decided it was safe to cross to the King David, the tram started to do the full 'U' turn from Colston Street into Park Row. I stopped at the junction with my ill-balanced and weighty burden, with 8 ft. 6 ins. blocking one pavement, and 9 ft. 6 ins. blocking the other.

The weight of the pole was now too much, and I realised that I would be in trouble if it fell, and I felt I could not hold it. I sallied forth like Don Quixote, tilting at a windmill, and made it to the other side – well almost.

Actually, I did get there accident free, and turned down the hill towards Jamaica Street, and Stokes Croft, and had just swung my burden into a reasonably harmless position when a gentle thump indicated that my luck, or someone else's had just run out. Propping the pole against a wall I turned round to see what ailed us. Some unfortunate celebrant from the King David, walking backwards, whilst waving a fond farewell to his mates (disappearing up Park Row), had backed his head into the pole, and now lay sleeping peacefully on the pavement, out of this world, but smiling so happily.

A shopkeeper appeared, "S'Alright, son," he said, "get going. These boozy buggers are a nuisance. He's not hurt."His assistant flicked dirty water from the bucket he had been using, for the floor, over the injured party, who flatly refused to show any kind of life, except an angelic smile.

The assistant helped me to pick up my pole, and off I went down the hill towards Jamaica Street. I was puffed when I had only got as far as the B.R.I. so I sat on the steps leading to Alfred Hill. This was uneventful except for the clever clogs who, showing off to his companions, said, "If that is for the B.R.I. take it to the tradesman's entrance, up the steps and round the back."

I managed a solo lift this time. I was beginning to get the hang of it, and made steady progress along the front of the B.R.I., past the Brewery, and on to the open spaces of King Square. This, I decided was now the time for my next puff of Woodbine.

It was dinnertime for the workers of Cridland's and Comac's Shoe factories, and I became the object of the attentions of the female operatives, sunning themselves in an early burst of Spring sunshine. They whistled, they cat-called, and their comments and conjectures, as to the disposal of that pole were interesting, but surely impossible. I decided that I would have to move on, when a very large policeman appeared. Policemen were always large in those days; they never walked anywhere, they 'proceeded'.

"Where did you get that pole, son?" he asked.

"From Luffmans," I said.

"Oh you nicked it, did you?" he said.

"No," I said, "I'm taking it to ----," I faltered. I had forgotten where I was going.

"Oh," he queried, "Where are you taking it?"

Put off by the attentions of the girls, I forgot completely about the details tacked to the pole.

He fumbled with his notebook pocket, "I need to know a bit more about you," he said, "there's been a lot of flag poles nicked around here lately. I think that you had better come down to the station. Better still, if you do come from Luffmans you can come back with me and get identified."

I felt shattered at the prospect.

"Come on lad; pick up the pole and get going in front of me. Back to Luffmans."

I felt that it was not my day.

Suddenly, I detected a faint grin, "Carry on with your delivery, son," he said, "but truth is I thought I saw you smoking, and you're not old enough for that."

I was so relieved that I managed another solo lift, and staggered off at a rate of knots, towards Stokes Croft, like a fore and aft rigger.

Once out of Jamaica Street and I was in trouble again. Traffic and pedestrians had increased, and there were fewer setting down places. The Academy Cinema was guarded fiercely by a Ruritanian General (called a Commissionaire) who kept the forecourt and steps free of all non cinema goers, and I definitely would not pass as a potential customer, with that flagpole in tow. But it was all houses, with long gardens, and shops, up to Arley Chapel, and I had to rest before the Chapel.

Staggering on a few yards past the General, resplendent in green, I spotted a house which had a long garden, but with a low wall fronting on to the main road. I set down my burden with one end, resting on the gatepost, and the butt end in line with the wall, on the pavement. One person fell over it, and he was not too well pleased, but as he spoke in a foreign language, he obviously didn't count.

Solo lifting again, I carried on and got to the road crossing by Arley Chapel. Whilst negotiating this crossing, I was approached by two cars, one from the main road, and one coming down Arley Hill. I realised that if either of them hit the pole, that I would spin round like a top, and finish underneath the pole. The one from the main road, mounted the pavement, and went on his way. The one coming down Arley Hill mounted the pavement and left some lamps and things lying on the footpath, after he had hit the wall. I was unscathed.

One more peril had to be faced; the Zetland Road crossing; always a blackspot. Traffic here was always busy, and mishaps frequent. This day was no exception. I had got into a good stride, after leaving the Cheltenham Road arches, and was dismayed to see a fair sized crowd milling around at the approaching junction. I realised that trying to get through that lot was almost as lethal as looking for a gas leak with a match. Just as I despaired of getting through, I heard a heavy tread, like a policeman "proceeding" somewhere, and the click of a Sturmey Archer three speed, when the bike is being wheeled. It was the policeman from King Square.

"Follow me, son," he commanded, and I was glad to. He strode truly majestically through the crowd, parting them right and left, like Moses and the Red Sea. I struggled and panted to keep up, but made it. Safely on the Parade in Gloucester Road, I lowered the pole and regained my shattered composure.

"Alright, son," he grinned, and went off to help sort out the traffic.

I made it eventually to the house in Shadwell Road, where the lady rewarded me with a cup of tea, and a ginger biscuit. Refreshed, I walked back to Gloucester Road and caught the tram back to the Centre. As I went through Pipe Lane and down Frogmore Street I could see Sid; and he was not pleased.

"Werss thee bloody bin? I bin waitin' fer thee," he greeted me. Apparently, during my absence the boss required some urgent jobs to be carried out, and Sid had been the only one around to do them. He didn't like it. May, (the lady machinist) stood behind Sid, signalling me not to make any reply, by shaking her head and pointing at his back. I remained silent.

The next day, Wednesday, my third day of employment, I arrived at 07.25hrs, hoping to mollify Sid and just in time to see the Carter Paterson driver deliver an 18ft. flagpole. Later that day Sid made out the local delivery dockets.

On the Thursday, at 07.30 hrs, I started work at John Somers box factory, in Pennywell Road. Here, at least, they cut wood down to a reasonable size.

If anyone should ever find a spare flag pole in Frogmore Street they can deliver it when and where they will, and in any manner they choose, with my blessing.

A TEN YEAR OLD REMEMBERS
BY BARBARA BOULTON

A gas mantle splutters and spits above the large family table. Outside the wind lifted the glass on the lean-to. The old marble clock ticking away on the over-mantle, high above the black lead grate, from where I reached to the hob for the brown enameled tea-pot, pouring the now almost black liquid into a cup and adding a teaspoon of condensed milk, I sunk into the armchair, feet on the fender, shifting to make myself comfortable from the many muddles pushed under the cushion.

The heat from the fire burned my cheeks, as I sat contented, my cup of tea clasped by both hands and surrounded by familiar sounds. I gazed searching for pictures in the flames, afraid of the blue ones, the Devil in the fire. Gosh! It had been a good day; my mind travelled back over the day's events, which started with meeting Gertie, my friend, at the police station on Jacob Wells Road. She was waiting with her dad's home-made wooden barrow. We were to go to the gas works on the Docks and fetch one hundredweight of coke.

Saturdays saw loads of children queueing along the docks for coke.

"Can I sit in, Gertie? You push, then you can ride and I'll push."

"Dirty, inn't?"

"That's all right, I'll run over 'Snooks'is' and get a bit of cardboard for a cushion." Off we went to join all the others at the Docks.

In the afternoon we'd gone across from Mardyke Ferry to Bedminster. It was 2d each way. In the week it was filled with workers, for Wills tobacco factory, it was a quick way to Bedminster.

On the evening, as every evening, we'd sit on the wall around my house waiting for the lamplighter. There used to be railings all around the wall, until one day a gang of workmen came and took them all down, to melt into weapons for the Second World War. All that was left was stubs embedded in the wall.

Promptly at six o'clock we'd follow the lamplighter with his long pole and watch fascinated as he lit the gas lamps. We'd say "cheerio" to him as he'd disappear into the darkness of 'White Hart Steps'. This night we had the joy of sitting in the night watchman's hut, by the bombed buildings. A row of houses had been bombed, and some of the house contents were strewn around.

I remember one had the mantelshelf and fire place still intact and even after all the bombing a statue of the Virgin Mary remained upright on the mantelshelf. The night watchman was a kind of security man and we'd sat there with him around the glowing brazier. In an oxo tin on the seat he had a thick slice of toast, a piece of bacon, and an egg to cook

Barbara (centre, middle row) aged 10

over his fire for supper. No one came to call us in, but we knew just when our time was up.

Yes, it had been a good day. I snuggled further into the chair enjoying this time all "Catch" brothers and sisters were out.....peace....a voice broke into my dreaming. "C'mon now, outside and wash yourself and away to your bed."

"Oh Dad, 'tis terrible cold outside in the wash-house!"

"Aah c'mon, you'll soon warm up washing in cold water."

The candle stub in the saucer lit up the peeling distemper, but the corners remained hidden. To my feet the flagstones struck cold through the thin piece of matting. A single brass tap sent water cascading down into the yellow stone sink. The bar of 'Lifebuoy' made a lovely suction noise as I released it from the wooden draining board. I washed myself from neck to feet.

Candlelight flickered on to the enamel bowl, where the dried fish lay soaking, for Sunday morning breakfast; I hated it! But t'was that or go without! There was a lot of discipline in the family which was, until this day, to prove its worth in all of us.

Guarding the flame from the wind, I hurried through the dark yard to the 'lav' and sat in the dim light trying to read from the newspaper squares hanging from their string on a nail behind the door. Returning through the yard the candle spluttered and went out, just an opaque blurp in the bottom of the saucer.

Going up three flights to bed I remember saying, "Touch wood as I go up the stairs, touch wood when I'm up there." The wooden bannister representing to me the Wood of the Cross.

It was very dark in the bedroom as I felt for my candle by the bed. "It's **not there**! S'mbody pinched it, our John, **I bet**!"

I was awakened some hours later by a thud and a shout of pain! My eldest brother had the habit of undressing on the landing, throwing his clothes in the room and following them with a flying leap onto his bed – **but** one of my married sisters had come up that day, given his bedroom a good clean and moved – his – bed! I stuffed the sheet in my mouth to stop from laughing – well, serves him right for pinching my candle!

Barbara and brother in 1944

I MEET FIRE
BY GILBERT CROKER

For all its horrors, its bloodshed, the last World War gave to the unemployed employment, and to the unskilled the opportunity to become skilled. In its early years I was 'snatched' from the military 'grasp' to don the darker uniform of the defendant Fire Service.

As a boy I had gazed through the glass-fronted doors of a fire station and wished that I was that peakless-capped figure polishing an already-shining engine. Even when I had grown to man's estate I felt admiration for a crew of men whom I saw jump from a fire-tender to enter a garage from which smoke was issuing. Nothing on earth would have made me, at that time, do such a thing with all the inflammable and explosive hazzards that I felt existed in such a place.

Had anyone told me then that I would, later, become a fireman I would have gaped, unbelievingly, at them so remote seemed the possibility of my doing the work of those brave figures. Had they repeated it in the 'Depression Thirties', as I searched the streets for work not to be found, I would have taken them to be on some exercise from a mental home.

But daily reports of the 'Battle of Britain' losses found me, with others, dungaree-clad in a requisitioned tramway depot imbibing the basic ideas of how, and with what, to fight fires. It could only be guessed at how widespread, and deep, these fires would become. Only certain was that, needed to fight them, a great manpower trained in the work of the existing peace brigades. So, for some two to three weeks we 'auxiliaries' imitated the acts and listened to the words of one who had been a regular fireman.

Apart from this fundamental training, with some drill in the carrying-down and rescue of trapped people, little else was given us at this time. We visited fire stations, sometimes rode to fires. That the Fire Service regarded our fitness as necessary we found too, for plenty of physical training was in our curriculum. Lectures were few as they developed, later, in their subject matter and necessity as the war's requirement grew.

So, this vital 'schooling' finished, we tin-hatted 'auxiliaries' were sent, with gas-masks slung, to either a peace-time fire station or one that was newly established. These latter were arising in all the Cities of England in garages, large houses and requisitioned buildings.

An annexe of a church hall was where I had to commence duty. I first saw it when reporting to a yawning, uniformed man sat at a utility table. It was seven o'clock in the morning. This darkened and seemingly empty building was far from my conception of what a fire station should have been.

He bade me, with a nonchalant gesture, to go through to another longer room where I would find the inevitable cup of tea! My passage through there I can still bring vividly to mind for the impact it had upon my senses. Ranged each side of it were wooden bunks. These contained fully-blanketed, reclining men. It was a shock, indeed, to think of these heavily-snoring figures as the ever ready heroes of the fight with fire. My nostrils were heavily assailed by the unwholesome smell of many manly expirations in a badly ventilated place! For many years to come, the morning 'cuppa' was to be associated with such an odour.

Of the memories of those years some stand out in the mind. No admiring eyes of children, or adults, saw the wartime firemen going to their fires. Lights were forbidden as they sped at night. All were denied the polished, adorned helmet and many knew not the gleaming brassy engine. For them the lorry, or car, was requisitioned often to pull a pump near to its own weight.

In those days fire-crews were dispatched to action-points upon the warning of approaching enemy planes being sounded. If ever it was considered, then, that the more classy car would be better to ride in than the prancing, shaking lorry but a few yards would suffice to reverse that thought.

Trying to dress in such a confined space to the accompaniment of the rattling, bumping towage was a terrifying experience. Saws, spades, heavy metal standpipes, rolls of hose all demanded space in a vehicle certainly not made for such nightmarish journeys. The pain and the bruising of those days I can still bring back as I think of how those sharp-edged heavy objects, protesting at all the shaking and the noise, struck out to make the nearest fleshy contact!

Then the 'bane of contentment' of those days was the weird wailing of the warning sirens. Upon their undulating note firemen, not on duty, had to report at once to their stations being permitted to leave when the 'All Clear' sounded. Many were the false scares of enemy planes approaching and many were the unnecessary journeys of bicycling, tin-hatted firefighters. One meal I once started, at home, was interrupted, resumed, interrupted, resumed and yet again interrupted and resumed all within the space of some forty minutes!

The tenseness of those first months of war was equalled, perhaps by the absence of the expected aerial bombardment. Auxiliary firemen, keyed and trained to the needs of war, enthused little over the paltry rubbish fire and expressed disgust at the false alarm! Then the 'regulars' were just a little annoyed at this mass infiltration into their almost-closed profession. But there was to come a time when these two-week trainees, whose entry standards had to be lowered to meet the times, were to fight fires the like of which had never before been seen. The professionals had never even dreamed of the proportions to which these were to sear and spread.

The evening of Sunday the 24th of November 1940 was a usual one of fading church bells and emptying streets. Its quietness was, for some seconds, shattered by a pump attending a small fire in a telephone kiosk but one hundred yards from the station at which I was on duty. The paper that was involved there was soon 'tackled' by an extinguisher and we quickly returned.

At the time that we were dealing with this rather insignificant incident preparations were going on, unknown to us, somewhere in Europe to make the coming night one of fear and sleeplessness. But some hours later we still looked upon the transmitted coded-colour warning, of enemy planes approaching, as continuing in its monotonous and harmful routine. Even when the wailful sirens followed almost at once, none of that fire station's hearts felt the dreaded, sinking feeling of thereafter nights and days.

The first knowledge that I had of anything irregular was from two, or three, colleagues who had, inquisitively, gone outside the station. As this bordered a deep railway cutting it was possible, looking westwards, to see the greater built-up area of the city. Strange indeed was the colour of the horizon's sky!

"It's the Centre! They're hitting the Centre!"

The dejected note in this informative cry brought more of us out from the building.

"Look! See! It must be in Town. O Hell! That's heavier bombs!"

Split now with shots of more glowing flame the very sky seemed to be on fire!

"But 'tis incendaries mostly. Why, the whole place must be blazing!"

"Then this is IT!"

That short snapped-out sentence declared the dreaded truth that so many of us had, for so long, hoped not to face!

Inside the station much movement now went on as men were ordered to go to the iron-sheeted garage to standby, their ready appliances having already been warmed-up. Across each chest gas-masks were braced, at the ready, as upon each head sat a tin-hat. These small-rimmed steel basin-like things were so far removed from the familiar elaborate fireman's helmet. But, surprisingly, they gave one enormous confidence.

How long we stayed there talking, smoking, fidgeting no one knew. But the expected summons came!

"A Major pump! To report to Inspector Potts at Bridge Street."

The fireman in charge of the wanted appliance jumped into the cab of the lorry whose engine was now roaring into life. His crew, clambering over the wooden sides behind, searched for some softness in that great open deck where they might get off their feet. They found that, amongst all its equipment's hard metal, the tightly-rolled canvas hose laid flat, and coiled, gave the most comfort.

Their station set towards the fringe of the city was, as yet, untouched by this visit of the enemy. Suddenly cut from its wealth of human companionship, did it take a nerve of supernatural proportions, possession of which none of us had any knowledge, or no nerve at all to respond to this incident right in the centre of heavy concentrated bombing with all its fears and unknown terrors?

Somewhere at the back of our senses, still dazed from the initial shock, was the overiding feeling that we were members of an emergency service responding to a call. Thus we rode along between the dimmed, hooded lights of the lorry and the bumping jerking pump that it was towing.

The familiar streets through which we drove showed, at intervals, more tin-hatted figures. These were on watch after their shepherding work of moving people to shelter. Some were shouting at the occupants of a car which was making an unhurried progress along the road. Obviously they were returning from a visit to the country unaware of the air-raid warnings. Yet humans do strange things in never-before-seen circumstances. It could have been that they cared not, one fig, for the power that was above them and were adamant to go their usual pace homewards.

Our route, so quiet and darkened at its outset, took upon itself more of the yellow light and frightening heat of our fiery goal. Crossing Bristol's bridge we all blinked our eyelids at the great surgings of fire that stretched far to the right. Entering Bridge Street it was as if we had to pass through some hot 'Gulliverian' oven! The lines of fairly-aged buildings, ranged each side, were as old gas-burners some of whose jets had fired whilst others stood inflammatory.

So hot was it that I and the others around me started to undo our top coats. In so doing we displayed, beneath, multi-coloured scarves that the slightly-relaxed discipline of those days allowed. Johnny threw off his coat altogether to resemble more the many almost shirt-sleeved firefighters beneath.

The long corner shop known so well in more youthful days was, with its scholastic contents a 'sitting target' for all this rampaging fire. Halfway up this street, between a side-blazing gap in the line of shops and over still-smoking rubble, ran two fat lines of hose. Flame-coloured water was being pumped through them from the river by a boat. I had noticed it, below, whilst crossing the bridge. Down those same wooden steps and from that same small jetty pleasure-trippers used to go down to Keynsham in happier times!

The sky right over us and now deeper red was fringed by the misty shafts of the moving searchlights. In one, for a brief second was seen, as some silver insect, an aeroplane. It darted, quickly into the darker sky. This led us to believe that it was one of the enemy that had failed to follow its group into this hidden safety.

"But they'll be back! You see!"

The shouted words came from Jim, next to me. It voiced all our fears that somewhere above lingered the enemy desiring not to get caught in the great light that their dastardly work had created.

Somewhere in this place of swirling smoke and shattered glass, where the noise of collapsing buildings sickened and fiery sparks rained down, was the one man whom we sought.

"Inspector Potts? Where can we find him?"

Many figures there were in that illumined 'picture'. Lit most was an extended, and large, ladder that arched a stream of water into a great store whose large stock of highly inflammable gramophone records was so much 'food' for the huge flames that rose from it. But of those human beings who stood against forceful jets with their feet in dirty fire-contaminated water there were others who were bent to the strain of moving heavy hose. From neither did an arm direct or reply come.

So our large vehicle, with its heavy towage, jogged on past whirring pumps. Where the street was half-blocked with the piles of debris and the water-soddened contents of the ruined shops, it swerved to make the standing-up in its long, wooden deck of greater comfort to us. Then as it tugged, and jerked, over pressured, snaking hose it brought forth unmentionable comments from sweating firefighters!

At the top of the street, flames, that came from behind its fronting building, were rearing up against the turretted Norman tower of St. Peter's Church. It seemed as if, drunk with all this power over fairly-modern creations, fire was now daring its strength against a centuries-old construction. As we turned into Peter Street the ornate and ancient frontage of the neighbouring 'Hospital' was scorched and smoke-palled.

On the other side of the road a large basin-like hole in the ground told that more deadly things than the truncheon-shaped 'incendiaries' had fallen from that sky above. The debris of smashed stone and woodwork, that, almost filling it, belied its true depth, was left to burn itself out.

"What the **hell** are you doing running around as on some sightseeing tour?"

The voice came from a large, uniformed figure whose so-red face was not all due to the surrounding heat. Reg, our leader fireman, touched the rim of his helmet to Inspector Potts!

"Station C.8. reporting, sir."

"About time! You should have been here an hour ago! But then nobody could have got within fifty yards of this place it was so damned hot! Keep going!"

Jumping on to the step of our lorry the inspector clung to its framework and continued with his orders.

"Now get down to Woolworth's! But not for 'nothing over sixpence!'

Greeted with silence this remark lost its intended humour. But its creator gave no sign of any loss as we went past engines that stood dangerously near fire-ravaged buildings. Steel pipes, thrust in holes in the roadway, still fed the precious water into hoses from the, as yet, undamaged mains. One large jet was almost overbalancing two firemen against whom it was striking. Either it was cooling them or was too difficult for its handler to direct!

Chaotic clamour continued its intrudence into the night's usual quietness. Human voices shouted orders, stung the air with blasphemous oaths or screeched warnings of danger. In a crescendo of clatter tin, china and metal was smashed and plate-glass shattered. Pumps pulsated heavily as they gulped-in and threw out, gallons and gallons of water. The roar of rampaging fire accompanying the thunder of fallen masonry was so vastly 'nightmarish' compared with the lesser and more peacful noise of the previous evening's shopping throngs.

That evening was destined to end an era of those fair-like week-ends! Then shop-gazers packed the pavements. Shop-seekers laughingly thronged the roadway enforcing their ancient right to walk in it to the retardation of vehicular progress. At intervals crowds milled around a road-side stall whose contents were lit by a hissing naptha flare! Then the many-coloured goods on display outside the shop-fronts made up a little for the rather poor street illuminations!

The so-popular rendez-vous then was now being attacked by the fiery enemy as our banging pump was at last halted.

"At the bottom, there, you can get down to the river. I want all that b---- water brought up here!"

The gesticulating officer released his clinging hold on the cab's side and moved away satisfied that his short and blunt phraseology was understood and that its meaning would be carried out.

Queen Street was just wide enough to let our lorry through. At the bottom we all dismounted to unhitch the big pump and manhandle it towards the river. It took the six of us to persuade it, with the adroit and occasional use of the handbrake, to go to where it was required. The pathway led through a hauling-way of a flour mill where willing hands helped us, eventually, to set it on a concrete platform some twelve feet up from the water level. With suction pipes in the river, rolls of hose, with more grabbed as the lorry was passed, made two lines up, and into, Castle Street. There they provided, from another pump, jets upon three and four storey buildings.

Jim and I set another line, from the pump's outlet that ended in the narrow street and Woolworth's side-wall.

"Quick in here!"

He jerked the spitting jet, and my arms, to his left as a sheet of fire shot out from a shattered window. But one stream of water was so hopeless against many spurting flames. Soon their reaching made contact with the inflammable wood of the opposite building.

"Here, can you hang on to this?"

I passed the full weight of our pressured hose on to my colleague as that roof of fire grew.

"I'm getting another length. We'll get out into Castle Street. 'Tis safer there!"

With Jim's acknowledging nod I ran down to the river's edge and shouted, with cupped hands, to the pump operator. It was necessary for him to cease his noisy pumping for the short time that I was hastening back and adding another length.

Of course, while we waited for our renewed supply we were subject to the vented annoyance of the nearby pump attendant. As his engine started to splutter and the canvas hose behind him collapse, "Is the b---- river as dry as my blasted throat then?" he managed to get out before his hose started to fatten once more.

Now we could look up and down Castle Street. Strange was its appearance! Its two lines of storeyed buildings, some of ancient construction and some of new, lay cut by uprising smoke and fire. Where this had found some untouched part great flames of orange colour shot up or out. Or where it had found some more inflammable substance flames of blue and violet. Then, where it had consumed huge gaps of charred framework still dripped water on to the piled, smoking debris below. The large Woolworth's building seemed destined to that end as we strove to hold steady, on it, our jets. These we even used to demolish, further, great sheets of plate-glass that we might lessen the risk of its flying splinters!

Time, when thought of amidst all this utter chaos seemed some far-off thing. The outward picture of that dirty firefighter, near us, handing others mugs of tea was misleading. His senses were as paralysed as were all of ours by the amount of amazing noise and needless burning destruction that they were expected to take in. Above all, and overiding in its horror, was the subjugation of so much to fire. As human hands did what they could eyes strove to impress upon the brain the obvious inevitability of the night's inhuman work, with which

Time would have no connection!

Had it done so it would have seemed to have stopped, with one's heartbeats, as another sound could now be heard. To the imaginative mind it was as if a fleet of paddle-steamers was pounding their way up the river!

"T--thr--ump!" "T--thr--ump!!" "T--thr--ump!!!"

But to realising thought the ear was transmitting but one thing. That regular and approaching note, from the east, meant that the enemy planes were returning!

Now to the confusion of noise and colour upon the ground was added more above it. The grey shafts of the searchlights speeded their search of the clouds as gunfire opened up in green flashes. Incendiary bombs, whose fuses went off prematurely in their swift descent to earth, burst in varied colour. Others 'rained' down on us to split in an ultra-violet flame when striking the roadway, to fall into the holocaust that the previous ones had made or to pierce through more unprotected roofs to set alight other fires. Where one dropped uncomfortably near a boot often dispatched it. Where a forceful jet could be spared for a few seconds others were short-lived.

"Look out!"

More than one voice shouted this as an accelerated 'whistle' could be heard speeding from the sky! For one indefinable second the shocked humanity, near, remained unmoved! Then in a clatter of noise intermingled with curses all dived for what small thing instinct told them might give shelter as that screaming 'whistle' landed 'smack' into a great pit of fire! The flames of this, ravaging a building, were blasted out by a vivid light that shot great chunks of smashed masonry and charred woodwork high into the air!

Crouched beside that pile of debris or pressed against the side of that fire-engine we were given a little shelter, too, from the cutting shatter of plate-glass. But its frailty was such that we could not linger in either of these places. So the down-thrown and still-outpouring branches were taken up again and the pumps re-accelerated. No respite was there in the tumult upon the earth nor in the farther-off sky. Neither was there any lull in the great gulf of space between.

To our left our ears picked up another fiendish 'whistle' swiftly descending. Again with bent frames and every nerve tensed and braced for the resulting blow we heard a great

"Swo--oo--sh!"

Then, amidst the surrounding din, a consoling voice,

"That one landed in the river, thank goodness!"

In our relief we made 'play' of the obvious nearness of our pumping colleague at the river's edge.

"Bet he is nearly drowned with all that water coming up and over!"

"Or washed down the river, lucky chap!"

Our particular fire, Woolworth's was getting out of hand. It was obvious, before even this second raid, that salvage work could not be done here had we the necessary manpower. So when another heavy bomb fell higher up the street Jim and I sought for a safer position.

"I think that if we get down to the bottom of Queen Street again we can still throw a jet to the side, here, whilst having cover from that flour mill."

Understandably other fighters around us moved to other positions. Some, I heard later, had found good shelter in the old ruined Banqueting Hall of the former Bristol Castle. This was behind and had built into it, a confectionery shop, but this, like many other erections in that street, had been destroyed.

Down through the narrow and terribly hot street Jim and I dragged our hose. No sky could we see for fire, above us, blotted it out. Nearer to a higher building, but one of concrete construction, we again directed our jet. Proffered tea by some of the mill's occupants we asked of our riverside colleague and found that he had not been touched by a drop of water for he had dived beneath his broad appliance.

Now that we were more enclosed in, it seemed that the 'rain' of incendiaries was easing off. Less did we see their landing bursts of threatening flame and hear that queer, yet awful sound as the unexploding bomb hit hard rubble or metal. Reg, our leader, came to ask of our circumstances before leaving on a similar mission to the river's edge. What had happened to the other member of our crew we knew not. We had not seen him since that combined effort to get the heavy suction hose connecting river to pump before he left us together to 'run out' the delivery line. Evidently he had been 'caught' without some piece of equipment in his hand and had been 'snatched' by some harassed officer to help get some other jet going on those reaching, rearing flames.

But that was how the night's work was done. Water was so urgently needed on all this fire that pump operators, branchmen, officers all got going to this end. The individuality stressed upon us in the days of training when we were numbers one or two of a crew had long since 'gone by the board'.

These blazing buildings did not call for the sweep of the firemen's branch from side to side as is required in damping-down operations. The continued direction of a jet in one position and for lengths of time was necessary to try to 'flood' these persisting flames. We both found it exhausting to keep an high-pressured jet so fixedly. I thought it better for us to lay it down upon a small pile of rubble and, while Jim kept its direction gradually ease off his grip on it with more bricks holding on top. When the direction did slip a little a slight pressure of a foot and leg we found would hold it.

It was when straightening-up from this operation that I found Jim, too, had been wondering about our missing colleague.

"Jack, where ------"

He got no further. A thunderous roar, at the top of the street, that came and went with the speed of lightning shook the ground under us! We both jumped back having no time to seek shelter. Jim, with his arms shielding his face, flattened them against the outside wall of the mill as if he would press his whole body into that rough concrete! My back finished against that same wall as my eyelids slammed down in protection against the vividness of the following light-flash!

But opening again they were held by the terrifying scene that I had to take in! The windowless wall of the three-storeyed building, near which we had stood, was enveloped in a sudden uprising of smoke. Then the top of it leaned outward and hung as if for seconds before it collapsed straight down in that mass of smoke with the rest of the wall!

As if it, too, had been affected by this horrifying blast our jet of water now disappeared from the end of our branch. Moving to seek the cause of this helped us both to recover. Whilst Jim looked for any obstructing of the end length I traced the others back. Eventually I found that our pump had stopped and its operator explained why.

"It sounds crazy to ask for petrol with all this fire around. But this 'thing' wants it and that's that!"

Now some officer had to be found in all this fiendish work to ask if he knew of some brave fellow who might be running around with a 'load of dynamite' in his petrol wagon! It was all so frightening and yet crazy! But coming out of the mill I hardly trusted the sense that seemed to tell me that, somehow, 'things' were quietier! The roar of flames and the din of crashing storeys continued but now accompanied less by the 'thumps' of falling bombs.

Jim had rightly guessed at the cause of our vanished water for he said that Reg had been down and he had passed on his fears to him.

"In the meantime we've got to move up again into Castle Street to see what we can do there."

Over the 'mountain' of debris at the top we now struggled into the broader but almost cremated thoroughfare! Here we found water flowing from branches that were only too quickly handed us by similarly sweating, dirty men. But wasn't there now something of change in their manner and tone of voice? My partner felt it too for he came out with "The 'All Clear' will go soon!"

It seemed hours after this, when in fact it was just within one, before his heartening prediction came true. In this time still the flames ravaged and persisted, still depressed was every eye at the sight of so much destruction. Then the ear, too, was still being attacked by many other noises. But it was this that first received the welcomed wailing but steady note of the 'All Clear' signal. Then relief was seen to clear anxiousness from many faces.

That Jim and I were lucky, when Reg came along with some good news, we were told by many spitting throats.

"Haven't been here five minutes! Now they're going back!"

"What about all this bloody fire?"

"Any vacancies at your 'jammy' section?"

To these 'departures' we moved away to regroup our former crew. Jack had been found and Ron, at the pump, was glad to get away from his 'charge'.

We were indeed most fortunate to come away so quickly from that nightmarish scene. The stroke of midnight was but minutes off and some of our colleagues would be staying there until reliefs were organised for them or until they could be found as individuals! But some half-a-dozen would never leave that place of unprecedented fire. They had laid down their lives beneath a collapse of masonry just above Bristol's bridge!

NEVER A DULL MOMENT FOR A BUILDING WORKER

BY FRED MOSS

It was now March 1942 and I was sent to Bath. Our job was to build an underground electrical furnace. The idea of the furnace was to twist the blade propellers to a correct pitch and also to erect a building for engineering work and also a new canteen for the factory workers. There was a large mechanical digger there to excavate a very large hole ready for the building of the underground furnace. Everything was going to plan, many tons of dirt and rubble were excavated and taken away to the tip, we were working twelve hours per day and six days per week.

We had been working there for about five weeks. I must state that we had a rather large workforce on this particular job as the work had to be finished as soon as possible, everything being needed for war requirements.

We finished work on Friday the 14th of April at 6 p.m., but on that particular weekend the German airmen blitzed Bath including destroying all our work and damaging the mechanical digger beyond repair. All the huts and every workman's tools were destroyed.

A land mine had exploded right on the front of our site creating absolutely enormous damage. There were about twenty rolls of reinforcing wire stacked near where the mine exploded. Now each roll weighed about five hundredweight, each of these rolls was blown up onto the roof of the factory next to our site. Houses all around our site were severely damaged and many people killed or injured. It was a terrible sight to behold. We set to work to salvage whatever we could concerning the tools, but we found very little. Some of us concentrated on unravelling the rolls of re-inforcing wire from the large asbestos roof of the factory. It took us a week to disentangle all the wire from the roof, it meant that many new roofing sheets had to be fitted.

The Ministry of Works supplied the firm with a brand new mechanical digger. The job had to be finished on time, some of us were asked to work extra hours and that meant working Sundays as well. All told I was working ninety hours a week. All the trenches were excavated for the concrete foundations including larger holes for concrete bases for stanchions made of steel to be erected. I worked many weeks at ninety hours per week and of course my turn in firewatching. None of the workmen grumbled, they knew and I knew that a job had to be done and we did it.

In February 1943 I was sent to Saltford just outside Bristol. It was an experimental job in concrete. First of all there was a great deal of excavation work to be done, all the trenches and bases for stanchions

were all dug out by hand. We were all doing what we termed as 'bonus work'. We were paid at so much per cubic yard. We picked up excellent bonuses. After all the examination was completed we concreted the trenches and bases still on bonus work, but we received very little bonuses on concrete work.

Right opposite our building site there was a large factory-type building that was taken over by the American Army. The building was used as a food store; guarding the foodstore were black Americans and they were a very happy group of men. We thoroughly enjoyed their company.

At twelve p.m. we would have a break of one hour for lunch, while we were having our lunch some of the Americans would come into our hut and have a chat about the war and they were very concerned about our food situation. There was a sergeant who also wandered into our hut, he was black; six foot three inches tall, he was also very broad shouldered, in fact he was a very large man. He was a very intelligent man, a devout Christian and he worshipped his mother. He would do a little preaching in between conversing on other subjects. We really enjoyed their company and it lasted for many weeks.

Now everything that was to go into the building of an enormous shed on this site was made on the site. First of all the stanchions with an extending arm to carry the roof had to be cast on site, the cages of reinforced wire were made to the shape of the stanchions. All these cages were boxed in with timber and concrete was poured into the cages and vibrated with a specially made vibrator. The vibrator was used to solidify the concrete and force every bit of air out of the concrete.

A firm of steel erectors was employed to lift the stanchions into their positions. This particular firm had the right lifting tackle to do the job. Eventually everything was lifted into its respective positions, now the bricklayers could do their job of building the brickwork between the stanchions. As soon as all the brickwork was finished the next job would be concreting the floor. That job was finished after about two weeks, but I did not see the job finished as I was asked to go to Wotton-Under-Edge to demolish an old 16th century woollen mill wall. The rest of the mill had gradually crumbled away, leaving an end wall twenty five feet high with a chimney stack at the top of the gable end wall. There were two men already there, but they were too nervous to tackle the job so that was why I was asked to help them. Of course I had already been demolishing dangerous house walls that had been left in a dangerous condition through the blitz. I looked around the wall and made up my mind that the chimney stack would have to be demolished first.

The man in charge of the job, whose name was Fred Davidson, was concerned about the danger in doing the job. I told him that I would do what I could to avoid anyone being injured. I climbed a very long forty two rung ladder. The ladder only reached the lower part of the gable, therefore I had to climb up part of the gable to take a look at the chimney stack. The stonework was falling part, and freestone was coming away from the stonework. It did look very, very dangerous, but I

Fred Moss (back) at work in 1939

decided that I could demolish it, but the man in charge was still concerned. Anyway, I told him I had made my mind up on what I intended to do. There were lengths of four by three timber lying around, so I chose a seven foot long piece.

I climbed the ladder, Fred Davidson followed behind. The other workman looked very nervous, but he stayed on the ground. I climbed part way up the gable and asked Fred to hold onto my feet. I intended to push the stack over by pushing the timber into the stack. I pushed and kept pushing at the stack. Fred was holding my legs firm. I gave one huge push and luckily the whole stack fell away from us down into the stream. So the danger was over. The three of us sat down and enjoyed a cup of tea. It was guite easy now to demolish the wall course by course of stone. The stone was a beautiful Cotswold stone. As we were demolishing the wall we came across a honeycomb of bees in one of the chimney flues. We carefully exposed it and carried it down to the ground. It measured three feet tall by eighteen inches wide and was full of hibernating bees. On one warm day they flew away. We finished demolishing the wall and then once more I was on my way back to Bristol.

Fred Moss (centre front), 1961

MY ST. PAULS
BY E. L. L. SHADDICK

I only knew St. Pauls for three months in the middle of 1944, but I grew to love it.

I roamed around on a bicycle, all hours of the day and night, during the wartime blackout, and never had cause to fear anything larger or more sinister than fleas which abounded a plenty.

The three months was the culmination of my training before qualifying as a State Certificate Midwife, St. Pauls was part of my district, St. Werburghs was the posh bit. Many of the streets and Bristolians' homes have disappeared and it is virtually impossible to recognise any landmarks when coming off the M.32.

Memories are not so easily obliterated. Some parts could produce sights, sounds and smells to rival the reconstructed Viking village at York, but the natives were real enough, earthy, witty, kind, poor, and generous.

It had been dinned into my head before being turned loose on the Public at Home, that patients in hospital were guests. On district, things were different. I should enter a patient's home by invitation, I should be the guest.

My Sister tutor took me around on the first day to introduce me to all my charges and mothers to be.

It was a revelation.

She breezed into a small terrraced house, giving a perfunctory tap on the door.

"Morning, Clara. I've brought Nurse Shaddick along. She'll look after you from now on."

Our Hostess, obviously an old hand at the game, was propped against the mantelpiece, firmly anchored by one elbow. One handed, she was deftly stoking up her youngest, (it wasn't going to be her youngest much longer) with bread and milk while it was jumping up and down in its high chair.

Clara took time off to survey me.

"Arh. An if theece dusn't suit I, theece'll get the arse kicked out of it."

I could not blame her. She must have had a longer procession of pupil midwives practicing their doubtful skills upon her than I'd had hot dinners.

The Sister tutor had also seen it all before. She was small, dark, Welsh, and her eyes did not miss a thing behind her pebble lens spectacles.

It was my turn to make a contribution to this oft acted farce.

"I hope you won't have to do that, Mrs..." I was cut off in flow.

"Who the Hell dust think thee art, calling I Mrs...I'm Clara, and you'll call me Clara."

For the record, Clara was a very good tutor. She knew far more than I did, and she made sure I did things proper like. When her time came, it came quickly. She did warn me.

"When I had this little bugger," indicating her offspring, which, as far as I was concerned, was still unsexed, "I only turned to Ma, and said 'Ma, pass the custard' and before she could, he were there."

Clara would be well over eighty now. I've often wondered how many more she had, how they grew up, what they would think of St. Pauls now. There must have been a Mr. Clara somewhere, but I never saw him.

Accepting gifts from patients was not encouraged, especially in war torn Britain, but on one occasion, I was presented with a treasure beyond price. It was the fourteenth day after the infant's birth, and my last visit.

"That's to wipe the dirty look you gave me off your face when I called you out in the middle of the night."

I felt guilty, but the call had been a false alarm, and not the only one. And my treasure? A tablet of Lifebuoy toilet soap. A truly generous gift in austere times.

I started by saying I never had cause to feel fear. That is true as far as the area was concerned. The combination of schoolgirl type nurses' hat, navy blue raincoat, black shoes and stockings and traditional little black bag, was a safety passport to anywhere at any time. But there was one night of terror to remember in St. Pauls.

Delivery by gaslight was not ideal, having been used to all mod cons in hospital labour wards.

This particular middle of the night, things were coming along very well. Citizen 1944 had delivered as far as the eyebrows when the gaslight gave a despairing dip and expired.

"Don't push. Strike a match. Get a candle. Turn off the gas tap. Somebody DO something." I couldn't do anything but hang on.

Mother pushed. The head was out.

"Please God, don't let the cord be around the neck." It wasn't.

"Please God, let the shoulders rotate." They did.

"Please don't let them stick." They didn't.

Nature took over.

The infant yelled, so I had not let it drown.

The mother contracted, so I had not let her bleed to death.

After an eon of eternities, a match was struck, and a stump of candle produced. It might have been a tiny flickering flame to the Universe, but it was a beacon of salvation to me... and a warning. I managed to scrounge a couple of inches of candle and a few matches, and made sure I always had a few coins for meter feeding until I could afford to buy a torch. My salary worked out at a bit less than £5 a month at the time.

Forty or more years on, custard, candles, and soap reminds me of St. Pauls.

‘FAIRYLAND’
BY MARGARET REDISH

“We’re going on a picnic to Fairyland.”

‘Fairyland’ was the name given to the wooded area of the Downs just before the Sea Walls.

Our mothers would be waiting outside of St. Johns School with baskets containing tea and sometimes balls, and skipping ropes. We bounded across the playground and out of the gates, glad to be free of the restrictions of the classroom; only to be marshalled across the road via the belisha beacon. Then we were free – to race all over the daisy, dandelion covered grass and to feel warm breeze on our faces.

On our way to ‘Fairyland’ we would pass ‘The Dumps’. This was a very popular spot as it involved a lot of running up and down the grassy slopes. The steepest of these only being tackled by the more adventurous of the group. We felt we were really ‘mountaineering’ as we struggled to get a foot hold on the loose dry soil. We might discover a den, its entrance hidden and overgrown with brambles.

On arriving at ‘Fairyland’ we would have our picnic amongst the trees. As soon as we had finished eating we would dash to see if we could see any ships coming up the river. There was the excitement of seeing the steam train emerge from its rock tunnel, smoke billowing all around it. We would also watch the cars travelling along The Portway, looking exactly like our Dinky toys at home.

In the autumn, armed with baskets and walking sticks we would hunt for blackberries.

When the war came a lot of the Sea Walls area was cordoned off with barbed wire. I can remember seeing American soldiers playing baseball. There were also cairn like mounds of stones standing guard ‘to prevent enemy planes from landing’ we were told.

There was also a large barrage balloon, hanging like a silvery Dumbo in the sky.

I saw several of Shakespeare’s plays performed amidst the trees, which made a marvellous setting.

At other times the Fair would arrive – I would have saved up 3d or 6d for a ride on the Golden Gallopers and would wait until I could get an outside horse – you could see so far and I would imagine I was really galloping all over the Downs.

There was a bandstand behind the water tower. When not in use we would clamber up the wooden steps, swing on its rails and perform various acrobatic feats such as handstands and balancing precariously on its narrow ledges.

I have been privileged to live all of my life, within a short distance of this childhood 'Fairyland'. My children took their first unsteady steps on its carpets of green, played endless games of cricket and football – and now I am again sharing its magic with my grandson as he plays hide and seek amongst the trees and grips my hand tightly as we venture down the steep path in The Dumps to see if we can find a 'Fairy House'.

ON SUNDAYS AUNTIE LOU BECAME A LADY BY JANET ILES

She was walking towards me wearing a rather battered hat, which was perched on top of a mass of untidy curls, with clips hanging on to an odd strand of hair here and there. Her coat looked as if it had seen better days, as did her shoes. She carried an old shopping bag in one hand and clutched a bulging purse in the other. I asked some children nearby who she was and I was promptly told that she was Auntie Lou.

Having just moved along with nine other families into our new homes, I was keen to explore my new surroundings. I discovered at the end of the cul-de-sac a pair of wrought iron gates surrounded by a solid grey wall, with a lane leading down to the railway track and a road below. I remember peeping through the gates at the cottage inside, which I discovered was Auntie Lou's home. She lived there with her husband and unmarried sister. Known as Uncle Joe and Auntie Mary to all the children.

In no time at all she became a friend of the family and popped in to see us almost every day. I soon realised that her personality was outstanding. She held very strong views on just about everything and would cut anyone down to size if they tried to contradict her. Even as a child I was aware of the inaccuracies of some of her stories. But I wouldn't dare to voice my opinion, such was the power of Auntie Lou that one withering look was enough for me to shut up!

Unfortunately, she had a habit of expressing herself most forcefully by swearing and one day I used some of her swear words during an argument with my sister. My father took a dim view of this, as he hated bad language. He told Auntie Lou that she wouldn't be welcome in our home unless she stopped swearing in front of his children.

She was offended and it caused an unpleasant atmosphere for a while, but it soon passed and she began to visit us again. Trying to keep her expressive language in check.

One thing I noticed about Auntie Lou and her family was the extraordinary teeth they all had. They were very long and thick, rather like horse's teeth. Eventually Auntie Lou succumbed to toothache and announced that this particular tooth had to be removed. We were amazed to hear she had always removed her own teeth, as she wouldn't allow a strange bloke, meaning the dentist, to put his hands in her mouth! That remark was punctured by her fist crashing down on the table. It wasn't so much a comment as a statement she made.

We were all horrified at the lengths she went to to remove her tooth. It would take weeks and many methods were used to loosen it. She would spend much time and effort moving it backwards and forwards, during which time she was in constant pain and eager to solve the problem. Eventually, when it was loose enough she jammed a fork underneath and hit the handle with her fist. She had to do this time and time again until she achieved the results she wanted. When she brought the tooth to show us there was a look of triumph on her face as she held the offensive tooth aloft. It had four of the largest prongs I have ever seen, then or since!

There were two sides to Auntie Lou. She could be immensely kind and caring or as hard as steel. An example of the latter side of her nature was revealed one day when my mother expressed her anger because my father had brought home a little kitten. Yet another animal for her to feed and look after. Some while after, this sweet little kitten disappeared. When asked Auntie Lou denied any knowledge of the kitten's whereabouts. However, someone had seen her taking it to her cottage. My father, who by that time had arrived home, confronted her and demanded that she should return the kitten. Unfortunately, it was too late, she had already drowned this beautiful creature in a bucket of water. That was her way of solving my mother's problem. This cruel act towards a ten week old kitten, who was old enough to be aware of what was being done, alienated her from our family for quite a long time.

On the other hand she was generous to a fault. She always gave my mother regular amounts of garden produce, which was always gratefully received. However, we felt less keen when she told us that the abundance was solely due to the contents of her chamber pot!

She loved having visitors, as much as I loved taking my friends to see her. We were always made to feel welcome and she obviously enjoyed showing a first-time visitor around her lounge, which was filled with antiques and various knick-knacks. No-one ever left without being given a small gift of some sort.

Auntie Lou became many people when she needed to add to her voice of authority. One day she was disgusted to see a little baby sat in a pram without a bonnet on, something she thoroughly disapproved of. She left the young mother in no doubt at all that she felt the baby was neglected by this oversight. An argument ensued that was ended by Auntie Lou's raised voice telling the young mother that she would see her at the Clinic on Friday. Again she emphasised this statement by slapping her purse down hard on the edge of the pram. The young mum hurried away feeling quite sure that she had a position of authority at the Clinic. She had completely overlooked Auntie Lou's dishevelled appearance.

My mother was constantly reprimanded by Auntie Lou, because she felt we all bathed too much and any illness we had was due to the fact that my mother kept us too clean. In fact, our resistance was washed away!

Auntie Lou and her family had one real wash just once a week. She would stand in a large bowl of soda water, which had been placed in the middle of the kitchen floor, and sponged herself from head to toe.

This ritual usually took place on a Saturday night, so that she was clean and wholesome for Sunday. The rest of the week she just swilled her face with cold water first thing in the morning.

There was another ritual which took place soon after breakfast on Sunday. I can picture her now removing the clips one at a time from her untidy curls. She would then meticulously comb each curl to perfection which would then be clipped firmly in place. After this was done she would cream and powder her face. On Sunday she always wore a navy dress with a lovely pearl necklace with matching earrings. On Sunday Auntie Lou became a lady both in appearance and by the way she spoke. Her voice was more refined and the absence of swearing was quite noticeable. There was also a tremendous ladylike quality in her voice when she told me stories from the bible, and in the same breath of how, when she was kneeling in the church receiving the blessing after taking her marriage vows, the sun shone in all its glory through the window enveloping Auntie Lou and Uncle Joe in its light. She told this story with such reverence that it obviously had some miraculous significance, but of what, as a child, I was not quite sure. Except that something very special happened on Auntie Lou's wedding day.

On one memorable occasion, she wandered into our house whilst my father was playing 'The Holy City' on the pianola. Suddenly with great dignity she folded her hands in front of her and began to sing. She had an astonishing soprano voice which was strong and crystal clear. The whole family listened in awe to this beautiful voice. When she had finished there was a few moments of utter silence as we all digested that the voice we had just heard belonged to Auntie Lou. Then much to her delight we clapped and showed our appreciation in a number of ways, all chattering at once. It was several hours later when she left our home, having sung almost non-stop.

We enjoyed many such occasions after that night. I always felt so excited when I knew Auntie Lou was coming to sing for the evening. I was even more in awe of her when she told us she knew Dame Clara Butt and Eva Summer who she met again when the famous singer visited Bristol.

Sad to say Auntie Lou became senile as she grew old. During the last months of her life she had to be confined in a hospital, because she was constantly found wandering around in a confused state. Whilst in hospital she would still display her individual character, and wasn't above giving the staff a clout if they upset her by ordering her around.

Uncle Joe is ninety seven years old and he too is senile and resides in a nursing home. Auntie Mary died when Auntie Lou pushed her over in a fit of temper. My mother mopped the blood from her face and generally took care of her. Unfortunately she had a massive stroke that night and died several days later.

Auntie Lou was totally unaware of her sister's death, as far as she was concerned Auntie Mary was directing traffic at Purdown in all winds and weather. She would often stand at the top of the lane shouting obscenities at her!

I have only to put one of her beautiful embroidered cloths on the dining room table, and my thoughts take me back into another world. I can picture myself in her tiny sitting room being taught the intricacies of embroidery surrounded by her beautiful antiques.

Gas was the only form of lighting downstairs and candles and oil lamps were used upstairs. No one who saw her during the week in her shabby coat and untidy hair could ever guess at the richness of her home.

But most of all, whenever I hear 'The Holy City' or 'We'll Gather Lilacs In The Spring Again' I'm hearing the haunting voice of Auntie Lou. Because in my eyes they were, and always will be, her songs.

'OUR RON, THAT CHLÖE'
BY RON GLADE

A few days before Christmas 1933 two grubby little urchins, a boy of 11 years and a girl of 9 years were to be seen, noses pressed against the window of Maynard Sweet shop in Old Market Street oblivious to the crowds and traffic. All they were interested in were the lovely decorations and mountains of sweets and chocolates, knowing full well they would be lucky to get even a small Fry's Selection Box for Christmas. The sensitive boy still blushing with shame at the thought of a few days before when at school he was called out in front of the whole class and given a new pair of boots from the Lord Mayor's fund, yet there in front of him seemed to be enough sweets and chocolates for every little girl and boy in the whole world, and a lovely big box of chocs for Mum.

Poor Mum was looking so tired these days scrubbing office floors, washing and ironing for his six sisters and two brothers. Dad was always drunk and beating her, and horse-whipping his older brothers and sisters. Thank God Dad had deserted us again, we were happier without him although he never hit us younger ones.

Suddenly there was a hand on the boy's shoulder. Forgetting the goodies in the window he looked up to see a handsome well dressed grey-haired man, who took the children by the hand, the boy and his sister Eileen and marched them into the sweet shop. He said they could have anything they wanted. They were poor but well brought up and only asked for some assorted sweets. Then the man took them to a fruit shop and bought them apples and oranges. To their utter amazement they were rushed over to the Star Restaurant with lovely faggots and peas being cooked in the window, the tempting smell wafting all over Old Market. The man ordered Chicken dinner for three including Xmas Pudding and by this time the children were beginning to enjoy themselves and feeling lovely, warm and cosy. Leaving the restaurant the man escorted them along Old Market Street to the Kings Cinema where they saw an exciting film about a man called 'George'. All the beds and bathrooms appeared out of the walls at the touch of a button, the dining table and chairs came up from the floor, it was so exciting; like a miracle! The man never said much but smiled and had a lovely soft voice when he spoke. "Oh Lord" the boy prayed, "why can't we have a Daddy like him." It was dark outside when they left the cinema, the streets were crowded with shoppers and workers on their way home. Fortunately they only lived a few minutes walk away in St. Thomas Street, Redcliffe. The nice man walked them to the door of their home, gave them a lovely hug and a kiss and disappeared into the darkness.

The boy never forgot that man, you see it was the first time he could remember being hugged and kissed.

My first memory was the smell of fresh baked bread, and going downstairs in the early morning to find every room, even the living room, stacked up to the ceiling with trays of hot cross buns, and a queue of youngsters with baskets waiting to deliver and sell them around Bedminster. This was in the late 1920s, before the poverty of those 1930's Christmases. My Dad was a master baker in Spring Street just off the "cut", near Bath Bridge. Dad kept some of his horses and carts in Mead St., and in stables on Redcliffe Hill between the cinema and Redcliffe Church.

I was only about 4 or 5 at this time and very shy. I especially hated it when people passed remarks about my platinum blond curls and brown eyes. But I loved to help myself to the delicious fresh cakes and hide for hours under the shop counter. When I got fed up I would go and play the enormous cabinet gramophone. No-one could understand how I knew every record yet couldn't read at that age! The gramophone didn't last long, Dad came home drunk one night and put his boot right through the lovely gold mesh front!

I remember how as children we used to go up to Victoria Park with old army blankets to make tents, and take bottles of cold tea or lemonade. We got into big trouble when we were caught making tents out of the sheets in the big double brass bedsteads. We would screw the corners of the sheets onto the four bed posts using the big brass balls, and then prop up the sheet with a broom handle. Of course the damage to the sheets could not be disguised!

A favourite game was in the back yard. Me and my three sisters would block the drains to make a swimming pool. Of course as soon as it got to a certain depth of water it would gradually run away. It was great fun though, even if it was muddy! The lady next door, called Mrs. Bacon, kept an ironmongery shop. Her favourite amongst us was our snooty sister Dorothy. In the midst of all the excitement in the 'pool' Mrs. Bacon leaned over the wall and handed Dorothy a delicious roasted pig's ear. All we younger ones got was the smell, we were much too common!

We were still in the Baker's shop in Spring Street which was a pretty little street with St. Lukes Church on the corner (now demolished) at the top end facing the river, the "cut" as they called it. There used to be a little Cul de Sac of lovely little cottages with front gardens just like being out in the country. I suppose we must have been quite well off compared to most people around there, but we didn't realise it at the time. Our home was very ordinary, the living room always full of bread, cakes etc. but we had a room over the shop full of lovely antique furniture which was always kept locked but one day we found the door open. That did it! In the centre of the room was an enormous round table and we found we could undo a screw underneath, then the top would revolve so we would climb on top and one of us used to push the others around and around. It was great fun especially when we found what seemed hundreds of pound notes in the sideboard drawers, so we used all the money like confetti showering it all on the ones going round on the table. It must have seemed like Carnival time! It never occurred to us to take any money, who needed money, living in a lovely cake shop?

We must have resented baby Doreen because we used to hide her away, she was always being found under beds, settees, even in a drawer of a chest. No wonder she grew up with a nervous disposition. Years later she grew up a raving beauty and was one of the first G.I. brides.

We hardly ever saw Mum and Dad, they were so busy. Mum did most of the work, poor thing, whilst Dad went out boozing mostly. We had a man who worked in the bake house at the rear of the shop, and a poor girl who I suppose was a sort of baby sitter, I didn't envy her having to look after us wild lot.

Our older brother and sisters were out until late at night delivering the bread, it must have been a hard life. Dad was like a stranger to us young ones. I can only remember once he took us out to Paulton to see Mum's mother Granny Poole, it was lovely clip clopping through the country lanes, so peaceful with hardly a motor car in sight in our little Pony and Trap. Of course, he had to stop at all the pubs on the way, which spoilt our outing – it made us afraid of him.

I can't say it was a happy childhood because Dad was such a monster, always beating mother and the older children. The terrible rows left its mark on me all my life and in the early 30's we lost everything. Dad deserted us and we were given a Council House in the newly built Donegal Road, Knowle West. The night we moved, in a horse and cart, I'll never forget, instead of England it was more like the Pioneer days of the Wild West. Wedmore Vale was still fields and not built on. The thunder and lightning on that dark night and torrential rain was frightening to a young boy and my younger sisters. They could not get the horse and cart up Donegal Road with all our furniture in the mud, so we all had to be carried up in some men's arms, luckily our new neighbours were very kind and we were all put up in different houses, sleeping in armchairs, etc. We weren't in that Council House for long. Dad turned up out of the blue, drunk one night, smashing all the windows on horseback. He brought the horse into the house. My brother nearly killed him. Poor Mum, screaming, "Don't, Bill, he's not worth hanging for." Then he rode off into the night, no saddle or anything. He could have showed John Wayne a thing or two. Anyway the police took 10 days to find him in Honiton in Devon where his people came from. He had ridden bare-backed all the way. The final blow came when a man came for us kids to put us in a home, a terrifying prospect in those days, we were all screaming, hanging onto poor Mum's skirts. I didn't know what was said but thank God we were left with Mum.

Over the years to come, Dad kept coming home and going off again, scrounging money for his drinks and never ever supporting us. He would take anything to sell for a few shillings for his drink, yes even our clothes, believe it or not. There was no Social Security in those days. Poor Mum went out scrubbing office floors to support us. What a life she had!

Once again, we had to move house. According to one of the older members of the family, we moved eleven times in twelve years – I presume, to get away from Dad. But he always found us wherever we lived. Apparently, Mother had a little insurance money when her mother, Granny Poole died, so after the dreadful experiences in Knowle

West, no doubt she was inspired to try her luck with the Fish and Chip shop in Bannerman Road, Easton. From what I hear it was another disaster.

Strange, but my mind is completely blank about life in the shop, I can't even remember what school I went to. But I can recollect the front window full of oranges stacked like a pyramid and on the shelves, a few bottles of Lemonade and Tizer, etc. There was a large open space at the side of the shop where there seemed to be dozens of handcarts, and someone used to rent them out.

When Dad came rolling home again, I remember he used a handcart to sell sawdust to pubs and butchers shops, with a small dog tied to one shaft and my lttle sister Eileen, sat on the other side. He was so cunning, taking that child and sitting her on the bar to sing. That way, he used to get free drinks and she had sweets bought for her. He used to call Eileen his little Gypsy Princess (because of her dark hair). I get so cross with Eileen even to this day, when she reminisces about Dad. She is still theatrical. Even now at 60, she does a fair take-off of Marlene Dietrich singing 'Falling in Love Again' and pulling a grotesque face, with one eye closed and just showing the white of the other. We were all 'Star struck'. I don't know where we got it from.

Our Ancestors were country folk, so where our theatrical influence comes from is a mystery. Maybe it's because we used to spend our lives in the Cinema to escape our poverty. Eileen and I could copy dance steps from watching Mickey Rooney, Judy Garland and Fred and Ginger. We were too poor to take dancing lessons, which was a shame, because we were said to be very good dancers. Dear old Mum was so proud of us showing off! Some rich American tourists once took a movie of us dancing, in St. Thomas Street, Redcliffe (we moved there after leaving the Fish Shop).

Did they film us because of our great talent, or to show the folks back home, the poor streets the working class lived in, in England? Remember, we were dancing outside the factory wall of Greenslade's, the Brush factory, next door to where we lived. It was very depressing.

The family had to split up because we only had a couple of rooms above a converted shop. An elderly couple lived on the ground floor and we four younger children had to go in and out through their living room to get upstairs to our own rooms. We felt like prisoners and it was all so embarrassing. Where our elder brothers and sisters lived, I can't remember.

St. Thomas Street was certainly more attractive than it is today, with all those dreadful warehouses. Despite Greenslade's Brush factory, there were some nice old Georgian houses and a beautiful old Inn called 'The Wheatsheaf' with a lovely arched entrance to a courtyard, where I suppose the stage coaches used to pull in.

Further down the road was another pub where my first girlfriend Barbara lived – at least the other children told me she was my girlfriend – we never thought of kissing in those days. I was about twelve years old and can remember playing Doctors and Nurses quite innocently under an old blanket we used as a tent. But her mother caught us just as I was examining her tonsils. She threw me out and the next time I visited I was hurt to find my photograph torn to pieces on the mantelpiece. That was the end of a very dull romance!

A few doors from Barbara lived a black man, with his white wife and about ten children. The man was extremely handsome and he was the first black man we had ever seen. He was so kind to us, always giving us pennies. He used to see us kids safely to school. We were all great friends and fifty years later I still bump into some of his family. Others have gone to live in the United States. One son and daughter, David and Evelyn Savis, have a stall in Eastville Market.

I then went to school in Victoria Street at Temple Colston School with my sister Dorothy. The younger children had to go to St. Nicholas School in Queen Charlotte Street. It was at Temple School that I nearly died of shame when I was presented with new boots from the Lord Mayor's fund in front of the whole class!

Life was still very hard for Mother. At one time she had three cleaning jobs to earn money to feed us, no wonder she was always worn out. There were no sponge mops in those days, or electric polishers. She had to scrub and polish on her hands and knees. Once she went to the Public Assistance Office in Jamaica Street for help – they threw half-a-crown across the table at her and told her to sell some furniture. But we had no furniture left!

Once again on the move, this time a place in Easton called the 'The Paddock'. I can't remember much about it except that it was a row of houses with long front gardens almost like a lane or Cul de Sac with no traffic.

One thing that stands out in my memory was a neighbour, an old lady that adored me and was always cooking garden snails for me and hugging me, she was a secret drinker apparently of methylated spirits. I walked into her house one morning and found her dead in bed, it wasn't a pretty sight, yet strangely it didn't shock me as much as some of the things I had seen with my Father.

Now happier times were ahead if only too briefly, perhaps a couple of years. We moved to a lovely house in Richmond Road, Montpelier which was a very respectable district in those days, all professional people such as school teachers, doctors, etc. The whole family was reunited and we all lived together for the first time in years. We had a lovely long garden and a large conservatory where I trained flowers on string up to the bedroom window. Next door was a beautiful large Georgian House out in its own grounds. They must have been very rich because they were nearly always abroad. However we found a way into their house through the basement where their children kept all their toys. We had never seen such expensive toys and had the time of our lives. Looking back, of course, I realise it was wrong but being poor and adventurous what child wouldn't be tempted? Fate was to intervene in the nicest possible way. One day we were in the house as usual, the few of us, Doreen, Betty, Eileen and myself, when to our horror we heard the owners coming home. Panic stations! We all flew, trying to get out the window all at once when Betty's arm went right through the glass, blood everywhere (she still carries the scar). We all thought we would be put away in a home and our Mother was worried out of her wits. However those people were so kind to us after that and gave us beautiful toys even, inviting us to play in their lovely garden and swings with their children. The house had its own drive-way up to the front door and a great heart-shaped lawn with gorgeous flowers and trees with huge walls. On special occasions they used to light up the garden and trees with fairy lights. After all the years of poverty we had known, it was another world to us.

The evening meal was always a very happy time. My older brother and sister, Bill and Dorothy were marvellous ballroom dancers and had won several awards. Very often as we were eating, Bill would rush in, push the table and all of us back to the wall and say, "Quick Dorrie, I've got a new step," and practice until they got it right. Their tango was a joy to behold. Bill belonged to a cycling club and had an accident so the club held a benefit dance for him in Prewett Street, Redcliffe at 'The Provident Hall'. Although we were only about twelve or fourteen years old Eileen and I went. It was our first dance and unforgettable with the round ball in the ceiling reflecting all the coloured lights, needless to say we showed off rotten, making up our own steps as we went flying around the floor getting dirty looks from the champions Dorrie and Bill.

One fly in the ointment was when big-hearted Mother took in a girl whose husband was always beating her when he was drunk, he found out she lived with us and kept breaking into our house but I was always ready for him. I slept with an axe under my pillow and made sure I locked myself in my bedroom, so brave?

My mother got me my first job in a shop at seven shillings and sixpence per week (35p) at a gentleman's outfitters from 9am until 7pm every day, half day Wednesday, and Friday until 8pm, Saturdays 9am until 9pm. I nearly died of boredom but we needed the money.

My next job was just as bad in a high-class grocery shop opposite Clifton Down Station. Same boring routine, long hours but this time I was grinding coffee beans. The manager was always nagging me so when I was up the tall pair of steps cleaning the windows outside on the busy street, something snapped, I just poured all the dirty water, the chamois leather as well, then let the tin bucket go, which fitted his head nicely (it must have hurt) then I ran all the way home. I must have been a good worker because he begged my Mother to take me back to work. I saw him talking to my Mother at the garden gate so I sneaked back up the road, called for another boy I knew and said let's walk to London, as if it was just around the corner. He agreed, so we started walking and got as far as Bath. One night we slept in a barn where a farmer found us next morning. He not only gave us something to eat but some good advice to go home where Mother welcomed me with open arms.

We used to play a lot on Montpelier Railway Station just minutes away from home, it was so pretty in those days with window boxes and hanging baskets of flowers. It's so sad to see it now all vandalised and dirty, like so many railway stations. Of course in those days staff were on duty day and night and trains seemed to run every few minutes.

A year before we moved to Montpelier and I started working for a living, we had moved to Queen Charlotte Street, leading from Baldwin Street to King Street and Queen Square, a most exciting district full of fruit warehouses with all the fruit and vegetables displayed out on the pavements. I was thirteen years old.

It had a village kind of atmosphere almost something like Covent Garden in London. We had the wonderful old 'Theatre Royal,' fondly known as 'The Old Gaff'. The public houses like the 'Llandoger Trow',

'The Old Duke'. The smell of fish and chips filled the night air, as did hot chestnuts baked on a shovel by men with little portable fires on wheels. Piano accordians being played outside pubs.

The 'Theatre Royal' had reached its lowest ebb, they could only afford to put on third rate musical shows or Variety. But Oh what fun it all was! Being working class, we didn't want high class plays or Shakespeare, all we wanted was comics, singing and dancing and chorus girls etc. No one seemed to notice us kids as we sneaked into the pubs flogging half price tickets for the show. One of our passes would get you into the Gallery for two pennies instead of four pence. The 'Gods' as we called the Gallery, stunk of orange peel and empty lemonade bottles, sweet papers cluttering up the gangway to your seats. People used to line up all along King Street waiting for the doors to open. The street buskers were all waiting to entertain us with their different acts, the organ grinder with his monkey, and I can clearly remember two female impersonators, (they call them Drag Queens now) dressing in beautiful long evening gowns and big picture hats, tap dancing on the cobblestones. It was all so exciting to our young minds.

We lived in the little lane at the rear of the theatre leading to the Stage Door. We had the top two floors over an office on the corner. On the other corner was St. Nicholas and St. Leonard School where Doreen, Eileen and Betty went to school. Dorothy and I were still attending Temple Colston School in Victoria Street.

Mother had the chance to take in some of the theatrical people as lodgers so what was more natural than Eileen and I dressing up in their costumes, make-up, eye lashes, (the lot!), whilst they were out? In the hot weather the old Stage Door Keeper used to leave the doors wide open so Eileen and I used to sneak in and dance on an empty stage where we lived out our fantasies of being big stars.

1938. Age 16.

Happy innocent days were soon to be gone forever. I was now working as a painter's apprentice for 50p per week on new houses being created at 7th, 8th, 9th, and 10th Avenues at the end of Filton Avenue, working on scaffolding in all winds and weather, going to work on the fascinating old tram cars from Zetland Road. I would have enjoyed it if it hadn't been for the bully boys, so called men, always playing practical jokes on us young boys, stripping us of our clothes, painting and wallpapering our young bodies and encouraging us to fight each other, ruining the few bits of clothes we did have.

I was rushed to Ham Green Isolation Hospital with a strange complaint, covered in what looked like purple bruises all over my body. The doctors asked me if I had been horse whipped or ill-treated at home or if we kept birds. Of course I hadn't been ill-treated and we certainly did not keep any birds. Looking back now, could it have been the paint and wallpaper paste? Of course I never told tales to my Mother, but one day she found dead field mice in my overcoat pocket, which I never noticed, crawling with insects and creepy crawlies, and my clothes all torn. That did it.

To my amazement my Mother appeared at the same building site and put those men to shame. I was so proud of her, she was so ladylike and dignified about it, telling them how she had to bring up nine children with no man beside her, what with the price of clothes, etc. Just prior to my illness I had a second hand black leather coat almost down to my ankle (would have been fashionable today). Anyway, the bully boys painted that coat all colours of the rainbow. Being mad on the cinema I used to go to the Cabot Cinema at Filton straight from work. People would come and sit by me in the dark, but within a few minutes would start sniffing and move away. It amused me so much, to have about two rows of empty seats to myself.

Mother was having trouble, as usual, with her finances. She was so soft-hearted and would take in anybody with a tale of woe, so half the time the lodgers never paid their rent or would promise it next week and do a moonlight flit. History repeats itself. I was to be the same compassionate fool 40 years on. So of course Mother was getting behind with the mortgage payments, and to our amazement she got involved with a lodger named Bill. Now, being only forty five years old and very attractive, and with the life she had had with our drunken father, no doubt she was lonely, and who can blame her for trying to find a little happiness? But because of the wonderful way she had brought us up, of course we were disgusted, and no doubt jealous, because we had always had her to ourselves. I think if he had been a more caring man we might have learnt to accept him, but he made our lives a misery, except for baby Doreen who was about eight years old, by spoiling and fussing over her. No doubt it helped his case with Mother. The older members of the family all left home. No more dancing lessons at tea-time. No more brother Bill's cycling club members coming to see us on Sunday mornings. So at sixteen years of age, I felt deserted, lonely and betrayed. I was devastated. It's bad enough being a normal teenager, and a sixteen year old today is far more mature than I was. Where could I go to live on 50p per week?

The final blow, was coming home from work and finding all our furniture and belongings out on the street, the younger ones crying and screaming and the neighbours all on their doorsteps. The dreaded Bailiffs had completed their dreadful task.

We all ended split up, staying for a while at different addresses, until Mother managed to find rooms in Cumberland Street near Stokes Croft. It was so depressing, after the lovely house and garden we had just been evicted from.

After a while, I could stand it no longer. Bill the lodger made his dislike of me so obvious, he would never talk to me, only to find fault and just stare at me all the time, with those awful small beady deep set black eyes of his – he frightened me to death. I just had to get away, so I found lodgings at Southmead with a family, but left a few shillings with young Doreen to give to Mum.

The new lodgings didn't last long. I was so confused, poor and lost – the next few years were hell, I ended up in Doss Houses and Hostels around St. Judes, Wade Street etc. Filthy damp sheets, with drunks and drop outs, fleas and bugs, were my constant companions and the smell of stale urine. You didn't know who had slept in the bed the night before you – and always so cold. What amazes me is that in spite of all this poverty I never turned to crime.

Over the next few years, including the beginning of the War I must have worked in every Hotel in Bristol, which included accommodation, living on the job, which of course was cheap slave labour, but at least it was a roof over my head. The hours were so long and the food disgusting – many of the staff went down with food poisoning and tummy upsets. I did every job under the sun – cleaning hundreds of pairs of shoes for the guests and working in the filthy kitchens scrubbing pots and pans, then graduated to Hall Porter and waiter – all hard work. Where all the Health Inspectors were I don't know?

There were of course no unions to help us. I remember working for two different so called ladies who owned small Hotels. They made us eat food left over from guests' plates, always telling us how lucky we were to have jobs and we suspected them many a time of stealing our meagre tips from under the plate. The lovely food they put down for their cats and the rubbish we had to eat. I remember a Vicar giving me a Farthing tip. He knew it wasn't a sixpenny piece!

One of these so called ladies had a lovely sitting room with a glass partition overlooking the main staircase, where I had to sit up half the night to see the last guest in and lock up. All I had to sit on, was a hard chair under the stairs where she could keep an eye on me. I could see her living in luxury, sipping her Port and eating her chocolates. Why couldn't she lock up and let me go to bed? I had to be up at 6am to stoke the boiler and clean the shoes. I stormed out one night, I couldn't take any more, she begged me to come back later. Strange, all these Hotels were always glad to have me back again. "Oh Ronald, you naughty boy, please come back," she said. I didn't have much choice!

3rd September 1939. On a lovely Sunday morning at 11am, millions of people like myself were sat around their radio sets waiting for the dreaded news that we were at war. A thrill of both fear and excitement went through me. What did I, a young man of 17, know about war?

Around this time, my Mother had found a garden flat in Miles Road, Clifton. Up with the nobs mind you! Clifton was very posh in those days – big houses with their domestics and so on. How Mum found that flat I don't know, but anyway in she moved, along with Bill, her lodger and young Doreen and Eileen. The rest of the family split up and moved all over Bristol. I was living in lodgings in a big house opposite Brandon Hill Police Station with a big jolly plump woman and her brother Joe. What Joe lacked in physical beauty he more than made up for in character. The two of them were always playing jokes on me when I came home late at night. Often I would find white sheets draped over mops and brushes on the dark staircase, as well as coins in my bed under the sheets! I was always "game for a laugh"!

At this time Eileen, then 15, was developing into a real beauty – so vivacious and cuddly. We were inseparable – we went everywhere together arm in arm. We were more like sweethearts than brother and sister. We loved all the compliments we used to get – and the wolf whistles. When we weren't working late we used to go to dances nearly every night. We were very popular at the dances because Eileen used to teach all the girls all the dance steps in one corner of the dance floor at Church Hall whilst I taught all the blokes in the other corner! We picked up all the steps, including the jitterbug, from all the latest Hollywood musicals. I can see Eileen now, the Belle of the Ball, in her smart little flared cotton dress which she brought for 4s. 11d (now 24p) from Marks and Spencer.

Eileen worked in a posh restaurant called Dunlop Mackies in Baldwin Street, where she was a waitress. She used to do very well in tips there – all the businessmen adored her. She wore a black uniform with a white frilly cap, white cuffs and frilly apron. She also wore black silk stockings and high heeled shoes.

I managed to get a job in the new American-style milk bar, the Farmer Giles, in the centre of town next to the Hippodrome. I was fascinated by all the fancy equipment, the liquidisers and waffle toasters. I was proud to be known as the 'Soda Jerker' like they had in all the films! Most of our trade seemed to be in the evenings when we were crowded with teenagers and cinema goers. I managed to get Eileen a job there, but she worked upstairs instead. She proved very popular. I was very proud of her. Eventually the manager built an outdoor ice-cream kiosk and Eileen would work from that in the warmer weather. She did a roaring trade. The manager was no fool – he realised how popular Eileen was with the customers.

Older readers will no doubt recall the little island in the centre where the trams used to terminate. They may also remember that there were a large number of people working in domestic service at the large houses in Clifton, Redland and Cotham. The slang word for a maid in service was a 'skivvy', hence 'skivvy's island' where they all used to meet their boyfriends.

In spite of the war, these were happy times. There was a wonderful atmosphere then. Maybe we all thought that we would live it up. We never dreampt of what was to come, what with the Blitz and all that.

I used to love all the jolly pubs in the Market Place – like the Rummer. We used to dance the Conga, which was a new Latin American dance craze, on New Year's Eve. I can remember leading what seemed like hundreds of people in a long line behind me weaving like a long snake all round the centre. Being at the front I had my hands free of course, free to bang together two ash bin lids. I came, I saw, I conga'd.

Bristol our beloved home town was never going to be the same after the night of Sunday 24th November 1940. Whatever possessed me to hold a party on the Sabbath I don't know, because it just wasn't done in those days. However, about twenty of us teenagers arranged to meet at The Chessels, Bedminster Down. Irene, my eldest sister, a proper sport, had sort of promised we could hold the party at her house, I think it was someone's birthday, I can't really remember.

Anyway, the Air Raid sirens at 6.21 pm that evening couldn't stop us, not even Hitler himself could have, we were young and out for a good time, just innocent fun with a knees up etc. I had persuaded Freda, my sister, who had a young baby, to come; her husband was away at sea so she was housebound with a baby to care for. It would do Freda good, a night out, so our young Doreen did the babysitting.

When we arrived at Irene's there appeared to be a family dispute so we discreetly made our way to a large Air Raid shelter to hold our party with the help of a great accordian player and hoping to go back to Irene's house later for the real party. But fate decreed otherwise. Suddenly whilst we were singing and dancing all hell broke loose. We

Clockwise (from top left), Dorothy, Eileen, Betty, Doreen, (inset) and Doreen with husband Grover, Ron and Dorothy

heard the German planes coming over and the terrible explosions, we dashed out of the shelter and there below us was a huge ring of fire which seemed to engulf the whole city. It was a terrifying experience. The whole sky was lit up by the flares the planes were dropping as well as the incendiary bombs and the explosive ones. One of the girls started screaming hysterically, I gave her a good shaking which calmed her down. Freda was saying that she must get home to her baby. At that time she had a flat in York Road, Montpelier, miles away from where we were. The buses, etc. had, of course, stopped running, so Freda and I started what was to be a nightmare journey of running and walking through deserted streets, except for the Police and the brave Air Raid Wardens.

We seemed to be the only two in the world, laughing through the blazing streets, no time to be afraid. Through West Street, North Street and East Street, Bedminster all ablaze. The Police kept pushing us into Air Raid shelters, but we would keep sneaking out again. We had to get home to Doreen and baby Joan. One thing I can still see clearly is all the goods blown onto the streets from shop windows and the flames reflecting in the jewelry and broken glass laying in the gutter. On through Redcliffe Street, all ablaze, over the Halfpenny Bridge up Tower Hill on to Old Market Street. The heat was so intense we thought we were on fire ourselves. Castle Street and Broadmead were burning fiercely. We didn't see another soul at this point, every time we heard a bomb coming down we would duck on the ground. Next to the Empire Theatre was a corner shop with a large window, Wil-Sam-Mors the paint and wallpaper shop. Just as we arrived there we could hear this bomb coming so I pushed Freda to the ground and laid on top of her to protect her. There was a terrific bang and I had the whole shop window on top of me (now the Holiday Inn). Forty years later Eileen tells me she was within yards of us that night looking for her boyfriend, and her Nylon stockings melted on her with the heat!

How we survived that night I will never know. We were nearly home now, thank heaven, just through the back streets to Montpelier where a tearful young Doreen greeted us with baby Joan safe in her arms

Living in a squalid bedsitting room in Hotwells, just an iron bed, outside loo and gas-lighting only, or a candle, those were my worst memories of those days; I was always cold! Of course working class people only ever had cheap linoleum and maybe a small rug. Their bedrooms were always freezing. The only carpets I ever saw was in the Posh Hotels I worked at.

Mum was working early mornings and evenings cleaning the Air Ministry just round the corner, a large old house with extensions on the corner of Pembroke Road and Guthrie Road, she was apparently a cheerful sight going to and fro to work with her ginger cat who followed her everywhere.

Mother managed to get me a job as a messenger boy and Porter at the Air Ministry. I was so thrilled because I saw her and the ginger cat every morning instead of visiting her at home, because of Bill the lodger who I couldn't stand. I hated and resented him, jealousy no doubt but I blamed him for the break-up of the family. I only hope that the short time they were together he brought her some happiness, she deserved it, heaven only knows.

So to the fateful morning of the 12th of April. It was freezing cold with snow on the ground, pitch black. I started work early before the office staff every morning to find and file all the different files from different departments. The Night Watchman gave me a strange look when I arrived and started work. Expecting to find Mother and Ginger the cat on one of the floors after a while I asked the Watchman where mother was? I froze when he said, "haven't you heard, son? Your home was bombed last night!" I flew running, sobbing and praying all at the same time. As I turned the corner what a dreadful sight greeted me as it was beginning to get light. The bomb had struck the top floor of the house at the rear – ploughing its way downwards bringing the three floors down to the front garden. The roof was almost intact. I nearly went crazy thinking of Mother, Doreen and Eileen buried under all that rubble or debris. I started clawing at the rubble begging the Air Raid Wardens to help me. They calmed me down, then I noticed Bill the lodger lying dead on the grass. The men told me that a woman had been taken to the B.R.I.. I ran all the way to the Infirmary where injured people seemed to be everywhere, but they had no one brought in by our name. In desperation as no buses seemed to be running I spent the rest of the day in a daze cadging lifts from cars or lorries to the General Hospital, out to Southmead and every hospital I could think of, convinced that Mother, Doreen and Eileen were all buried alive in that house, it never occured to me to phone around all these different hospitals as I was in such a state.

I can't remember much else about that day except why, I don't know, I went back to the B.R.I. at 6 pm and mentioned Bill the lodger's surname and there sure enough was poor Mother tucked away in the corner of the ward, still covered in dirt and dust with serious head injuries. She had been buried for thirteen hours under 16 ft of debris, she was barely conscious but was able to put my mind at rest. Doreen and Eileen were alive and well having stayed the night with relations when the Raid started. Apparently the rescue men had heard Mother's cries, hoping she would not lose consciousness, having her voice as a guide to her whereabouts saying in broad Bristol accents, "Alright, my love, we'll take thee for a drink when we gets thee out." I hope those brave men never found out that it was their shovels that caused poor Mother's head injuries. It may have worried them all their lives if they had known that she was to die in six months. No one could possibly blame them for doing their duty. All I could think of at the time was that Mum was alive and after we found a home somewhere possibly all the family could get back together again? Five people were killed in that house that night, Bill and the Banker's family, by some miracle the little baby was thrown clear and uninjured, so now forty four years later, he or she may be married with a family of their own? Life goes on.

Here we go back in time again to 1942. Dorothy, Eileen and I were living at St. Johns Road, Clifton. Betty had left Bristol to work in the catering business, Restaurants etc. Out of the blue, our eldest sister Irene and her husband had decided to move in on us – what a shock? Irene was outrageous to say the least, a proper Tomboy. Maybe it was a good thing at the time because it helped us youngsters to get over the shock of Mother's death. Irene was so unpredictable though, and before long we were all fighting and squabbling. What a noisy lot we were, all wanting to be on stage and in the limelight at parties. I was quite mad, I used to imagine I was Fred Astaire tap dancing all over the furniture, the sideboard, even our cabinet gramophone. The trouble was I danced on it whilst it was playing (the fool) then I wondered why all my records were scratched and ruined. Not forgetting the cabinet. From childhood we had always called Irene " Our wicked Rene", she loved it, and it had always made Mother laugh. Now I am not saying our Rene was wicked, mind you, but she would have given Alexis Carrington in 'Dynasty' something to worry about! Ah! ah! what a personality she had: Thank God the Americans had arrived and billeted around the corner at Clifton College. What fun we had with some of them, going to their dances. One of them was destined to become young Doreen's future husband.

Doreen started working for Hornby's Diaries (later Unigate) delivering milk with a horse and cart. We were amazed because she was so shy and timid, but the male staff and customers alike, thought a lot of her. I couldn't handle a dog let alone a horse and cart. Finishing her rounds early she would take her daily pint of milk, a book and sunbathe on the Downs.

What a revelation one day, I looked at her and couldn't believe she was that plain child, our baby sister. The sunbathing had lightened her hair, her teeth had dropped evenly into place, her lovely rosy cheeks, were complimented by a wonderful suntan, and those gorgeous blue eyes. She had grown slim and elegant, and walked nicely (I should have been her agent, eh?) Seriously, no photograph ever did her justice. Grover, her G.I. boyfriend, came from a Preacher's family from Louisiana, U.S.A., way down South. He had a lovely Southern drawl when he talked (Honey Child) and was very polite. Doreen's customers said they made a lovely pair, as he used to help her deliver the milk. What a laugh. I cornered Grover, man to man, to make sure his intentions towards my kid sister were strictly honourable. Sounds like an old fashioned Victorian melodrama, doesn't it?

Now one Saturday morning a C.I.D. man called from Redland Police Station. He used to call concerned for my Mother after her injuries and always had a cup of tea with us. "Ronald," he said, "this is not a social call, six months ago you should have been in His Majesty's Royal Air Force." I buckled at the knees. Apparently my calling up papers had never caught up with me! He said that I must report to base in South Wales and could I pay my own fare to Penarth. Not I, I said, what a nerve, if they want me they will have to send me a Railway Warrant. On the following Monday, I had a Police Escort who waved me goodbye at Temple Meads Station.

What a farce it all was. I felt like Norman Wisdom the comic. After three windswept rainy days at Penarth, no uniform, just an RAF cap and a belt on top of my civilian clothing, we took the oath to serve King and Country, then after three days marching around the town, it was more like the Church Lads Brigade, I was sent home again on deferred service. I was lucky to get my job back again. Unbelievable, isn't it?

One lovely summer's day I was walking down Park Street. Suddenly a hand plonked upon my shoulder from behind. It was the same Policeman. "Now Ronald," he said "I didn't think you were the type to desert." "Just a moment, Officer," I remarked and with a wonderful sense of power over the law I showed him my deferrment paper. I won't repeat the language he used. "After all the trouble we took to get you to Penarth," he said, then we had a good old laugh about all the red tape that the British Empire had no doubt been founded on.

In 1942 the R.A.F. demanded my service for real this time, so after eight weeks of square bashing and discipline, which I detested because all I wanted in life was to sing, dance and make people happy, I was posted to Blackpool of all places with all that expensive entertainment on 15p a day mind you! The added insult was to see the G.I.s or Yanks throwing their money around like confetti. We were paid fortnightly which made matters worse, we were always broke after a few days, spending our money mostly on food. Being in private billets eight to a room with bunk beds and an old skin-flint of a landlady. We went to bed many a night homesick and hungry, some of us used to flog our razor blades to civilians to raise a few coppers.

I was posted to a miserable windswept aerodrome twenty miles east of Edinburgh called East Fortune, an enormous air field where they trained pilots for new aircraft like the Mosquitos. Sadly of course there were a few aircrash accidents and I was always chosen it seems to attend the military funerals and fire my rifle over the newly dug grave. It used to break my heart inwardly at the sight of the weeping relatives. What was I doing in this darned war I thought, haven't I seen enough tragedy?

Now for happier times; being an aircraftsman second class, you couldn't get any lower than that, I was sent to work in the cookhouse. I was very popular because I, though very shy, dished up the food and gave them all enormous portions on their plates.

One day between meals and being very quiet I started fooling around and tap dancing of all places on the enormous hot plates from which we served the food. Over the tannoy system "Music While You Work" was on; I was in a frenzy so never heard the Commanding Officer and his staff doing their rounds of inspection. "Airman," he roared at me, "you are now in the 'Station Concert Party', report to the NAAFI Canteen tomorrow for rehearsals." I blushed to the roots of my hair, shaking like a leaf, I couldn't sleep a wink that night. I'm a star at last I thought, Jenny (a plump WAAF who was always molesting me on the rifle range) will be so proud of me!

I loved the rehearsals as it got me out of a lot of square bashing and parades. The other airmen used to cheer, or jeer, when sometimes the C.O. would give me a lift across the huge runways. I felt a little inferior as except for a sergeant the rest of the cast were all officers, but on with the show – called "East Fortune Follies" which opened with all the male cast including 'your little Ron' in hired ballet skirts and wigs doing a comedy ballet. My big moment came when we did a Minstrel show in striped suits and straw boaters with a big bow tie. We all linked arms singing such songs as "Swanee River", "Lily of Laguna", etc. Then I stepped out into the spotlight to do my soft shoe shuffle to the song "By The Light Of The Silvery Moon" while the men behind were singing and swaying. My tap shoes were killing me, butterflies in my stomach, but the sound of all that clapping and cheering was worth all the agony. I was told afterwards that I didn't look the least bit nervous, in other words I gave my all and lost another night's sleep with the excitement of it all; worst of all Jenny pestered me all the more! The next show was "Babes In The Wood" but I turned down a speaking part, I was much too shy. It was bad enough having to wear tights when they all whistled at my legs. Ah! ah!

1943. The Show must go on, so with a hired large coach packed with crates of beer and other goodies, we hit the road touring hospitals in Scotland with "Babes In The Wood" and "East Fortune Follies".

One hospital I will never forget was very large, for the mentally handicapped. To our utter joy it had an enormous professional stage, wonderful lighting effects and a gigantic safety curtain covered in old advertisments. In the finale of the show I led everyone on stage criss cross pattern singing "Happy Days Are Here Again" with much gusto. Like a fool I was soon too close to the footlights, someone off-stage was waving frantically at me, I thought what's that chump doing he'll have to wait until the show's over, I soon found out why he was calling me! As we sang the last bars of the song the safety curtain came crashing down hitting my head, nearly killing me, locking me out from the rest of the cast, so being quick-witted I went off stage doing a comic dance, the audience, bless 'em, loved it and thought it was part of the show. What a lovely audience they were, we noticed all through the show they either laughed or cried in all the wrong places. We mixed with the patients after the show, what fun we all had, they were just like children hugging and kissing us and trying on our costumes and wigs. An evening I will always treasure.

20th November 1943, a gloomy dark day at 2pm. Doreen married her American boy Grover, I managed to get weekend leave, so did brother Bill from the army and with Grover's G.I. buddies, also a lot of Doreen's customers. We caused traffic jams at the corner of Apsley Road and Whiteladies Road, Clifton. Everyone wanted to see the handsome couple, poor Doreen so bashful in her borrowed wedding dress and her Bridesmaids' dresses which none of them fitted properly, but no one seemed to notice. The name of the church? St. Johns Church, still standing. Sadly we only have a few dark snapshots of the wedding to remind us.

They had a nice reception thanks to those big hearted Yanks who brought enormous tins of Spam and Peaches and Doreen's lovely customers on her milk round, who clubbed together with their meagre rations and made her a lovely wedding cake. People were so kind in those hard days of rationing and sacrifices. I would like to remind younger people the shortages and rationing lasted almost ten years, well into the 1950s, but there was a glorious feeling of comradeship that we could do with now in these gloomy days; sad to think in forty years nothing's changed, what have we learned? It's still a world of housing shortages and the Haves and Have Nots. I can remember two of my sisters making very smart winter coats out of bed blankets and children growing up never even having seen a Banana.

Our Rene was only too pleased to give Eileen and Doreen permission to marry, so with Betty working away, our Ron in the R.A.F. meant that she and her husband had our flat to themselves. But what hurt me most was the fact that everything was sold up eventually which meant that when the war was over and I was demobbed from the forces, Betty and

I, the only single ones in the family, had no home to come home to, so I was condemned once again to living in lodgings or lonely bedsitter land. Meanwhile I had to serve four and a half years in the R.A.F. Most of the time I hated it, it seemed more like a prison sentence, except for the station where we did the concert party shows, but happiness is so fleeting it seems. I was soon to spend eighteen months in Iceland of all places.

With Mother dead, the family split up – 'Our Ron' in Iceland – there was nothing to keep Doreen in this war torn country of ours. Doreen told me recently that, if Mother had lived, she would never have met her GI American husband, Grover Stroud – she was quite happy staying at home evenings with her Mum. But at the tender age of sixteen and a half, she became a child bride.

After a brief weekend honeymoon in London, Grover was posted to Germany. On 22nd April 1945 Doreen was rushed in the greatest secrecy to Southampton, to a huge hospital ship called the SS Argentina. This accompanied a sister ship loaded with wounded GIs, each ship also carrying 120 British war brides. They were escorted at sea by a convoy of battleships to protect them from the German 'U' boats. What a frightening experience for a girl travelling all alone – 'U' boats attacking them with depth charges! However, Grover had unexpectedly been given leave from Germany and had hurried back to Bristol with two bottles of Champagne. He missed Doreen but rushed immediately to Southampton, but he was not allowed to see her. Just as well she didn't know he was on the dockside or it would have broken her heart (like a film script isn't it?) So he returned to Bristol to be consoled by sisters Freda, Eileen and Betty who helped to polish off the Champagne. What a thrilling welcome the brides had when they reached the safety of New York harbour, with all the brass bands playing, streamers and small boats whistling. They were the first shipment of GI brides. Rich society ladies from the American Red Cross took them on a tour of New York with exciting gifts. One beautiful girl tried to buy Doreen summer clothes for her long hot train journey to Louisiana but Doreen proudly declined and accepted instead a small box of candy, she had been starved of luxuries for so long.

After almost three days journeying 3000 miles by train, Doreen arrived at Lake Charles, Louisiana, a small town 120 miles from New Orleans, on the Gulf of Mexico. She fell into the loving, waiting arms of her in-laws who almost hugged her to death. They were amazed at her English peaches-and-cream complexion for, in the heat and humidity of Lake Charles, the local people had very sallow skin. Of course, after several years, Doreen's own complexion became the same as theirs. They all piled into several cars to drive home. Doreen was so saddened as they drove through intense heat with dust belching everywhere as the car tyres hit those dirt roads, through the Black section of town with unpainted wooden shacks – no doubt like Soweto is today in South Africa. This, of course, was in the 1940's, before the Americans had learnt the lessons of civil rights. Doreen found this so distressing, remembering the wonderful black family we grew up with in the 1930s in St.Thomas Street, Redcliffe, when the Father used to give us kids pennies and see us all safely through the traffic over Bristol Bridge to school. All this marred her 12 years of life in the States, and the heat, swamp lands, etc – I don't know how she felt about the alligators!

To return to Doreen's welcome: her mother-in-law, who grew to adore Doreen, lived in a modest six-bedroomed house with a pretty garden. On Doreen's arrival she presented her with a whole hand of bananas which she had stored under her bed after reading that the British hadn't seen a banana since before the war – how kind! Doreen couldn't stand the heat and humidity so her new 'Mama' lovingly powdered her 'beautiful' shoulders and skin to cool her down. 'Papa', a lay verger, was killed by a hit and run driver in front of Doreen's eyes just when he was crossing the road to buy them all hot dogs. This depressed her even more – she had seen enough death and destruction in the Blitz back home, with our own dear Mum's death.

Within a month of her arrival in the States, her beloved husband was demobbed after VE Day and the two were reunited; whilst most British troops, including me, had to serve until months after the war was over, missing out on VE Day, and the end of the Japanese War celebrations.

The young newly-weds lived with Mama for nine months whilst their own house was being built. Grover managed to get a well paid job changing records and servicing the many juke boxes all over town. At nineteen years of age, Doreen started their family. She had four little girls, including one set of twins, all within 5 years. We were living a drab existence at home in Britain with all the shortages and rationing, but we were pleased to see Doreen living in luxury. She sent us clothes and food parcels. All we could send in return were parcels of 'Bisto' – about the only thing that wasn't rationed here! She loved her English gravy – so did the Yanks. By now she was feeling very homesick for all of us and for the English countryside. So it was to our utter joy and amazement that in January 1952, she arrived at Southampton on the Queen Elizabeth, with her youngest daughter, Elizabeth, in her arms. I was working in London at the time and dashed to Southampton – like a fool I got mixed up with the First Class passengers, amongst whom was a film star called Gloria de Haven – some readers may remember her from MGM musicals? I mistook her for a waitress I worked with and said "What are you doing here?" I think she took a shine to me but I was too busy looking for my kid sister. Suddenly, there was Doreen in the distance – her magnificent penetrating blue eyes which seemed to stand out in a crowd of hundreds met mine. Then we rushed into each others' arms. Tears all round!

On the train back to Bristol, Doreen amazed me by confessing that for years she had watched me dancing with our Eileen and had dreamed of being my partner. Apparently, she had secretly planned this trip home and made herself a beautiful ball gown for the occasion – she insisted I took her to a dance. Well, you could have knocked me down with a feather! Actually, I had noticed our Betty and Freda were always squabbling to dance with me at parties. Between you and me, I never thought I was that good a ballroom dancer – I knew I could tap, and show off a little, but I had always envied my brother Bill who had nice long legs and big strides for ballroom dancing. However, we all have our 'hang-ups' so on with the show! Doreen and I went to a dance at the Corn Exchange. I was surprised at her choice of colours for her ball gown – black velvet and gold, which I associated with older people, but

Clockwise (from top left), Keith Mills, Chlöe in action, Ron 'under arrest' in Weymouth

she looked ravishing. Of course in the 1950s, we were still starved of glamour. Here was my sister with perhaps the first gown in Bristol made from what seemed to be hundreds of yards of petticoats and underskirts. What a sensation she caused when we made our entrance! Doreen was trembling like a leaf because she was the only one in evening dress and, of course, the poor English girls were still having to watch their clothing coupons. She attracted a lot of envious looks from the women, and admiration from the men, who were afraid to ask her for a dance. It seemed that when she sat down, the skirts of the gown enveloped her face almost. I was so proud of her. I had to beg the men to dance with her, explaining to them that I was only her brother.

We slipped out of the dance hall and did a tour of the pubs in the St. Nicholas Market Place. Some of them were the 'Gay Bars' of the time where all the Boys raved about her, fussing with her hair and one or two wanting to try on her dress. Shy Doreen loved all the fuss and attention. We returned to the ballroom slightly intoxicated, danced every number, and the men actually plucked up the courage to partner Doreen, some of them like elephants putting their feet through her net skirts. On the way home, her gown in shreds, Doreen said it was one of the happiest nights of her life, and believe it or not 35 years on she still treasures the remnants of that gown which she had made herself – I am proud to think that I was part of that memory. Doreen of course had to return to the USA, but things were never quite the same between her and Grover, her husband. She was alone so much while he was at work and, when they started rowing, she divorced him in 1958 and brought her four daughters home to England rather than bring them up in the troubled atmosphere such as we had known ourselves as children. I think she was very wise, if only for the children's sake. I only hope they and the 'Terrible Twins' appreciate the sacrifices their mother made on their behalf.

After demob and work in London where I was very lonely I came back to my beloved Bristol, to loving caring friends. For the third time I returned to work at The Royal Hotel, College Green. At the time, "Guys and Dolls" was being premiered at the Bristol Hippodrome with the Broadway and Film star Vivienne Blane; what a little darling she was. To me anyway. I had worked there in the 1930s as Linen Porter – the work nearly killed me. The laundry was in the basement, my mate and I had to load this enormous lift, almost as big as a modern kitchen, with the clean sheets and towels and pull it up five floors to service the chambermaids who then returned the dirty linen to us, but what fun we had going down in that lift with me tap dancing all the way, till we landed in the basement with a mighty crash. Very dangerous but fun.

Prior to that, at 6 am, half asleep, I had to polish scores of pairs of hotel guests' shoes. Now from every floor you could look down on the wonderful Victorian Dining Room, with its beautiful white marble pillars, huge potted palms and ornate balconies. All the great stars used to stay at the Royal, so my biggest thrill was spying on the famous guests eating below, people like Gracie Fields and handsome matinee idol Ivor Novello.

The Cocktail Barman confided to me that his stocks of Guinness were disappearing mysteriously, a poor cleaning woman was found to be burying the bottles beneath her dirty water after scrubbing behind the

Bar. I felt so sorry for her as jobs were so hard to find. She was sacked of course.

The 1950s were drab. The pubs were run down. Bristol was still nothing but a pile of stone, like a ghost town, a miserable place, no singing in the Pubs, no nightclubs, so my mate Keith and I, in our small way, were determined to bring a bit of life and laughter back to the Pubs around St. Nicholas Market Place, especially to the centuries old Inn 'The Rummer'.

The licencees were a Mr. and Mrs. Baily. He was a perfect gentleman, but we all dearly loved Mrs. Baily, what a character! Dear soul, she was so tiny, and always dressed in little girlie dresses, with layers and layers of make up, blonde curls like Shirley Temple or at times Bette Davis in "Whatever Happened To Baby Jane?" Mrs. Bailey used to sing to us at parties up in the L-shaped room above the Bar, where she posed on a red quilted settee which she told us was part of the set when she starred in "The Desert Song". At times she would change the light shades to match her dress, to make her entrance down that wonderful staircase which is still there today.

During the war with bombs falling we used to shelter in her wine cellars. All the years I drank at The Rummer I never heard a malicious or unkind word about the lady, even though she sang to us all the wrong lyrics of the songs. I still don't know if she ever was on the stage or just liked living out her fantasies. The world today is very short of characters like her, and a sadder place.

Now The Rummer had become a very seedy place, dirty and run down. We always washed our own glasses before pouring our light ale. It became a haunt for all sorts of people including the local prostitutes, bless 'em. What fun they were, rough and ready with hearts of gold, ready to help anyone down on their luck, all with exotic names. One slipped me £5 when she heard I had to sell the furniture to exist. £5 was a fortune then.

Any visiting famous star in Bristol would always come to visit Mrs. Baily. She was famous indeed and always called us her boys. She called me "Con". Why I never knew!

I always felt different from other children with a terrible sense of inner loneliness, a terrible shyness, so have been mentally scarred all my life by numerous occasions of sexual abuse, which no doubt in my later years accounted for my bouts of severe depression and guilt complex. I became very restless, always pacing the floor thinking, my brain almost exploding, compelled to read and watch the News and cry inwardly for the tragedies and wickedness of Man's inhumanity. Maybe this urged me to the bright lights, and parties, to escape my poverty. How I envied placid, gentle people who seemed to live their lives on an even keel. I was either deliriously happy or very low with long bouts of depression, but never showed it to anyone, very difficult to live with.

My Doctor used to pat my bottom and say, "It would be a very dull world without people like you, young Ron." What consolation was that? All I wanted to do was sing and dance and make people laugh, so when I met a chap called Keith Mills – his professional stage name – in the chorus of a show at the Empire Theatre, we decided to team up as a double act. Keith was very different to me, he was very hard and resiliant, I was always the soft touch, easily hurt and disillusioned. In fact many people used to say I was the one with the heart, but how I envied his business sense. He was ambitious.

Our careers, if you can call it that, started in the drab 1950s in the dirty run down Rummer. All the years of our act we never made a penny out of it. I did it for fun, but later Keith turned 'pro' and made a very good living. It happened quite accidentally really, no stage props, no costumes, no musical accompaniment. We did a little patter, jokes, etc and would end up singing popular songs to Keith's very clever witty naughty lyrics. We started using bits of drag, like old lace tablecloth, mop head wigs, etc. We decided we needed stage names as Keith was the beautiful one in drag. I was the ugly comic one with a boxer's nose. I always loved an old comic record by 'Spike Jones and His City Slickers' called "Chlöe"; on the record there were fire engine sirens, the sound of marching boots, and scrubbing boards, motor horns, etc. – the singer shouting and coughing "Chlöe, where are you, you old bat?" I used grotesque make up to look rough, where Keith was the pretty girl. We decided our stage names should be 'Chlöe and Katie'.

Our fame, if you can call it that, spread by word of mouth to housing estates such as Barton Hill, Withywood, Hartcliffe, Southmead, Knowle, Kingswood and then young tearaways would come in to cause trouble and heckle us with names like "Queers, Nancy Boys, Pansy Boys". We used to retaliate by calling them "Bums, Suckers, Peasants" and "With a bit of luck you'll be a man before your mother." Of course, we were sacred stiff really, but we would not show it. Amazingly, at the end of our shows they would all come and shake our hands and call us "good uns", "our mates", and they would take us to parties all over Bristol, showing us off because we had "Guts".

We were never threatened and the few fights were protecting us from other gangs. We were proud and amazed and taken home by many to meet their Mother, wives and sweethearts or they would come to The Rummer.

The Rummer and Mrs. Baily did good business out of our free performances. My life became an endless party, night after night for years. But ouch! The mornings after! The hangovers and having to do a day's work soon caught up with me. However it was all good clean fun. Of course we were all smoking and drinking too much. I think we had invented the gaiety of the 1960s back in the 1950s.

During the 1960s Fortune smiled at me at last. I had a new job, bought a cheap run down house and at forty years of age my first holiday, a cheap trip to New York, USA. Broadway was just like it was in the movies. I worked in a furniture warehouse, now demolished, in Temple Way, here shop keepers used to send their customers. I was confident and outrageous. Many customers were told to ask for me, where I many helped a shy young couple furnish their home. Selling beds was a scream, the couples would shyly touch the mattress. I used to jump on the beds and make them lay beside me and say "I am sure the three of us will be very happy on our honeymoon." The other staff would fall about laughing at my antics. I was the only salesman who used to get pieces of Wedding Cake, from grateful newly weds. That thrilled me so.

We had a young van driver with a dark beard who several times sang on HTV. I told him he would never get anywhere with that music, he sang. I am glad I was proved wrong. That young singer and composer became world famous and very rich now living in Nashville, Tennessee. Remember that famous hit record with black singer Madeline Bell? I think it was called "The Melting Pot". His name? Roger Cook! Now I am a fan of his, of course.

The 1960s came with a bang, everyone suddenly seemed to be vibrant and alive. New buildings were going up all over town, full employment, Rock and Roll music, and those marvellous mini skirts. These were the happiest years of my life, without a doubt and we all had a few pounds in our pockets. They say life begins at forty, well it did for me anyway. I was never more at ease with life.

Keith decided to turn professional as a solo drag artist touring the country. When he had some Bristol bookings gangs of us would go along to cheer him on. And we were amazed how talented he was. The wonderful gowns he wore costing hundreds of pounds could rival Danny La Rue anytime. I never had the dedication, confidence or discipline to be a pro-artist myself. I was more of a comic, I could only perform in my local pub (now near Jamaica Street) where I could feel the genuine warmth and affection. A big cheer would greet me as I made my entrance dead on nine o'clock every night. I felt loved at least. Most evenings it was a battle of wits, not a performance.

I was always dressed in everyday clothes, but at Christmas, birthdays or Halloween, I would appear in drag with my boxer's nose. I could never look pretty so I made myself up to look and dress more like a Dame or Ugly Sister in Pantomime. Every act was different and impromptu, no rehearsals. It came naturally to me. Dear Pat and Joan Sullivan who kept the Hillgrove Pub became very dear friends and joined in the fun. We would have a slanging match across the bar and Pat would so say "ban me" every night, his part of the act.

They were a marvellous crowd from all walks of life. We had some fantastic parties at my home. The name "Chlöe" stuck for ever, some times to my embarrassment people would shout it at me across the streets, from car and lorry drivers wherever I went. Even today that still happens.

The young tearaways soon found out my new local and came in droves, but never caused any trouble. I had many 'minders', some lovely girl friends, one in particular, an attractive blonde called Elaine. The boys would all make passes at Elaine. What a sport she was! I used to tell the boys that she was a drag Queen and had to shave twice a day. She would, with a twinkling eye, play along with me and keep stroking her beard!

Now even though my performance may have been a little blue or vulgar deep down I'm a bit of a prude, so my parties were always innocent good fun. I kept all my bedrooms locked and told them "no hanky panky", if I wanted to make my house a brothel I didn't need their help. Of course the bathroom always seemed engaged and heaven only knows what went on in my long garden!

Sex always embarrassed me and I hated being mauled about by people; hang up from my childhood no doubt. I hated all bodily functions, strange I know. I was engaged to be married once, and could have been married dozens of times. I preferred spiritual love and loyalty. I couldn't live with people yet couldn't live without them either. Typical male logic, because I was always surrounded by lovely girls. The boys always said I was either a great lover, the girls were lesbians or I put them on the game. We always kept them guessing – all part of the fun.

For ten years my life centred around that homely Pub, The Hillgrove, I rarely went elsewhere, but if so we would have fleets of cars following us or sometimes we would travel in open lorries screaming round the streets of Bristol at breakneck speed. There were no drunken driving laws then. Now I think back with horror of the times we could all have been killed. I can't drive myself. Ah! impetuous youth.

I never saw any signs of drugs, except maybe Pep Up Pills. The warmth and respect I had from all those people of all ages, I was like a gang leader and had to make any arrangements. Anywhere I went they just followed, it was wonderful. And don't forget I was in my forties. The few times I go out now I very often bump into middle-aged people who rush up to me with affection and say: "Chlöe, you were part of our teenage years. We'll never forget you." That thrills me. I get a lump in the throat.

Of course I had my love affairs like anyone else and my live-in lovers, but it never lasted. I was too tense, too theatrical and temperamental. We always parted good friends. Marriage was not for me, having had the home life I had. And with six sisters I knew and understood women. I am not afraid to admit my faults, I had to be the boss. I retired gracefully from the fun scene in 1978 due to ill health.

I have a few home movies to remind me of those mad days; everyone seemed to bring their cine cameras. In a favourite film of mine the girls put me in a black cat suit, a tatty black wig, Wellington boots turned down to the ankles. What a sight! All this was in broad daylight – I climbed the scaffolding around my house at the time and was running all over the roof with a twelve yard long Indian Sari waving in the wind above my head. I must have looked like Batwoman. I could mention dozens of incidents such as this.

Now what comic hasn't at some time in their career dressed in drag? Taking off Carmen Miranda? Why should I be an exception? Some friends of mine kept a Public House at Weymouth with Bed and Breakfast facilities. They begged me to visit with friends and bring my drag. We had a wonderful weekend, the weather gorgeous, the town full of sailors and our Pub packed at lunchtime.

I was dared to do my stuff. The cheers as I made my entrance, then started serving behind the bar pulling pints for a wonderful audience, all my poppet beads and lucky charms from enormous long earings flopping into their pints. Of course I was getting as drunk as they were and at closing time about a dozen sailors grabbed me and marched me on their shoulders down to the beach, the holiday makers following us and joining in the fun.

What a sight I looked! All that horrible greasepaint and false eyelashes, on a hot sunny day. I was getting a little worried about the jolly sailors, I thought at least they would throw me into the sea, but they were perfect gentlemen. We ended up paddling in the sea, whilst they were singing rude Naval songs. A weekend I will never forget. I have a couple of colour slides to remind me of 'Carnival Time'. I was very worried when arrested by the Naval Patrol and thrown into a cell, but it was all a joke. We spent the night, all of us drunk and singing. If only you knew the agonies and discomfort of dressing up, but worth it all to make people happy. Where did all those years go!

I am still called "Chlöe" sometimes, or Chloris (lavatory cleaner), Cleo or Leo, and one quaint compliment I treasure in broad Bristol dialect: "Chlöe, thee's look class in a Tate and Lyle sugar sack!"

ACCIDENTS
BY GILBERT CROKER

Reporting for duty one evening with a mind most unconscious of hazards, or accidents, I was detailed to go with a crew for 'damping-down' operations at a fire that had started in the mid-day. Merrily we rode, in a van, to a large three-floored building that was gutted by fire.

Amongst the tricky, slippery network of fallen debris upon weakened floors I remember pouring a jet of water upon 'pockets' of fire that persisted here and there. Then I was ordered to another part of the building and followed a colleague to a small roof where a bricked parapet lay, in one place, but some eighteen inches from a framed skylight.

Why I never got past that skylight or what attracted me to it I know not to this day. The next thing that I remember was waking up, as if from a long, deep sleep in a hospital bed with a terribly sore head and an aching stiffness of body limbs. My first reaction on the realisation that I had had a bad accident was to move my legs to assure myself that they were alright. I remember, even now, the thankfulness that ran through me then.

But came the thought of what effect this shock would have upon my loved ones, especially my wife. I heard later that, in my unconscious hours she had spent a most anxious time near me not knowing how things would be in the hospital ward. With the comfort that my regaining consciousness gave to her she was most apprehensive as to the state of my head. This was most bruised and in its unnatural shape not pleasant to look upon!

I had fallen through that skylight and, in a 20 foot drop, had landed across a metal bench. My head had taken the full blow for my only other injury was but a slight cut across the side of a little finger! Apparently, in that fall, I had lost my steel helmet or it had saved me from even further trouble.

But a frontal head fracture, near to a vital spot, and a severe dizziness kept me for two weeks in that ward bed. Then, for a further twelve weeks in which time that puzzling dizziness gradually lessened, I was home-nursed by my wife. By her complete care I was able to return, once again, to those with whom I had worked and who had shown, to me, much consideration.

At another time I found out, if I had not known before, the purpose of the 'coxcomb' on a fireman's helmet! The interior of a large store was badly damaged by a fire of great heat. At its entrance it was found to be advantageous to remove the slate roof-tiles for ventilation purposes. Consequently, from a ladder, slates mostly broken were falling to crash in pieces upon the ground.

After working inside I felt a need for fresh air so I decided to come out of that only exit. What made me keep my, so hot, helmet on until I was well out I know not, but passing that ladder I suddenly felt a head blow that forced the helmet further upon my head and temporarily stunned me with its intensity.

Helped to the seat of our appliance by a colleague I gradually regained my normal senses. Wondering what it was that had struck me I took off my helmet and received a further shock! For almost the depth of its 'coxcomb' a cut had been made! Obviously I had passed beneath a descending slate-tile that had fallen with the force and position of a guillotine-blade!

THE HOUSE OF POWER
BY GLADYS POWER

It was June 1951 when our family came to live in Charfield Road, Southmead, to a three bedroomed non-parlour type house; the rent being the princely sum of twelve shillings and sixpence (old money). Having five children, the eldest nine years and the youngest eight months, we could only just manage with the room available. When our belongings had been delivered, I heard my husband ask one of the children if he liked the house. He replied "Yes Dad. Now let's go home."

We found the area very friendly. All the streets at that time were spotlessly clean. There were always road sweepers to ensure they stayed that way. There wasn't the continuous traffic of today. Hardly anyone had a car. Folk usually got around on bicycles. One or two had a motor-cycle, but they were few and far between.

It was just like a country village. Any traffic noises came from the main Pen Park Road. Nothing like today's standards. I did my shopping at the prefabricated stores, situated beside the dairy which happens to be still there. I still recall the assistants sending the bill and money to the cashier on an overhead wire. A receipt and any change was placed inside the cup and triggered back to the assistant. For five pounds in those days, I could fill my baby's pram with groceries and still have change. Beside the dairy was a piece of waste ground which was the plot for a more solid building to be erected at a later date.

In a few years, our family had grown by two and it was decided that we should ask for a larger house. So once more we were on the move to Ashburton Road. With each child came their friends. My house and garden were always full of children. They would have their squabbles and leave but five minutes later they were back again. If it was cold or raining, I'd sit them around the fire with slices of bread and jam and cups of tea. Those who couldn't find a seat would sit on the floor and I'd sing to them at times. There was no television in those days. As they grew they still came. Even today I number among my friends those men and women who were no more than babies when I first met them. There was one instant, years later, that stands out in my memory. My husband came home late one night the worse for wear and explained the reason being was because he'd met a man in the pub who had been so thrilled with the atmosphere in our home that he'd made up his mind to pattern his own family life on ours, and for the happy hours he'd spent with us he wanted to say thank you by buying him a few pints. I replied, "I see! I do the work and you have the reward." For all that, I appreciated the sentiment.

I now did my shopping at Arnside. It was a retail store then with a shoe shop, men's, women's and children's clothes and hardware. The

grocery part was as you entered from the door either from the road or the butchery department. The assistants were friendly and helpful and whilst being served, we exchanged the happenings in our lives. The manager at that time, Mr. Stone ran the store like the captain of a ship, everything in its place. I miss the personal touch since it became self-service.

My husband worked for Bison Flooring Specialists and was away very early in the morning, and home very late at night. His work took him all over the country. When it was too far, he and his gang of men would have to get digs until the job was finished. I looked forward to the times when the contracts would be for Bristol and the surrounding towns. Some of my happiest times were when the Broadmead Shopping Centre was being built. It was not without its tears, even then. There was the time when a man fell from two storeys high and was left with severe head injuries. Then there was the time when Fred Short fell from the top floor of Boots and was killed. When you think that they were walking on only a few inches of steel, it is a wonder that any of them survived. What I had not known then was that my own husband, a few days before, had fallen, but being athletic had managed to hang on to the ropes until he was hauled up. I wondered why his trouser leg was ripped from ankle to waist, but he hadn't wanted to worry me at the time!

Now came one of the saddest times of my life. At only forty-five years of age, my only sister died. I had to travel to Ipswich for her funeral. When I arrived, my Father (who lived there) had already been joined by my brother. After sorting out my sister's personal business, as she was a widow, i.e. disposing of her belongings, etc., we were discussing different points, when her young son said, "Auntie Glad, will you have me?" My first reaction, when I thought of the bursting seams of our house, was to say, "There's no room." But looking at the poor little fellow I said, "I'll send a telegram to your Uncle, and if he says "Yes" I will, of course. The reply I received was "Bring him for Mae's sake." That is how Freddy became one of the family. Having my own son of the same age, he never looked back. They went to the same school and he soon settled down.

One day my husband was given a live cockerel by a friend, who thought he would be pleased to have a fresh meal. My beloved had a notion that instead he would get some pullets, and who knows? ... One day he may have a poultry farm! He always dreamed if ever he won the Pools that is what he'd buy. As he said "Oak trees from little acorns grow". But as most of his great ideas, it didn't come to anything. After buying six hens, they turned on poor Charles (the cockerel) and pecked him so badly that he had to be put out of his misery – but the children enjoyed fresh eggs for a time.

I was always getting hints on how the children would love a puppy. Of course I knew it was the eldest child (my husband) who really would. As I also knew, it would be me who would have to do the honours when the novelty wore off, I wasn't too keen. Sure enough, I opened the door to a small boy who was holding a bundle of fur. "Mr. Power's puppy," he said. "Oh yes!" I thought, "You think you've won." Putting the pup in the kitchen I set about seeing to the dinner. As soon as he came home from

The Power Family of Southhmead, 1954

work, I said "You can take the pup back to where he came from." When I saw the poor little thing cowering beneath the chair, I felt so sorry for him that I cuddled him and he licked my face. What I didn't know was that my husband winked at the children behind my back as I gave the pup a saucer of milk.

Of course, from that day he entwined himself around all our hearts. He was fielder for the boys when they were playing in the fields or in the garden, though he was reluctant to give up the ball. Many were the balls he retrieved from neighbours' gardens to save the boys a ticking off. He lived to be fourteen years old and was like another child to me. It broke our hearts when he died.

The years were slipping by without me being aware of it. I had my washing machine and all the conveniences to make life easier. Although one girl was married and one boy joined the army, there was still plenty of cooking, cleaning, patching and darning to do. Also along the way, my Father had moved from Ipswich to live at Lawrence Weston in Holly House. I travelled twice a week to do his shopping, etc.

In 1970, two of our girls were married within three months of each other. This house rocked! There were all the preparations; the excitement of the fittings for the bridesmaid dresses and page-boy suits and the church arrangements. I didn't think the house would ever be normal again. Like always the day was perfect and the house was missing two more people.

In 1971, Mike decided to enter the Aborfield College in Reading as an apprentice in the Army. Shortly afterwards Freddy decided to follow suit. We went to see them pass out and worried when they were posted to Northern Ireland. Then Mike decided to leave the army, but Freddy stayed on.

Now came the time when Terry decided to work on the Kibbutz in Israel. After much preparation he departed.

In the coming years we saw the last of the family married. We travelled to Scotland to see Freddy marry a Scottish lass.

In 1980, my dear husband died, leaving me with my memories. Sometimes when listening to a favourite piece of music and I sit with my eyes closed, I can see and hear them all. I hear again the thudding ball and Sandy's bark. I hear the squabbles, the tears and the laughter. I think of the friends – the many we had made through life.

Each time my grandchildren come, the sleeping house opens one eye only to sleep again when they go.

JEAN'S STORY
BY JEAN McKENZIE

My name is Jean Rosemary Mckenzie. I was born in 1937 in Knowle West in the City of Bristol. My father was from Ahdrossan in Scotland and my mother is Bristolian. I had two older brothers and a sister.

My mother remembers me as being a lovable little girl, full of curls. My dad went to war when I was three and my mother found another man. My mother thought a lot of him but he didn't like me. As a result I was sent into care to a home in Porlock. My father knew nothing of me being sent into care.

I do not remember much about my early childhood, but I know I was very unhappy at Porlock. I used to be nervous and wet the bed and was smacked for it. I remember the bombs dropping nearby and going to a shelter. Afterwards I was given a teddy bear (which one of the staff or my mother had given me) as I wanted my mother. The girl in the next bed to me had a glass eye which she used to take out at night and put into her glass of water. I was once accused of stealing a handkerchief and felt frightened as a teacher there threatened to call the police. I remember also being frightened when older girls used to push me into the paddling pool after they had finished swimming.

About 1943 I was moved to a home in Downend for about two years until I was eight, when I returned home. This was the first time I had seen my mother since leaving home. My mother's common law husband wanted me to call him 'dad' but I refused. I was even more unhappy at home than in care and used to runaway from home and school. My mother was always a bit cold towards me. My step-father once drowned some kittens, which he tied up into a bag and put into some boiling water. I tried to grab the bag of kittens but he pushed me away.

Within a year I was back at Downend, which my brother also went into a few years later. During this early period of my life I do not remember being naughty so much as being rebellious. I used to be jealous of other children with mothers and fathers.

I was in Downend until I was 10, when I went to approved school for stealing apples. Fourteen of us went 'scrumping' at St. Nicholas Market and I stood on some boxes to take apples from the stall. I was caught by a policeman who said, "Alright lad, come down, bloody hell it's a girl." It ended up in Juvenile Court with Lady Inskip sentencing me to five years at approved school. They sent me to Ploverfield in Hampshire. I thought I had been very wrongly punished and was feeling bitter towards everyone. How was I going to do five years away from my home town of Bristol? But I had to do it and that was all there was to it. I was very unhappy for the first three years at Ploverfield and kept trying to run off. I was called a "home brat" at the nearby junior school I went to and ended up smashing the classroom and hitting some of the kids. When I was about twelve I ran away with another girl from the home and stole £40 from a bag on a postman's bike. We made our way to Southampton hoping to catch a train back to Bristol. But we were caught by the police and they found £38 stuffed in all parts of my clothes and underwear. I was given a caution for this – the postman didn't want to press charges as I was already in a home.

My life brightened up in the following years through having foster parents during the holidays. One day a nurse visiting the home saw me upset because the other residents had all just left at the beginning of the holidays. She told her parents about this, who thought they could help by giving me 'love and understanding'. The parents were both magistrates, fairly well to do and had four children. They all took me in as "one of the family". I was very happy with them, sharing the children's toys, going swimming in the evenings and being taken out for dinner and events like the scout meetings which the mother ran. One of my elder foster-sisters added lace to my drab clothes to make them look more like those of my little foster-sister. My foster parents were religious but didn't force it on me.

So at last I began to settle down, only to be told when I was fourteen and a half that the school was closing down. It once more meant I was on the move. I learnt from the School Governors that I was to go to a hostel in London which did not please me very much, but off I went on my travels.

The hostel turned out to be run by Methodists in Doughty Street in Holburn. I used to have to go to church. Dr. Soper (a Minister well known on the media and at Hyde Park Corner) came to speak; I liked him in the afternoon when he spoke at Sunday School. As the hostel was for working girls, I left school when I was fourteen and a half. When I was fifteen I got a job as a canteen assistant on one of the newspapers off Fleet Street. Here I made some good friends among the office staff who I served with their lunch. I got very fond of a few of them who invited me to their homes at weekends. After a while I changed jobs and worked at a Customs and Excise office. Amoung people who came in was Gordon Pirie. I remember planning to run away when I next got my wages and telling someone I worked with about it. After that my wages were paid directly to the hostel.

I then moved to Bristol and stayed at the Salvation Army hostel at Ashley Road. I worked for a while at Carwardines in the Centre of Bristol where I was friendly with the Manageress. I broke my probation by staying away one night from the hostel and was sent back to approved school, this time in Seaton, Devon. I spent six months there and was fairly happy.

I returned to Bristol and got a job working at the Homeopathic Hospital. Here I was ready to settle once again with a live-in job. I worked as a dining room maid and looked after two doctors. I used to serve the doctors with meals and clean out their rooms. They were really good to me. I felt trusted and wanted and this made me happy. After about six months I made friends with a girl called Margaret. She was planning to leave and asked if I would go with her. Like a fool I did, so once again I was on the run.

I got taken back to court during this time when I was found stealing to feed myself. I had nowhere to go and no money. I spent days wandering Bristol and sleeping rough. I used to knock on people's doors asking for food but most of the time I went without. I was glad when I got picked up so I could sleep and eat. I appeared in court four times and eventually was put on probation with a condition of residence in a training home in South Norwood.

This was a large home run by the Salvation Army and was like a prison. I stayed there for a year and was very unhappy. I was made to go to the Citidel every Sunday and we used to have to go in groups to do our shopping. I had to work in the home every day and was not allowed out without a member of staff. I was in there with about 18 other young girls under 21. I only got eight shillings a week, that was to buy toiletries, writing paper, stamps, and anything else we needed. We were only allowed one shilling for sweets. Anyway I stuck it out for a year and once again got returned to Bristol.

It did not last long. I was in trouble again in 1957, when I was 20 years of age. I got two months in prison for breaking my probation. When I was discharged, I was only out a short time when I got four months for larceny. I was again discharged but for only one month.

This time I really landed myself in trouble, having stolen three pounds from my brother. This happened one day when I went home to my mum. I went up to my brother's room and took the money out of his drawer. I ran out of the house and was picked up a few hours later. My brother had charged me because he hated me and because of my previous record the police took a serious view. I got sent down for three years corrective training which was served in Holloway and Strangeways Prisons.

I was terrified of what was going to happen with the thought of me being put away for a long time. This really made me mad, I mean all I did was steal three pounds off my brother. I don't think I deserved three years for that.

I was in Holloway for two years. I used to be on the young persons' wing. It was a dreary place with all sorts of women from young to old. I was beaten up a lot and spent months in solitary. I was glad to be moved to Strangeways but it turned out to be no better. There were four wings for women and I was on H wing. When you first go in you are stripped, bathed, searched, and given a kit and put on a wing. We were only allowed out of our cells to go to work. The cells were badly painted and cold. The meals were served on tin trays and were disgusting. The place was bad enough to crack up any human being. Women used to scream and hearing some of the inmates getting beaten up just used to make me feel worse. I tried suicide but couldn't get away with it. I was watched like a hawk, eyes everywhere. I felt I would have been better off dead than stay there with those horrible screws.

I rebelled from the day I got to Strangeways. When you arrive the screws say to you that you can do it the easy way or the hard way. I was determined to do it the hard way. I lost all my remission for attacking staff and smashing the place up. The worst incident happened one Sunday night when I could not take any more and two of us barricaded ourselves into the chief's flat. We set fire to a cushion but it got out of hand and it ended up with the roof alight. I panicked when it turned into a blaze and ran down the stairs where two prison officers tried to grab me. I hit out at them, hitting them on the head with a steel vase and nearly knocking them senseless. It all happened so fast, I was just running wild. Anyway the male prison officers were called over to the female side as well as the fire brigade and the police. I was beaten up very badly by the prison officers and kept down in the punishment cell for three months. Then I went to court and got three years on each of the five charges, adding up to a total of fifteen years in prison. But I was now even worse and I was sent back to Holloway. So here I was, a girl of about twenty one or two, just sentenced to three years in prison.

I played merry hell in Holloway, attacking staff, smashing my cell or anything I could get my hands on. I did not care anymore, they had a hold over me. After I had been there three years, three men came in to see me. I was talking very nicely to them when one said: "Well, Jean, we think you have been locked up enough, we are going to send you to a nice place where you can go dancing, swimming and do other nice things." I didn't realise that these people were doctors from the Home Office. They couldn't find anything wrong with me so couldn't certify me themselves. They asked me to sign a form. I was drugged up and like a fool did not read it and signed it. The next thing I knew I had certified myself. The worst was to come, I had landed myself in Broadmoor.

It was now 1961 and I was 24 years of age. I was starting my first year in Broadmoor, one of many which were to bring sadness, violence and trouble. The first day that I was there I was taken on exercise by two nurses. I had been out for about 10 minutes when the sister came to the door and told the nurses to bring me in. I didn't want to be locked up. They gave me an injection which knocked me out and I slept through until eight o'clock. The door then opened and there was a gang of staff who had brought me some sleeping tablets. I didn't want them but thought that I might be better if I slept it off. So I took these tablets and slept until the next morning. When I woke up I wondered where I was. When I realised I started banging on the door. They told me to be quiet but I kept on. The doctor came to see me and said he was going to give me some electric treatment. I wondered what this meant and was terrified of what they were going to do to me. I was taken to a room with four beds and all the staff standing around. I didn't know what was happening and started struggling. They jumped on me and got me on the bed. I then saw these electric things like wires. They gave me an injection and I felt myself fading away. I tried to fight against it but it was no use as they had the power over me. When I woke up they took me back to my room and asked me if I wanted some breakfast. I said I was thirsty and they brought me a paper cup with tea and some bread and marmalade.

This was to be the start of my life in Broadmoor. The first three years were perfect hell. I was given electric shock treatment three times a week. I was only out of my room for short times and these times became fewer and farther between. The first Christmas I was there it was awful. I had only been there a short while and had no cards or presents. I felt miserable and left out. It was not long before I was put on all kinds of drugs. I was doped up so much I just slept all day and used to bang my feet against the door at night. I was kept in my room with no furniture. Just a matteress on the floor and had to wear a canvas nightdress. I had tried to strangle myself with the bedding and had also slashed my wrists. But they weren't going to let me die, they just wanted to torture me. Because I kept screaming and making myself mentally and physically exhausted. One day a doctor said they were going to put me to sleep. "Here we go again," I thought and for four weeks I was on narcosis. I slept all the time, only waking up to be fed and washed by the nurse. Then I would have more medicine and go back to sleep. This seemed to go on all the time, either being on narcosis or getting electric shock treatment. I thought I was getting better on occasions and asked to get up but was only laughed at. I was told, "If you get up you will only attack someone." I felt that I didn't have a chance.

The years were to pass and things just weren't going too great. One year I was found ill in my room. I was taken by doctor's orders to a room with a bed and bedding and found to have anaemia. I was very ill for about three months and was operated upon. I was between life and death. For about a fortnight my foster mother sat by my bed but I didn't know she was there until I woke up. One day I felt better and it was like a miracle. I guess I was not meant to die. They told me I had been very close to death. I was in bed for a few more weeks until I grew stronger. I was on all sorts of medicines and tablets. I was treated like a human being while I had been ill. But a short while later things had gone back to what they were before. I was again locked in my room and again things started to go wrong. One day when it was snowing I was playing up and they put me outside for punishment. I walked to the bottom of the garden, took off all my cloths and lay in the snow. I thought if I couldn't die any other way, I'll catch pneumonia. But they saw me and dragged me to my room screaming and shouting. I was seen by a doctor who said I was to be put in strict solitary. I didn't know what this meant but I was soon to find out. I was put in a room in what they called 'The Wing'. I was attended to once a day and no one came near me or spoke to me for the rest of the time. They gave me all my meals for the day in the morning, although at first I didn't realise this. I used to shout for water but was ignored. I thought I would go mad and felt like an animal. I used to bang my head against the wall and ran from wall to wall shouting "please someone come" but was ignored.

During my time in Broadmoor I rarely saw a psychiatrist. I felt that the doctors were mainly on the side of the staff. When I appealed for help or to get out they would put me on tablets or lock me up. There were very few older people among the staff, most of them were youngsters. Many started work straight from school and could become sisters as young as 28. A lot of the staff were related to one another, eg. mothers and daughters, and came from the local area. Some of them had been in the Police Force or Army. Many were spiteful and used to egg me on and gee me up. Most of the other patients never complained or anything and there would only be one staff in the room. As soon as I walked in there could be eight or nine. One or two of the staff were sympathetic. I remember one new girl broke down and couldn't lock us up. One night nurse used to lend me comics and take them out in the morning. I used to read The Readers Digest and Womans Own.

I hardly ever was allowed outside and spent little time in company. Most of the time I was with other people was in the Douglas Unit. These people were very mentally disturbed. They all just used to sit there, nod their heads and rock backwards and forwards. I didn't want to be with them most of the time, I felt they would drive me crackers.

I was on largactyl four times a day, which can make you burn in the sun. One day I was kept out in the exercise yard in the sun all day by myself. I was in agony and got badly burned and swollen. Ever since I have never liked the sun. When I had a bath I used to pull the female nurses in the bath with me. So the men started bathing me. They used to put me in a cold bath and duck my head under the water. I also remember banging my head for hours (in both Broadmoor and later in Rampton) until I got a hole in it. I used to put my finger in it and make it bleed. They used to call me an Indian because I had a red forehead. I also used to pull my hair out until I had bald patches on top.

In the last few years of my stay in Broadmoor things weren't much different. I was still treated like an animal. One day I had been behaving extra bad. My mate Davina was in the next room to me and I could hear her yelling and screaming "get off me." I knew they were fighting with her and then all went quiet. I heard them outside my door and I shouted to them. They came in and gave me an injection. I don't remember a lot but I remember kicking out. I heard a slight moan from someone and they all got off me. I could see them dragging someone out. I didn't think much more of it until the next morning when a gang of staff came to my room and started to beat me up. "What's that for?" I screamed. "For killing Nurse Cummins, you murderess," they shouted at me. I was just stunned. "I didn't kill her," I yelled. "Oh yes you did," they said. "You kicked her, she died of a haemmorhage." I was treated real bad then until one day the psychiatrist came to see me. "You can't stay here, you'll have to go to Rampton." I was in my glory. At last I was to get out of here, even though, as they said, I had to kill someone to do it. I was transferred in 1974. I didn't know what waited around the corner for me but anything was better than Broadmoor.

I was taken by van to Rampton with two female staff, one male staff and a doctor. I couldn't see out of the window and they kept me heavily drugged. The journey must have taken about four hours and I wondered what was going to happen to me. When I arrived I thought, "My! What a difference!" I was met by about eight staff and taken to a brightly painted ward. The staff were so much better. They said, "Come on, Jean! Let's give you a bath after your long journey." After my bath I was put into a room and told that a doctor would see me in the morning. When he came the next day I asked if I could get up. "Of course you can," he said, "the nurse will get you some clothes." Was this to be the beginning of a new life?

Things were beginning to get better. I stayed on the admission ward for three months and was moved to a block ward. Although the outside doors were locked and there were bars on the windows, it was very different to Broadmoor. We were up from 7.45 in the morning to 8.45 at night and could walk around the ward. We worked during the day and had our meals in a big dining room. As well as t.v. we had various entertainments like bingo, dancing and the cinema. I was settled for a while. But I couldn't get used to the freedom after how I had been treated at Broadmoor and started to get worse again. I used to wander around without anybody watching me and I used to become mischievous. For example I put a fist through the window, sometimes I was so drugged up I didn't know what I was doing. I ended up on the punishment block but it wasn't bad. Here I was put in an empty room with the light and fan left on all night. I called the nurse as I couldn't sleep and she gave me some medicine. I soon fell asleep. The next day I had breakfast and a wash and they said if I was good I could have my bedding back. I stayed quiet all day and they kept their promise. (Some people would go for weeks without bedding, they used to drop off on the floor in the end). That night after tea I had a mattress and blankets. It was my first of many times in the punishment ward. I stayed there for three weeks and got sent back to Mary Ward. I didn't mean to be bad and promised the staff that I would try to stay good as they were a lot more kind and understanding than the staff at Broadmoor. After about two years there I had a case conference. They asked me if I would like to go to a villa, I said it couldn't be any worse than Broadmoor. I was sent to Poplars villa but I didn't like it. Poplars was a house which was part of a village in the grounds with lots of houses and a green (which they used to play hockey on). I found it too open and wasn't used to windows without bars. I was sent back to a block ward where I had good times as well as bad. I was learning to enjoy life. I had been working on the ward cleaning floors, windows, corridors etc. It used to be very strict. For example, if there was a mark on a corridor we would have to scrub the polish off and re-polish it with about four lots of polish. This could take hours. I was then sent to work in the Laundry. I worked on all the jobs but mostly on the calander. I liked it here though it was hard work.

Years were to pass. One day a nurse said to me, "why don't you put in for a tribunal." I thought it would be a waste of time but I'd have a go anyway. I waited for about three months filling in forms and seeing doctors and a solicitor. The final day arrived and I was to go before my tribunal, feeling very nervous. It wasn't too bad. The chairman asked me what I would do if they let me out. "I would like to go home, Sir," I said which was the biggest mistake I had ever made. I went back to the ward telling the girls that I didn't think I had a chance. Anyway, three days later I went back from work and was called into the office. There was a social worker sat there with the doctor. "You are very lucky, Jean," they said, "You have won your tribunal." I felt thrilled. They really meant I was going to be set free. They sent a telegram to my mother. Three days later with a sister I was taken home. I couldn't believe it . But things were to get bad. I had been locked up for 20 years. My brother was cold towards me. I had only been out for one day and my brother asked me to do the shopping. I told him that I didn't understand the money. My brother replied, "If you don't pull your weight you can get out, we all pull together in this house." That's it I thought, I'm not staying here. So with the money my mother had given me for fish and chips I went off to London.

I was brought back to Bristol having been picked up by the London police. They sent me back home but it was hopeless as my mother and brother both got on at me. So I ran off again but this time I stayed in Bristol. I walked round Broadmead shopping centre all day then at midnight when I thought no one was around I chucked a dustbin through a Sainburys window. All at once there were police everywhere.

They picked me up, took me to Bridewell police station and next day I appeared in court. I saw the duty probation officer, John Nock who was to become my pal. I had a solicitor called Dudley Thomas who also became my friend. The Magistrate listened to my story and heard I had been sent home after 20 years with no help. He sent me to Pucklechurch for medical and probation reports. Three weeks later I went back to Court. The Magistrate was very understanding and said if John Nock could get me an address I could have probation. He found a place in Richmond Terrace in Clifton. I stayed there for a few days then decided to move. Once again I was on the road. This went on for 39 days and I was remanded to Pucklechurch several times having committed various offences which had landed me in court. This was when I met Doctor Reeves. In the end Dr. Reeves said the best thing that could happen to me would be to go back to Rampton. I was remanded for Crown Court. Three weeks later my case was heard and I was ordered to return to Rampton.

The next four years were to be better and I made a lot of progress. I thought if I kept good they might give me another chance. Everyone was pleased with my progress and I was a lot happier. I was sent once again to the villa ward where I was before but this time there was no trouble. I watched TV, read and played games and cards. I was sent to work in the sewing room but it was too quiet for me. I was then put on the farm (which was outside the main gate) and I enjoyed the work. Roma Dolby who was in charge of the farm suggested I put in for another tribunal so I did. It was going to be more difficult to get out as I was now under the Home Office. I had my tribunal and didn't hear anything for a year. Then one weekend my social worker, Peter Green came to see me. "We have got you a hostel in Bristol," he said, "now it's up to the Home Office to set you free." One day my doctor told me I was having a day out to see the hostel. So I travelled all the way from Nottingham to Bristol to see it. I didn't think I would like it but was willing to give it a go. Three months later I was told I would be visiting the hostel for three days leave. I enjoyed that and when I came back to Rampton a report was sent to the Home Office saying I had been good and would like to return there.

I came to the hostel on a three months trial but I did not stay very long. I didn't like it much so I ran away. The hostel wasn't like it is now. It was dirty, with no pictures, not very friendly and the wardens were too strict. It might also have been down to the fact that I was scared of being so free. I felt insecure and I was frightened of the big wide world after Rampton. I was picked up by the police after two days after smashing a window of an Estate Agents in the city centre. I was taken to Bridewell Police Station and put in a cell at about 5.30am. I screamed to be let out. About 9am the wardens of the hostel came to see me. I was very upset and wasn't nice to them. Later that day I tried to strangle myself with a belt from my dress, I was very disturbed. The doctor was called and he sedated me. About 3pm in the afternoon I heard the door to the cells open and saw these three women walk in. I recognised then as staff from Rampton. I screamed at them, "I'm not going back." "Oh yes you are," they said. It was about 6pm before they could calm me down. Anyway they drugged me and took me back. I got there at midnight and was put on the admission ward. On Sunday the sister told me to stay in bed and I slept nearly all day. When I got up the next day I was very upset about being back. Later that morning a doctor from the Home Office came and was very annoyed with the Police for sending me back for something so small. He said, "don't worry Jean, you will go out again." I was removed to the villa ward and in a fortnight was released and sent back to the hostel. "I will try and stick it," I thought which I did for about a month. One day I was in my room sorting out newspapers and the caretaker said, "what are you doing, Jean?" "Setting fire to the place," I said jokingly, thinking no more of it. Next day I went shopping with the relief warden. I came back very happy but was to be very upset by what was to happen. I was called to the office. "You are going back," the warden said. I wanted to know what I had done wrong. "For threatening to set fire," they said. I explained that I was only joking. "You might have been, but you have done it once and we can't risk it happening again."

I remained in Rampton for 7 months before I was allowed out again. The nurses were on a work to rule and no one was allowed to leave or be transferred. Time was slow and I began to lose hope till one day I was called into the office. The sister of the ward was there with the doctor. "You are very lucky," my doctor said, "you are going back to the Hostel on Monday." I ran out of the office, got hold of my pal and swung her round. "You lucky thing," she said, "please make a go of it this time." "I will," I said. I arrived at the hostel at about 1pm on Monday and saw the wardens. "Well, Jean," they said, "this is going to be your last chance. Did they ever tell you that if you go back again, it will be for good." I thought that I would have to try real hard. Anyway things went well for a few months and then one day I lost my temper, hitting the Assistant Warden. And you know what happened? Yes I was sent back to Rampton!"Well, you've had it now," they said, "You've thrown the key away, Jean, you will never go out again." I really regretted hitting Pam the Warden. Anyway I wouldn't give up. I thought I would ask them for another chance, although I thought it wouldn't be any good. I wrote to the Home Office, the Hostel and a few friends. Then one day Myna Briggs, my social worker in Rampton came to see me. "Would you really promise me, Jean, you would never come back if we got you out?" she asked. "Please give me a try," I said, "then if I do anything wrong again I wouldn't expect to go out."

Thank God! I was given one last chance and it has worked! I have been out for four years and I have made a lot of friends. I am going out with a lovely man named Ted and we are going to get married next year. He's really good to me and I am very happy with him. I feel having him is a great achievement. We share a room in the hostel at long last. I feel now that I have settled down and life is once again worth living. I'm now treated like a human being and not like an animal anymore. I used to hate myself, now I feel I like myself and have more of a liking for other people. I'm now a different person, I wouldn't hurt a fly. When I came out of Rampton I was on thirty tablets a day and an injection; now I am only on one injection a week and no tablets. I watch television (especially nature films) and I like reading. I enjoy watching Ted gardening. I'm sometimes called "Jean the Queen".

I'm now 49 but people take me for much younger. In some ways I've never had any worries like shopping, cooking, deciding what to wear, which might have kept me young! I've always been told what to do, even what time to go to bed and what time to get up! My mother is now 86. She won't have anything to do with me, nor do my four brothers and one sister. My foster mother, Mrs. Jolly, died before I came out. Mr. Jolly has died too but after I came out. I phoned him up from the Hostel and he was crying on the phone.

I have learnt a lot by what has happened to me. I have learnt to calm my temper which has always been my trouble. I have also learnt to cook, and understand money. I now understand people much better especially youngsters. When I was young I was a proper tearaway. I am now much more patient and not so quick tempered. My life has now changed a lot and I am very grateful to the people who have helped me. I am not bitter now about my 44 years in institutions although I used to feel bitter. I try to forget the past but it is difficult. Sometimes I have nightmares about being inside again and am relieved to find when I wake up that it was only a dream.

In future I would like to settle down with Ted and get married. I would like to keep house for him and look after him. I'm sure I'll be happy. At least I did all the wrong things when I was young!

If I had to live my life again a lot would be changed. I would never get into trouble and spend years locked up. I would have loved to have children and help young people stay out of trouble.

I want all young people to read this story. I just want to say please don't make the mistakes I have made. I too was young when I was put away and it breaks my heart to see youngsters locked away or homeless. You have a better chance than I had so please take care all of you young and old as well. I wish you all well in the future. Please take care if you are in prison or detention centres. Go straight when you leave – O.K. I hope this book will be of some help. All the best. Keep trying.

WHAT GOES ON BEHIND THOSE FACTORY WALLS?

BY STANLEY VANT

In the aero engine factory at Patchway, I first heard the saying "The difficult will take a little time to solve; the impossible will take a little longer". With these words of challenge in my mind, I began to get to grips with my new job at that factory in 1963 when the Concorde development programme was just beginning to take shape.

Luck has to play its part in life, and I was fortunate in being given the task of keeping watch on the financial implications of all the twists and turns in the course of developing the Olympus 593 engines which power Concorde, a project that was a major step in the history of turbojet engines for supersonic flight.

As it turned out, it was a success story but it was not without its trials and tribulations en route. Failure to achieve the objectives seemed imminent on several occasions but the Rolls Royce (RR), formerly Bristol Siddeley (BS) engineering teams always came up trumps in the end. The total number of Bristolians engaged on the theoretical and practical work must run into thousands, for the Development and Production period spanned some twenty years.

From the inception, which was actually before 1960, right up to 1984, everything was government funded and therefore government owned. My job was to advise on the way that the overall cost would be influenced by the hundreds of changes that had to be made to the simplified theoretical path of the original plans of the project.

The system of funding the project was tightly controlled by the government. Firstly, a master plan for the work involved, named the "Development Cost Plan", is produced as a condition of contract, and this is really a very broad estimate for the complete job of developing the engine to a commercially acceptable standard. In the case of Concorde, that engine standard was a Certificate of Airworthiness, a specified power output, and an engine life of 1000 hours of flight without overhaul being necessary. Any engine failing to fly 1000 hours was to be the subject of financial compensation, and this included the cost of any secondary damage caused by a failed component. The engines used for developing up to this standard could never be used commercially, so really the end result of the Development programme is merely a set of proven drawings for the Production Shops to utilise in manufacturing the engines for customers.

The master plan, of course, assumed ultimate success and within it, the projected estimated cost towards that goal breaks down into annual sums. These sums vary from year to year according to the changing nature of the activities envisaged, as the course of development progresses. The first necessary costs relate to building up a sufficient range of components for the first primitive engine to be constructed for a try-out on the test beds, in order to endorse the feasibility of the design. Subsequent annual estimated figures take account of the vast assortment of variant components that are made and progressively incorporated in the rebuilds of a dozen or so Development engines, on which the experimenting was to take place, during the five, six or seven years required to solve the problems.

In funding this and other projects, the government engaged their own engineers, some based at the factory and some at the London headquaters. During the development of the Olympus 593, a monthly meeting was held at the factory, the "Review and Authorisation Meeting", for the government engineers to consider the costs to date, what components had been made, what tests were carried out, and how far things had moved from the master plan. I attended most of those meetings and the information gleaned was usable in my reports on all the necessary revisions to the cost estimates of the original plan. These reports went upwards through two to three government officials to those holding the purse strings of the Treasury.

When things were well under way, and the rate of spend was getting towards £1 million per month, the mass of detail necessary to justify this level, was absolutely enormous, and complicated by the fact that so many components were incomplete and much of the cost related to work in progress. Although for the first two years I carried out my work single handed, because of the magnitude of the expenditure involved others were appointed to assist me in the tasks. I and my colleagues did not always endorse the BS or RR revised estimates and there were many arguments over our difference, although it should be added that a friendly situation always existed and each respected the other's views.

It may come as a surprise to learn that the final cost of the Olympus 593 Development programme (counted in hundreds of millions of pounds), was roughly five times the figure in the original master plan and estimate. Much of the difference is because of the rules under which such estimates are submitted. Only the economic conditions up to the year of submission are permitted, which means that the master plan cannot include anything for the effect of inflation. Over the twenty years of development, the average wage rate of the skilled men in the workshops moved from around 10/- (or 50p) to close to £2.50 per hour and, as to be expected, the actual costs incurred take all this movement into account. In addition to this economic factor, there were some rather substantial changes in design which made the final version of the Olympus 593 a much superior engine to that envisaged in the original master plan.

Some of the changes to the design were the sequel to advancing technology, such as in the electronic control system which initially used valves but ended up with micro-chip circuitry. Other changes were necessary in the elimination of unforseen snags of which, I suppose, the most serious was an early discovery of a titanium fire hazard. There was the possibility that the metal of the engine itself could catch fire!

This hazard came to light in one of the standard tests given to turbojet engines. The test is an attempt to burst the rotating core of blades through the engine casing. For safety sake, the rotor core must not burst the casing or else it would be back to the drawing board for a redesign. The development engine used in this particular test had carried out a lot of previous tests and was in need of modification to a later standard. The decision was made to wreck it instead by giving it what is termed a "Containment Test" in which a key component is caused to fail when the engine is running at full power. It is difficult to imagine the amount of power generated within an engine of this type, but it could be equated to that provided by 30 British Rail '100 horsepower' locomotives linked together and travelling at full throttle. Up to that amount of power rotates the rotor core of compressor blades within each of Concorde's four engines.

The rotor core with all its blades weighs nearly a ton, and at full thrust the blade tips are moving supersonically. It is at that point that the failure is triggered and one or two blades fracture. Instantly, rows of blades are mutilated as the damage compounds progressively. Nothing can stop that ton of metal rotating and even breaking from its bearings. In this particular engine, the frictional heat was sufficient to ignite the distorted blade remnants and great holes were burned in the engine casing before the momentum began to reduce. Nevertheless, the rotating ton was restrained from breaking out.

The test cell, which is something like a reinforced concrete garage, larger than the average house, was strewn with debris from the wreckage and when all had cooled down the inspection and inquest began. Every fragment was collected and examined, but quite a lot could not be found because it had simply evaporated in the inferno!

The result of the test might have been catastrophic, not for the test engineers who are safe behind their peep hole of armoured glass whilst operating the controls, but for the whole project. If titanium could not be used for the blades, it would mean reverting to steel with an unacceptable weight penalty. Fortunately, a new specification of titanium alloy metal solved the fire hazard problem.

POWER MACHINE
BY GRACE HEWSON

(Based on a real incident at Lyons Bakery, Brislington, in 1971)

Once upon a time, not so very long ago, nor so very far away, there was a huge factory, a bakery which produced bread and buns for nationwide consumption. And in that bakery there worked two hundred big, husky strong men and six women. The men doing the important work of mixing, kneading, baking. The women merely packing buns, sometimes sticky, sometimes flour-topped, four at a time into trays which were fed by conveyor belt into a cellophane wrapping.

Now one of these women was Gladys. She was the leader of the team so she wore a dark blue nylon overall, instead of a light blue one. Her husband Bert worked there too, in the Supplies Dept. For fifteen years now, they had been coming to work at 8.15, always through the rain or so it seemed,
Drip drip Drip drip
Heads down, dodging the puddles.
They'd meet the night shift coming out.
"See you tonight, love," to Gladys. "What's for tea?"
"I don't know yet. You'll have to wait and see."
Bye bye Bye bye
Into the cloakroom to the girls.
"'Morning Girls"
"'Morning Gladys" "'Morning Gladys" "'Morning Gladys"
"'Morning Gladys"
Overalls on and hats on and hair tucked out of sight.
Clip clip Clip clip
Queue up to clock in. Find the right card. Stick it in the machine.
Click click Click click
"'Morning Gladys"
"Quick you're late. Stick your card in or you'll lose a half-hour's pay."
Click

"All set at the machine then – Elsie lifting the baking sheets, I'll mind the cellophane. The others filling the trays. We'll change round in an hour. Switching on now. Off you go."
Hummmm Hummmmm
Clunk clunk Clunk clunk
Don't think of anything. Just keep your hands and eyes busy.

Coffee break at eleven.
Sip sip Sip sip

Lunch at one
What a day What a day
Washing's out Won't dry

More buns until four, when the first hooter blows

Whooh Whooh

Buy something for tea on the way home. Bert will be back by half past six.

And so it had been. Monday to Friday. For fifteen years. Except for Christmas, and two weeks in the summer.

Until one day, when a sudden change affected them. New baking sheets. Now that may not seem particularly momentous to you. In fact, no one had dreamt that it would be. But it nearly caused chaos throughout the factory.

Everything had begun as normal.

Drip drip Drip drip
What's for tea Wait and see
Bye bye Bye bye
'Morning 'Morning 'Morning 'Morning
Clip clip Clip clip
Click click Click click
You're late You're late
All set Off we go
Hummmmm Hummmmmm
Clunk clunk Clunk clunk

But then, after ten minutes, an unexpected moan was heard from the far end of the machine.

"Here," said Elsie, "Either I'm suddenly getting older, or these baking sheets are getting heavier."

"Ah," said Lil, "Twinging screws – gets us all in the end."

"No, I don't think so. Move over a minute, Val – you have a turn."

"She's right. They're much heavier – that's a real strain to get them off the top runners, Gladys."

Gladys thought for two seconds then with a burst of decisiveness, she reached for the switch and turned it off.

"Right, up to the canteen, girls. We'll have to see about this. I'm going to the office."

So it was up for coffee. At half past nine.

Sip sip Sip sip

Until Gladys appeared.

"I've told them. We're not packing any more buns if we have to lift those heavy baking sheets. They're tannoying the manager now. Give us all another coffee, love."

Sip sip Sip sip

Until the Man Himself came on the scene. The Man in the Dark Suit and the leather soled shoes.

Trot trot Trot trot
Up the stairs to the staff canteen.

"Now Gladys," he said smoothly, with a big wide smile, "What's all this? We've never had a problem with you girls, not in all the years the factory's been open."

"It's them new baking sheets – they've never been so heavy before. I'm not risking the health of my girls with them. It can do nasty things to women, lifting heavy trays."

"Oh I'm sure they're the same as we've always had. Just not so worn down. The old ones have been thrown out, anyway. Don't worry about it. You'll get used to them in no time."

"Oh no we won't, because we'll be sitting right here until something's sorted out."
This announcement followed by the departure of T.M.H..
Trot trot Trot trot
Back down the stairs to see what he could do.
Sip sip Sip sip
Trot trot Trot trot
"Girls," (the voice of T.M.H. was rather less smooth) "You must come back now. I'll try to do something for you but in the meantime there are five trolleys of buns waiting to be packed. None of the men will do them. They say it's not their job."
A hard stare all round.
Sip sip Sip sip
Trot trot Trot trot

What a day Such weather
Washing's out Won't dry

Trot trot Trot trot
"Gladys," (not very smoothly at all) "The two assistant managers, and myself have been trying to deal with the backlog, but the buns keep going everywhere, the cellophane has tangled up, we're losing nine out of ten packs to the reject pile. There's ten trolleys waiting and the bakers have run out of empty sheets so they can't cook the scotch baps ..."
The determined look all round.
Sip sip Sip sip
Trot trot Trot trot
"Nearly dinner time, girls."
Trot trot Trot trot
"Ok., Ok.," (extremely ruffled) "I've found a young lad – only temporary mind – a student. He was going to be helping out at the warehouse. He's on his way now. He'll do the lifting while you do the packing. Will that do for you?"
"In that case," said Gladys, very smoothly with a big wide smile, "We'll be getting back to work. At the usual time. After we've had our dinner."

The Man Himself disappeared from the staff canteen, from the smells of the sausage, beans and chips, extremely relieved, and headed straight for his double brandy and ploughman's lunch, saying to the bartender, "You know, it's been a very hard day so far."

Now this is a true story about real people, so I've cut out all the long-winded bits about the scenery, the character building, the descriptions of the damsels who could cope with their own distress, thank you very much, and all that rubbish. After all you know what real people are like, don't you.

As for Gladys, I've really no idea. But I have a feeling that when the hooter blew at four o'clock, she took a longer route home, browsed in the shop windows, sheltered from the drip, drip of the rain in a little cafe on the way, sat back in her seat and ordered a coffee and a sandwich, saying,
"He can get his own bloody tea tonight. I'm going to bloody well sit here until I bloody feel like moving."

THE INNER DARKNESS
BY GLADYS MEDCROFT

Much of my early life is now a blurred memory, but I still recollect the cold, the hunger and the constant moving from place to place as we sought for somewhere to live.

I was born in Totnes but shortly afterwards we all moved to London – my parents, sisters, brother and myself. We were living in squalid conditions in ex-army huts without furniture, but with blankets to keep us warm. As the huts became due for demolition, so our few possessions were loaded on to an old pram and we set out to try to find another. I can remember being woken by an official of some sort shining a torch on us and saying that we would have to go as the hut was due to come down. At one time things became so bad that we literally had nowhere to sleep and we all went into a prison for the night.

Travelling around trying to find somewhere to live we eventually arrived in Bristol where we lived for a while in an ex-army hut which was built on stilts. My father had a drink problem and when the worse for drink he couldn't negotiate the steps up to the hut and frequently ended up underneath it. Although as a father he was inadequate, he did his best. As far as I remember we always had food and blankets to keep us warm at night. However, when we had to leave our latest 'home'; there was nowhere else for us to go but the workhouse in Fishponds Road. We children were split up and I went first to Vinney Green Children's Home, and at a later date was transferred to Downend Homes as were the other children. I felt like a pawn continuously moved around.

We were all in No. 2 house. Years went by, my older sister left and we were all separated and moved into different houses, which really upset us. Every time I was missing I was in the nursery. I loved that. I had a brother and sister there. They were later fostered.

There was very strict discipline. At 6 am we were lined up and given our duties – bedmaking, peeling potatoes, mending and so on. There were so many different things to be done. Before we went to school we were again lined up like an army. A button missing or a hole in a sock meant we were sent for after school and reprimanded. Every Saturday we were given sixpence to spend in the tuck shop, but any misdemeanour meant we didn't get our pocket money. They looked after us well but it was nothing like a real home; love, there was none, and without that life for a child is empty.

While at Downend we attended church regularly and as I became older I was given charge of the young ones on Sundays. The staff never discovered that I often took them to a different church where I fancied a boy in the choir, who used to sometimes come to the home for functions like sports day. I enjoyed outwitting the staff and the little ones never told. Later I became very involved at our recognised church which I then attended regularly and I asked to be confirmed. As the classes had already started, I took them on my own. The day of confirmation arrived and I was very annoyed. It was a solemn occasion – we were all in white and the church was very quiet. Suddenly my mother and father who had come for the ceremony were fighting and arguing in the church. It spoilt my day. My father had bought me a skirt, but although I should have liked to have it, I wouldn't. I didn't know where he got it from; he could have come by it honestly, but I couldn't be sure.

Often at holiday times, and sometimes weekends, people would arrive whom we called aunties or uncles. They sometimes brought presents and sometimes took us out to tea or home for the weekend. No doubt their intentions were good and they were kind to us, but for me it was never a success. Where they had children of their own I found it impossible to mix. I felt so ill at ease and unsure of how I should behave with the result that I was very silent. I daresay they thought I was sullen and ungrateful, but they couldn't understand how I felt.

When I was about fourteen I went to a foster home, where I was very happy with my own little room, and I could watch television. I had now started working. My first job was at a drinking straw factory, which I didn't like very much but stuck at it because I was secure and contented. Unfortunately my foster parents were getting elderly and decided they didn't want the responsibility so I had to move to a hostel. Although I knew it couldn't continue I was vey sad as they had been kind, and understood children as they had brought up a large family. I kept in touch with them and used to go back to see them on Sundays after church, and have dinner and tea with them. Margaret – my foster sister – came too. After tea I went back to the hostel and so to bed. Each morning I got up – prepared my breakfast, usually cereal and toast, then off to catch my bus. The matron, when I was first at the hostel, was Mrs. Munroe. The money we earned we gave to her; so much she kept for board, some she saved for us for clothes and the rest she gave back as pocket money for make-up, toilet goods and the like.

I shared a bedroom with a nice girl called Anne – we got on well. It was a pleasant place and we had plenty of freedom to come and go. There were four bedrooms on the top floor, bathroom and toilet. One floor down was the staff room, and another bedroom with bathroom and toilet. Next going down was the big day room with armchairs and television. Also on this floor was the assistant matron's room and her office. The basement floor comprised the dining room and kitchen, store room and laundry. Our evening and Sunday meals were taken in a separate room, where there were four dining tables. If any of us were out of work we helped out with the meals, and those home earliest from work also gave a hand. After a while, Mrs. Munroe left and Mrs. Worgan took over. Miss Daw, or Marge, as we called her, was assistant matron. Mrs. Haines came in daily to help with the cooking. Miss Burgess, a dear old soul, used to do the cleaning – she brought her little dog with her.

As soon as I was working I tried to help my mother and father as much as possible, although I did not have much money myself. At this time they were living in two rooms in Bath. My father could not or would not get a job and they were constantly short of money. Most Saturdays I would go over on the bus, then to the food shops to buy what I could afford before visiting them. The one thing my father could find money for was face powder, which he made my mother use to cover up the bruises he inflicted. I should have preferred just to give to my mother, but I knew it would cause rows if I did that.

In the hostel we had a record player. They gave me a record of Elvis Presley's "Wooden Heart" and I was always playing it, much to the annoyance of the other girls. I used to go to the Glen dancing and on one occasion a girl stepped on my toe and I had a bad foot. I wouldn't get any treatment but finally I was forced to as it became poisoned. I had to have my nail off at the hospital and stay home from work, as I couldn't stand on my foot, and bathe it every day in very hot salt water. Wednesday we all went to a club and while my foot was bad my friends carried me up the stairs. We had some interesting speakers to teach us various things which we had never had any opportunity to learn about like dress sense and make-up. One time Shirley Bassey's make-up girl came.

I left the straw factory because the journey was too long and had a succession of miscellaneous jobs. After a couple of weeks without a job, the Labour Exchange sent me to a transport cafe. I enjoyed it there – I liked meeting the customers, but I found the money confusing and usually ended up charging less than I should. I could see it wouldn't be long before the manageress asked me to go; so I forestalled her by leaving there. In those days it was quite easy to get work provided one was flexible and didn't mind having a try at various things.

I enjoyed my next job which was in a paint factory where the work was rotated so it didn't become too tedious. Sometimes I was filling the tins, sometimes stamping the colour on the top, or maybe stacking or other work. While I was at the paint factory I made a good friend, Maureen. Four of us, Maureen and Bob who were later married, myself and Bill, went everywhere together. I was engaged to Bill for a year but decided I didn't want to marry him. Unfortunately from the day I started there was one woman in the same team as myself who was continually harassing and criticizing me. Now I would not let myself get upset by such a person, but then I was young and vulnerable. One day when she had been particularly vindictive I could stand it no longer. I had a tin of paint in my hand and I poured it over her head. That, of course, was marching orders for me.

So long as I was working the hostel staff didn't concern themselves with where I was, so when I left the factory I went straight into the Co-op Laundry and asked if they had a job for me. There was a vacancy so I started there right away. Here again I had various duties – sorting the laundry: pressing the sheets on large rollers: filling the driers, etc. After a few months I left as I found work at a printing firm which was not such a long journey for me. I couldn't settle for very long anywhere so I changed again and had a spell at a Corporation department serving dinners, and clearing tables.

I decided to have a change and took a post in an Old People's Home.

I loved the old people but the work was sheer slavery. On one occasion the husband and wife went away leaving myself. I was about eighteen then, and another girl – slightly older – and myself were left to look after the old people. After the owners had gone we found the only food they had left was biscuits and cheese, so that day we could only give the old people that for their tea, and the next day we had to buy food from our own money to feed them.

Much as I enjoyed the old people I couldn't stand the drudgery and so I left. I was by this time finding hostel life too restrictive and thought it was time I stood on my own feet, so I found a residential post at the B.R.I. There I lived in the maids' hostel. I cleaned the nurses' bedrooms, also the sisters' bedrooms which were in another block. I took them tea and breakfast in bed. Sometimes I also helped on relief in the matron's house. I still go back to see the ladies – it was a smashing place.

The painters came in to paint the nurses' home among them being a fellow called Ron. Although I was still going out with Bill, I started seeing Ron and at week-ends we went out all the time. Often we went to Dursley and stayed the night with Ron's brother, Bill, and his wife, Rosalyn. Ron could get all the work he wanted in the building trade, so we were able to go out and enjoy ourselves when we wanted to.

While I was at the B.R.I. the Sister of the Nurses' Home found out my reading and writing problems, also the fact that I had never had the opportunity to learn to cook or tackle things alone, and this was worrying me as I hoped to get married. She was very helpful and arranged for me to learn something about cooking in the O.T. department every Wednesday afternoon. Then on a Thursday afternoon I went to the Army School at Corsham where they had a class for soldiers with reading problems. It was interesting but I think I learnt more about guns, under-carriages, etc., than I did about reading.

When I was twenty, Ron and I became engaged and we married the following year. We had to wait until then as my father wouldn't give his consent – he had no reason for his refusal, it was part of his vindictive nature. We found a flat in Cotham and I moved in two weeks before the wedding to get it all ready. It was the middle flat with the living room one side and the bedroom the other. The bathroom was on the next floor up we shared it with the family there. The flat was in a terrible condition but Ron was able to decorate.

I was married at St. Michael's Church. I had three bridesmaids, two in yellow and one in blue. The material was satin and they wore white shoes and a flower in their hair. We gave them Prayer books as a present which they carried with them. I wore a long full white satin wedding dress with layers of lace on top, a matching headress and a floral cross of roses. We had a lovely reception which would not have been possible if the B.R.I. had not helped out with the catering. My uncle Fred made the wedding cake as a present as that was his profession.

I left the B.R.I. as obviously I didn't want a residential post and went to work at Bolloms in the canteen, preparing dinners and teas for the workers in the factory. We were eager to start a family and after about

Gladys and Ron Medcroft with children Brian and Linda at Chipping Sodbury

seven months I was pleased to leave as by then I was expecting a baby. In due course I had a baby boy, Brian, who was born in the Bristol Maternity Hospital. We were happy all the time we were married. We lived in Cotham for three years, then moved to a council flat at Withywood. Two years after Brian was born I had a miscarriage, but later I had a little girl, Linda.

Life went on day after day, month after month. Going to the shops, looking after the babies, taking them when older to school, preparing meals for Ron. We discovered that my father had cancer and he died quite soon afterwards. A few years later my mother developed cancer of the lung. We went to visit her at home as often as possible, first at the women's hostel and later a council flat until she died from the disease.

When I was a little girl I missed much of my schooling in the early days, so I had a speech problem including a very severe stutter. Years after, the doctor put me in touch with a speech therapist at Clifton. My speech problem was overcome, but I was still left with reading and writing difficulties. As a result of this I had a very unpleasant experience in a bank where I was accused of forgery. Needless to say, I have never been back to that bank. I learned to cope in various ways, not always very successfully, as I would, for example, arrive home with a birthday card with completely unsuitable words.

Ron woke up one morning and said, "I'm going to the Doctor, I've a lump on my neck which I think is a carbuncle." The doctor sent him to the hospital for tests and he was later admitted – neither of us realised how serious his condition was or what his prospects were likely to be. The doctor took me aside and told me he had Hodgkins Disease, which I had never heard of, and that his future was bleak and limited. I shut my mind to what he was saying. I was not in the room, I was at school, at home, anywhere but where my body was. His words meant nothing to me at the time.

I was told later tht he would live anything between six months and fifteen years. The doctor asked me if he should be told, but I said "No, I will tell him when the right moment comes."

In the event he lived for three years, in and out of hospital for treatment, but he didn't know until the last six months the truth regarding his condition, neither did he know that I knew all along.

So the nightmare began as his condition deteriorated and the treatment he was receiving produced horrific side-effects. Still not aware of how desperately ill he was, he was trying determinedly to lead a normal life – not realising that this was impossible. Each day brought its own problems and fears.

Whenever we went out in the car I wondered if disaster was ahead. Hanging on to the seat, shouting at the children and watching him for any signs of collapse which happened periodically and involved various parts of the body – eyes, hands and feet. Each journey seemed an endless hell. Continually watching his speed, shouting at him to go slower if he exceeded thirty miles per hour, him shouting back at me not realising why I was so scared, built up severe tension between us and the children.

He was on a limited diet, certain foodstuffs being forbidden. Without realising he was doing it he became very difficult to cater for. For instance, I well remember one day when he said he would like fish. I started cooking it and suddenly he said, "I don't want fish, I would like liver."

Episodes like this happened repeatedly. Looking back I realise that it was the effect of the illness or the treatment. At the time I couldn't see this, and suffered further strain and tension. What a contrast from earlier years when he was fit and well. Then as Sunday was my day off Ron cooked my breakfast for me, off I went with the children while he prepared dinner, afterwards cleaning up before taking us off to Weston or family visiting.

Now he started to have blackouts and the situation was similar to the experiences in the car. As I lifted him up, he usually came round and demanded to know what I was doing, having no recollection of having fallen and again we ended up shouting at each other. Bath time was another horror. Always he had liked a lot of water, and I tried desperately to persuade him to have less. Terrified that he might have a blackout while in the water I dare not move far from the bathroom yet prevent him from suspecting I was hovering near to rush in if needed. I had to help him in and out of the bath which he much resented and each time he had a course of treatment Ron became progressively worse.

When he realised the gravity of his illness his attitude changed. Nothing was said between us but he started buying more things for the house such as a washing machime to make things easier for me. He was also telling me not to hit the children and to look after them, and if I wanted to get married again I should do so. I made no reply but knew from his remarks that he was aware that he wouldn't be here long.

So the time went on until a day came when he drove to the hospital and was admitted immediately. Obviously he should not have been driving but he was so independent that he refused an ambulance as he had on other occasions, and his will power gave him strength to get there. I was with him and stayed with him and settled him in. Now for roughly a month my life revolved between home, hospital and school. In the evenings it meant taking the children to the hospital and they spent many hours in the library or corridors.

The day came when I took the children to see their father for what I knew would be the last time. The following night he was in a one-bedded cubicle. I sat for many hours by his bed: I must have fallen asleep and when I came round I was lying on a bed.

I went back in and stayed with him until he died the following afternoon. My first feelings were of intense relief for myself and the children. I felt in a whirl and didn't know what to do. After the intense activity of the last few weeks I had come to a full stop.

My mother-in-law had come to stay and Uncle Ted made the funeral arrangements. Flowers were sent to the house which was full of relations, who took charge of proceedings. I felt completely detached from it all and was thinking about other things. The day after the funeral my mother-in-law went home and I was left alone with the children.

About a week later I developed signs of hyperactivity which alternated with periods of complete inactivity. I spent hours watching television, identifying the characters with relations, but the bad characters I obsessively indentified with myself. Another symptom was that I sat for hours watching the clock on the stove looking for consolation.

I developed a terror of people and thought they were following me. Cars also frightened me, every driver had Ron's face, but I couldn't stop myself looking in them. I had a feeling of being closed in but was scared to go out. I avoided all people but men in particular terrified me, even to the point that I thought they were trying to photograph me in my bath and all the time the light bulbs were flashing. I thought I was being watched and photographed all the time. Sometimes I had spells of intense activity and danced wildly until exhausted before slumping into a chair and falling asleep.

I disowned my name and my ring. I still tried to go to work, but sometimes I couldn't bear the place or the people, although they really tried to help me. On one occasion I wrote a letter and gave it to a man at work, although I hadn't written it for him but for another dear friend; this particular work-mate never knew how he helped me just by talking to me.

I said many things which were true to me in my fantasy world, but had no real truth in them. Sometimes between whiles I realised what I had been saying but could find no way to rectify it. I felt guilty and stupid and stayed away from work more and more.

The money from the Insurance came through and I spent wildly but not without purpose. I replaced a lot of furniture – I didn't want any reminders of the past. I started taking the children out, using taxis in which I felt safe. I had to make myself shop for food otherwise the children would have gone hungry. The money was no object. I did not consider it was mine and was trying to get rid of it. We went on holidays, had meals out and generally spent the money until it was gone.

By now I was doing a lot of walking, but I was always looking for somewhere safe. A day came when I felt desperate. I went to the local churches – if they had been open, if I could have found someone to answer my cry for help, what happened next would have never come about. I walked all the way to the centre of the city, several miles, in a daze, and found myself eventually in the Lord Mayor's Chapel, an historic building in Bristol. Once there, I sat down and started to cry. I couldn't stop and I cried for three hours, hiding my face. There was a member of the chapel staff there, who tried to help me in my distress, but I couldn't express what was happening. Eventually he had to send for the police – he had no choice – but I thought he was against me, and I couldn't understand what I had done wrong. Once in the police care, I felt relaxed and safe and was able to talk coherently. They gave me a cup of tea and I waited until eventually a welfare officer arrived at Bridewell and took me home.

In my desperation I had started drinking, any time, day or night. I was drinking sherry and even took it to work with me concealed in a container. The doctor came to see me and prescribed tablets but I did not take them, I had enough sense to realise the danger involved in taking them while drinking heavily. A day came when I bought a bottle of whiskey, took it home and drank nearly the whole bottle. I can recollect gathering up the children's clothes and throwing them all out of the window. Neighbours thought I had taken an overdose and called an ambulance and I was taken to Southmead Hospital. When I was on the bed I heard someone say, "She's drunk." I was calling the name of a gentleman who had been very kind and helpful to me, but in my confused state I thought the doctor was this man. After a while I came home and cleared up all the mess I had made, the children staying with a neighbour for the night.

The following day relatives arrived contacted by my neighbour. I kept the doors locked and took no notice of their pleading to be let in. I was watching the clock; there was only one person I felt I could trust and he would arrive home at six o'clock. When he got home I asked for him to come in, but nobody else. I didn't want them and at my request he told them to go away, which they did. We talked for a long time and I felt calmer and more relaxed.

Things continued about the same: flashing lights, compulsive washing, fear of people in general, suspicion of neighbours. I had a strange experience when I went through all the motions of a pregnancy, continuing for nine months. My periods stopped, my stomach and breasts enlarged and I felt movements as of a baby kicking. Although I knew a pregnancy was an impossibility at the time, I didn't accept this and was quite pleased to think I was having a baby, and told people it would be at any time. At some point it all just drifted away and was finished.

On several occasions I made my son ring for the police who came to re-assure me and calm me down. Fear of going out continued. I couldn't bear to see his – my husband's – face revealed on the features of every man I passed.

One day I went on one of my long walks and went into a church at Fishponds. At first I just sat and looked at the altar; suddenly I felt everything was wrong. The Bible was open on the lectern so I changed the page, also opened the hymn books in the pews. Why? I don't know. I meant no harm. I left an offering in the box on the wall.

When I was in the house I would sometimes be impelled to gather up lots of bits and pieces, put them on the bed and try to make a crucifix from them. It was like a puzzle as seen before but not remembered. I had to try and put it together. I wouldn't let anyone else see me.

Finally things reached a climax. It must have been early morning with just enough light to see what I was doing. In the garden I lit a fire. I piled things on – all the things which had belonged to Ron – anything he had touched. It wasn't me, it was as if another personality had taken over, yet I was still in sufficient control not to destroy furniture or anything like that. Then I started washing, gathering up clothes etc., and bundling them into the machine. This half done I suddenly went upstairs ad said to the children, "Quick, get up, we must get out." I wrapped blankets around them and went out. I felt desperate to find a house showing a light. When I did I rang the bell and a lady came to the door, took us in, and made me a cup of tea. In the meantime her husband fetched the police. I wanted to go home, but they took the children from me and took us, separately, to the police station. Then a policeman took the children home after asking if there was anyone who would look after them – I told them my sister's and sister-in-law's addresses. I was really frightened.

Someone who said he was a doctor told me to sign a form which I did. I didn't know what I was signing, but I was consenting to be admitted to Glenside. They wanted me to go straight there but I insisted on going home first. I said the house was dirty and the fire might be still burning. When we arrived it was just smouldering and the house was, of course, perfectly clean. They took me back to the station and I heard them say, "she'll go to Glenside." I didn't want to go and struggled with them but, of course, it was no good. An ambulance came and picked me up! I heard them say, "she'll be trouble", but when we arrived there I got out and went quietly to Mason Unit. I felt safe and a great relief.

I was resentful and didn't want to do as I was told, or take the tablets prescribed. For the first few days I was not allowed out, but later, provided I asked for permission, I could, and I went for long walks. I was still suffering from 'visions' and confusions. I was running away, wanting to go home, but also to go back, although, actually, I was over the worst before I went in. I stayed three weeks. My escape from reality to relieve tension was through music and dancing.

After about three weeks, which seemed like forever, they said I looked a lot better and would I like to go home, so I went. The children came home. It felt very strange and I wanted to tell them to go away. I didn't feel it was time to see them. This was a first reaction which only lasted a couple of days.

My neighbours, an old lady and her son were very helpful over this period, but kept giving me soup which I did not want. I became very friendly with them and they sustained me over a difficult period.

They had asked me at the hospital if I worked and advised me not to go back for a while. However, I went straight back, although I dreaded going because of all the things I had said and done. In the event, although naturally they seemed a bit apprehensive about how I might behave, they treated me just the same. I had to get a doctor's note to allow me to return and then everything was as it had been before.

When in a depression one is liable to say or do things which you don't mean at all, but can really hurt someone and drive them away. If people could ignore it, sit and say nothing – which I know is very hard – they would do a great service. The outburst is beyond control and afterwards you want to say, "I didn't do or say it", but of course you did. It is very difficult afterwards to overcome the effects of an antagonism aroused in this way. If only people would accept that it is all part of the illness. It is as though for a short time another personality dominates you, taking over control. This may only last a few minutes but it may be hours or even days. This is not the real 'you'. It is a terriying experience – you wonder if you will ever recover your normality. I shall always be grateful to the people I work with for helping my recovery even though they may not be aware that they did.

LIFE BEHIND HORFIELD

Wednesday 20.2.85

Like Mad dogs

Lunch time. The front door knocks. This bloke says he's a plain clothes copper calling about an unpaid fine. He has either come to collect the outstanding £100, or take me to prison.

"Bit late, aren't you? This is nearly two years old."

"We can't keep track of them all. There's thousands and thousands. And a new computer has had to be installed to trace the backlog. Unemployed are you?"

"Yes."

"Best you paid it mate. Or they'll come and arrest you in the early hours of the morning. Might frighten the wife and kids. It's your turn this weekend. But if you can't pay come down to the station and I'll get you taken up Horfield. Come at your own convenience. I don't suppose you'll want to come now?"

"No."

"Okay. But don't leave it any later than this weekend. They come like mad dogs some of our blokes."

"I'll come down Friday."

"Okay mate. See you Friday."

"Cheerio."

Friday 22.2.85 Day 1.

Bring Out The Wogs

1400 hours. I walk into Bridewell. Nobody seems interested. Told to wait. A policeman appears at 1500 hours and interrupts my reading. We walk over to Broadmead Courtroom Cells. I am jailed. I meet the Wednesday plain clothes copper again. He offers me some food. Two hot pasties, apple, and a packet of crisps.

"Do you smoke?"

"Yes."

"Take this packet of twenty. Make the most of them. You'll get none up there."

"Thanks."

I smoke a fag, then stretch out on the seat. I go to sleep. Am woken by the sound of heavy machinery and a lot of shouting. Am surprised at the fact that I have slept for almost two hours.

The prison bus has arrived, and the driver is shouting for his passengers. He is extraordinarily fat, and has a truncheon that he keeps banging on the side of the bus.

"Bring out the wogs!"

Can hardly believe my ears or eyes. Surely such people only exist in American movies. But he knows how to use that truncheon. **Likes** using it too.

I've never been in a prison bus before. It has small cells both sides, each capable of holding just one prisoner. I can hear the other prisoners shouting and yelling. Through my little tunnel I can see the streets of Bristol that I am so familiar with. People stare as the bus passes by. Oblivious of the many other eyes upon them.

Horfield Prison. Bristol. More shouting.

"Shut up and get out you bastards."

Processed into the reception area. Waiting in a large room with about twenty other prisoners. The old con brags he's spent thirty years in and out of different prisons. But this is going to be his last 'stretch'. He's too old to keep doing time now. He moves into a corner and rolls a couple of strands of tobacco into something resembling a cigarette. I bring out my packet of 19 and light one up. The old con stands dumbfounded. The room falls silent. Prisoners stare at me. Someone asks for a cigarette. I offer him one. And another. And another. I am crowded back against the wall in the surge of prisoners coming forward to get a cigarette. I become frightened. Suddenly everyone in the room seems to be smoking. There are three cigarettes left. The old con moves forward.

"First time inside?"

"Yes."

"Any left?"

"Yes."

I offer him one. He tells me no one brings fags into prison. The screws take them away on entry reception. In his full thirty years of prison experience I was the only man he had seen enter prison with a packet of nineteen cigarettes.

We are at reception for what seems like hours. Gradually we filter through. I am asked my religion.

"Atheist."

"Look. There are only three religions. Catholic. Church of England and Non Conformist. Which do you want?"

"Atheist."

"Right. Non conformist."

He writes it down. Shower. All personal belongings removed. Uniform. I am now prisoner number F17662. Location 135. Sentence 20 days.

I am taken away and placed in a cell with another bloke. He is from Bedminster. Ex Army. Served in Northern Ireland. Discharged with alcoholism. Coughs blood. Tells me his name is 'Sketcher' Smith, on account of the sketches he draws so skilfully, which plaster the cell wall. Has four children whose pictures are also on the wall. Was 'nicked' forgetting to pay for two bottles of whiskey, and some groceries for the kids on leaving Tesco's. Sentenced to 40 days for resisting arrest. His wife has left him for another man. When his time is up he will torture and kill her. In the night he cries to see his children.

Saturday 23.2.85. Day 2.

Double Breakfast

The harsh cell light wakes me up at 0600 hours. The cell window gives no chink of daylight. It has been blocked up with a blanket in some sort of double glazing method against the bitter cold outside. 'Sketch' is doing another drawing.

Razor issue. Each one methodically issued. We are allowed half an hour to shave. Then with military accuracy they are collected again by the duty warder. One missing sets off an emergency alarm and throws the whole prison system into panic. 'Sketch' returns with his breakfast. Routine is meals are collected and taken back to cells. I never eat breakfast. Just coffee and rolls.

"If you leave it too late..breakfast will be gone."

"I only want the coffee and rolls."

"Can I have your cooked breakfast?"

"Yes."

"**All** of it?"

"Yes all of it."

"**And** the porridge?"

"Especially the porridge."

"Will you collect it for me? It's not allowed to go twice."

"Yes..I'll collect it for you."

I join the breakfast queue and bring one back. It is two small sausages, beans, and a piece of fried bread. While eating it 'Sketch' starts singing a little song he has made up.

"I'm a King.A King,
A fucking King.
I eat two breakfasts,
When the birdies sing."

But I'm not in a singing mood. Wonder if I can do my 'stretch' without cracking. Christ, I was even beginning to think like a prisoner. Two or three days ago I would have used the word only in its correct context.

"Er..I expect you'll eat all your dinner?"

"Yes. I expect I'll eat all my dinner."

Rattle of keys. Cell door bursts open.

"Follow me."

"Where?"

"You must see the doctor. Wait there."

Beginning to think prison consists of an endless round of waiting there.

"In you go. See the doctor."

Am flanked by prison warders. The doctor sits at his desk some distance away also flanked.

"Are you suicidal?"

"You tell me. You're the overpaid expert."

"I am a doctor and you must answer my question!"

"Are you a real doctor?"

"If you do not co-operate, I will place you on a charge."

"Your probably more experienced at doing that than practising medicine!"

"Take him away!"

I am placed on a charge to see the governor Monday Morning. Back in my cell 'Sketch' becomes worried about the incident and warns me to be careful. He doesn't want to lose me as a cell mate. For the rest of the day he absorbs himself in his drawings.

It is my first whole day in prison.

Sunday 24.2.85. Day 3.

Church and Television

Slop out the bucket. Mop out the cell. Doors are left open until church service is over. It is voluntary – except for the young prisoners who are kept segregated on their own wing. They move everywhere on the double – even to church. And have to call the warders 'Sir'.

Some of the men on my wing tell me they attend church service for somewhere to go. For a prison is a sickening and unhappy place and most prisoners will jump at a chance of a few hours change of scene. A good opportunity to walk around the wing and talk to other prisoners. Meet some who are here for peace activities.

This is called the Bed and Breakfast wing, as it is only for short termers. Seems as if 'Sketch' knows everyone in the place. Manage to get some old newspapers and a couple of books to read.

Two hours evening recreation. There is a noticeable increase in warders. (I refuse to call them officers). This is a dangerous time as prisoners use it to settle old scores, either amongst themselves or with warders. But it's generally quiet on this wing. Though disturbances have been known to break out over which television channel should be viewed.

Most horrible is the height of the landings with the safety nets stretched between them. The nets were put there long after the prison was built, officially to prevent prisoners committing suicide. There are those who claim more warders have gone over than prisoners.

I get some up to date TV news about the miners strike.

Monday 25.2.85. Day 4.

California and Cartoons

I see the Governor who dismisses my charge but warns me to 'behave' myself in future.

'Sketch' is happy about me remaining as his cell mate. Talks of re-joining the Army when he gets outside. After he has done his job on his wife he may on second thoughts move to California where he will work as a movie cartoon artist.

Has the ability and enthusiasm for both jobs.

Tuesday 26.2.85. Day 5.

The Treatment

Two warders outside my cell can be heard intellectually discussing the miners strike. One would end it tomorrow by bringing Scargill inside and giving him 'the treatment'. He knows how to hurt people without causing bruises, and would give a month's pay to see Scargill inside.

'Sketch' asks me who my favourite cartoon character is. I tell him the Pink Panther.

Have now completed a quarter of my sentence.

Wednesday 27.2.85. Day 6.

Wednesday. Bloody Wednesday

Four prisoners refuse to leave the exercise yard, and the Alsations go for walkies with about 40 warders.

Someone didn't like the drinking chocolate, and threw it away in a warder's face. Maybe that's why it's always served cold.

'Shotgun' farmer Backhouse arrives for the next 35 years, leaving his wife and her lover behind him.

I've read all the books in the cell, and 'Sketch' has only got comics.

I hate bloody Wednesdays.

Thursday 28.2.85. Day 7.

Part Of The Punishment

Outside pipes frozen. No water to flush slops away. Place overflowing and stinking. Cynics say it's part of the punishment. I do not think an epidemic of cholera would confine itself to being just 'part of the punishment'.

Would want 25% reduction in a house price before considering one in the Horfield area of Bristol.

Friday 1.3.85. Day 8.

The Liquid Cosh

Warder attacked by someone from the 'fours' (upstairs). Takes four warders to carry him away. Two other prisoners joined in the action. Saw most of this from the cell door window. Better than watching TV.

Even 'Sketch' left a drawing to view it. Tells me that violent prisoners are given a hyperdermic injection. The liquid cosh.

This place is a ticking bomb.

Saturday 2.3.85. Day 9.

Night Screamers

New warder replaces one badly attacked yesterday.

Someone upstairs screaming all night long. Other screamers join in with verbal abuse for the whole establishment. Sleep difficult to obtain.

Place reminds me of a madhouse more than a prison.

Sunday 3.3.85. Day 10.

Half Way

Half my sentence now completed.

Wednesday 13.3.85. Day 20.

Summary

I did the whole of my 20 days sentence without remission, and upon being discharged the £100 fine was considered 'spent'.

In pure financial terms it meant – in theory at least – that I was paid the equivalent working rate of £5 per day. A warder told me that it cost the taxpayer £300 to keep me in prison, and that there was no economic sense in imprisoning the unemployed for unpaid fines.

Inside I mixed with many different people, for a prison is not a complete segregation. And contrary to popular belief there is not a colour TV in every cell.

When I left, 'Sketch' was coughing increased blood, and 'waiting there' for a medical examination. In return for 20 extra breakfasts he insisted I accept three drawings of The Pink Panther, that he had worked on for many hours. I hope that he will not carry out his dreadful promise to the woman he married, and informed him that if he did, his chances of returning to active Army service, or moving to California, would be somewhat negligible.

On the whole the food was not bad. And I had eaten worse with the Commandos. But the indignity and monotony of prison, confirms that containing men rather than rehabilitating them is its sole function.

That which I hated most was the dreadfully unhygenic practise of slopping out, which has already been described by so many people.

I did not go to prison to investigate conditions, and I do not wish to convey that I have any great knowledge of the inside workings of Horfield Prison. I do know that I have no particular desire to return.

But I had belted a Social Security clerk whom I considered to be unnecessarily abusive and rude. I was fined. It was the non payment of this fine that landed me in prison.

Under the same circumstances, I would take exactly the same action again.

Anonymous.